The Boss
Always
Sits In The Back

by
Jon D'Amore

Advice & Legal Stuff

Hard Cover ISBN: 978-0-9853000-0-5
Soft Cover ISBN: 978-0-9853000-1-2

Jon D'Amore and The Boss *Always* Sits In The Back are represented by Howard Frumes of the law firm Alexander, Nau, Lawrence, Frumes & Labowitz LLP.

Cover art designed and copyrighted © 2012 by Irene A. LoPresto, Reflex Graphix, LLC & Jon D'Amore.

Layout and formatting for print by Steven W. Booth of Genius Publishing, and Jon D'Amore.

Published by Jon D'Amore
Printed in the USA by Bang Printing Inc.
First Edition

Table of Contents

Acknowledgments

A lot has happened in my life during the writing of this book. All I ever wanted was to bring pleasure, entertainment and a smile to the world...and to have a comfortable, relaxing life for myself. But nothing is ever as easy or as simple as that. Know what I mean?

Had it not been for my father, Carmine '*Rocky*' D'Amore, and my cousin and Godfather, Jerry D'Amore...this book never would have, nor *could have*, been written. I love them and will miss them always.

Thanks to: Al Certisimo, for numerous insights into the things that went on around me when I was too young to know; Johnny D, for not whacking me when he was pissed off at Jerry, and for his friendship and trust; Anthony Tarantino, for looking out for me while remembering that at the time I *was* just a "kid" in a *tough guys* world; Al & Carole Battisti, for being there with their kind hearts, humor, compassion, and for allowing me to have their home in paradise to write the majority of this book...and for Al's knowledge of the Italian language; Alan, Helaine, Cary, Derek and Jordan (my godson) Wohl, for giving me their unconditional friendship and love; Lisa Tracy, for her love and talent to push me to turn something good into something great; Lois Isenberg, for taking the time to guide a stranger in a strange land to a safe harbor in a stormy and treacherous sea called Los Angeles, for the multiple late-night double-features, and for being my friend when I needed one just like her; Shashi Harrie and Nanette Wolff, for giving me the energy and insight to learn from the past, live for the moment and plan for the future; all the cleaning ladies over the years for coming to my residences and keeping me clothed and my living spaces habitable.

Stuart Aion; Glorie Austern; Gail Borges; Tony Caputo; Sharon Coleman; Melicent D'Amore; Rose, Filomena & Joey D'Amore; Connie D'Amore-Ruel; Patti D'Amore-Steele; Peter Flora; Denise Gautier; Gail 'GB' Geoia; Richard Hartman; Carol Kadlic; Ray Koonce; Patty LaVeglia; Karen LeBlanc; Rene LoPresto; Robin Luxenberg; David, Michele & Alison O'Connell; Paul Peragine; LouAnn Rounseville; Tom Sullivan...true and caring friends and relatives for life.

What are *normally* titled "Chapters," I've called "Rounds." A handful of people within this story started out as boxers. In homage to them, I've used the same number of rounds as in the heavyweight fights of yesteryear. The Epilogue can be taken as the referee announcing the judge's decision (if that works for you).

The remaining space on this page is left for "industry people" who deserve some ink: The Writers Group of Studio City, for making my Wednesday evenings worthwhile, giving me the moral and creative support to believe in myself and my writing, and for inspiring me to bring each and every high point of my creativity to a higher level. Ashley Rogers, she believed... and asked for nothing but my friendship in return, and knew I'd take care of the rest. Howard Frumes, my legal representative and a dedicated believer who stood at my side knowing it would finally happen. He's truly one of the good ones.

Dedication

Jerry D'Amore

July 3, 1937
to
June 6, 1999

"As long as you trust me...I'll take care of you.
There's things I'll tell you, because...just because."

John Lennon

October 9, 1940
to
December 8, 1980

"You may say I'm a dreamer,
But I'm not the only one..."

Preface
A few things you need to know

For starters; this is not a memoir. It's not an autobiography. And it *most certainly* is not the story of my life. *That* would take volumes.

This is a fictional story based on some guys I knew and some things I heard and saw.

Oh yeah...and all of their names (except anyone named *D'Amore*), and a few other things have been changed.

I use *italics* and *ellipses* (such as: ...). Why? Because *that's the way we speak!* They are there to alter the way you read.

Italics *emphasize* the specific word.

Ellipses are used as a timing rest...while staying on the same subject.

The Boss *Always* Sits In The Back is a story primarily about Italians, who, as everyone knows, are *very* animated in the way they speak and the way they emphasize their words. The italics and ellipses will make the reading of this story more enjoyable...and bring the characters to life.

We all know *something* of the big cities named in this tome - Los Angeles, San Francisco, Las Vegas, Chicago and New York City - but the *real* stories take place in New Jersey, or *Jersey* as we tend to call it...around Hudson and Bergen Counties.

Hudson County is named after the English explorer, Henry Hudson, who, in 1609, "discovered" the river that bears his name. Of course, the fact that the Lene Lenape Indians were living along its banks for more than a thousand years and had *their own* name for it didn't mean anything to the explorers, mapmakers and historians. The Mohicans, who lived farther north in what is now upstate New York, called the river *Muhheakunnuk*, which meant "the great water always in motion."

Whether Henry Hudson disembarked from his ship, The Half Moon, and actually set foot on the river's most southwestern landmass, we'll never really know. But, in typical Anglo fashion, the river, county, numerous streets, avenues and boulevards were named in his honor.

The bulk of the county lies between the **Hudson River** on the east, and the **Hackensack River** on the west. Both rivers run in a north-south direction and join at their southern ends in New York Harbor and Newark Bay. The resulting peninsula consists of (from its northeastern point to its southeastern point along the Hudson River); **North Bergen, West New York, Guttenberg, Weehawken, Hoboken, Jersey City and Bayonne** (which I'm told translates to *On The Bay*); inland and land-locked is **Union City**; to the west along the Hackensack River is **Secaucus** (pronounced by the locals: See-caw-kus). Up until the 1950s, Secaucus was a very small town known for its swamps and the smell of pig farms, while being only minutes from midtown Manhattan. On the *other side* of the Hacky (the nickname for the Hackensack River) are the towns of **Kearny** and **Harrison**.

Hoboken, Jersey City and Bayonne are at the southeastern point of the peninsula, and provide magnificent views of the Statue of Liberty, Ellis Island, lower Manhattan and the New York Bay. Just north of Hoboken, a drive along Weehawken's Boulevard East, day or night, was *always* breathtaking…thanks to the majestic Manhattan skyline and the Empire State Building in the center of it all.

As the migration from Europe continued throughout the first third of the twentieth century, those who made it through Ellis Island's immigration process had the option of three transit routes to their new paradise. One shuttled the travelers to the Lower East Side of Manhattan, not far from Little Italy. Another route went around the southern tip of Manhattan to Brooklyn. A third came to the port closest to Ellis Island: Hoboken.

For many of those without family in America, and possibly intimidated by the early skyscrapers of Manhattan, when it came time to make a decision as to where they wanted to go…they chose the green land to the west…they chose New Jersey.

Hoboken, though only one square mile, was the hub of industry from the late 1800s through the 1950s. But as the century reached its midway mark, the factories, shipyards, trucking terminals, Bethlehem Steel and the docks (where *On The Waterfront*, with Marlon Brando, Rod Steiger, Eva

Marie Saint and Lee J. Cobb, was filmed) were slowly closing down. Still, the town held onto its title as home of the first professional baseball game and the birthplace of Frank Sinatra.

Then there are Hudson County's three lifelines to *the city*, two of which were bored through the bedrock beneath the Hudson River.

The Holland Tunnel, completed in 1927 in Jersey City, empties onto Canal Street on the west side of downtown Manhattan. It's a little known fact that the tunnel is not named after the country, but for the engineer who designed it, Clifford M. Holland.

In Weehawken, a couple of miles north of the Holland Tunnel, is **The Lincoln Tunnel** (named for the obvious), which, when its first of three tubes were completed in 1937, made it possible to get into midtown Manhattan within minutes from *anywhere* in Hudson County.

The **Bayonne Bridge** is on the southern tip of the county, connecting Jersey to the borough of Staten Island.

Together, they made Hudson County the primary gateway, making access to New York City easy and quick. They also brought countless jobs, not to mention traffic jams, to the region.

From the 1940s to the mid '70s, Union City had become The Textile and Embroidery Capital of America with its mills, dye houses and manufacturing factories along its side streets. It wasn't unusual to see Italian housewives doing *home work* (the cutting of small embroidered patterns to be used in the apparel manufacturing process) to make extra house money...after they cleared and washed the dinner dishes and while their children were doing *their* homework (of the grammar school variety).

Sure, a large number of Italians settled in Brooklyn, and many went to Manhattan's Little Italy...but the number that came to Hudson County and spread throughout each of its communities was staggering.

The proximity of Hudson County to the city allowed certain opportunities for the original *le cinque famiglie*...the Five Families. Because of the waterfront, the trucking terminals, warehouses, ships, and manufacturing plants, this was a prime location for the original *boss of all bosses*, Charlie '*Lucky*' Luciano, to pick and choose his territory out in the country...in Jersey.

He knew that by controlling the ports he'd get a piece of everything that came off or went on a ship. The dockworkers, the truck drivers, the laborers in the factories...they *all* needed someone to look after them... and to speak for them. For that, the unions took a small slice of everyone's paycheck and called it *dues*...and thus, their *members* were looked after.

By putting a weekly salary in the workers' pockets, the Average Joe had money to buy bootleg liquor and bet the ball games or the horses...or *the numbers*. And if he got in too deep, he'd be able to borrow the cash, along with a weekly *vig* (of course), to pay his gambling debts.

By the way...*vig* is slang for the word *vigorish*, which, in the *mob* vernacular means *interest*. It's a derivative of the Ukrainian "vygrash" or the Russian "vyigrysh," which first appeared in the United States around 1912. You'll see it a few times throughout the story.

During Prohibition, several Italian entrepreneurs built distilleries in the swamps of Secaucus. The local police weren't worried about the liquor because they knew it was headed out-of-state...besides, they were well paid to look the other way. By having direct access to the Hackensack River, a boatload of alcohol would be ferried south to the bay and then up the East River for distribution to Staten Island, Brooklyn, Queens and Manhattan.

This Jersey...it was a good way for the mob to make a living...away from the bright lights, notoriety and high profile of New York City. It was also a good place for them to live, go to church, raise their families and become upstanding members of their communities.

Bergen County is the northern land mass attached to the Hudson County peninsula. A handful of towns line the eastern edge along the Hudson River (from its southern point, going north; **Edgewater, Fort Lee, Englewood Cliffs, Tenafly and Alpine**) up to the New York state border. Inland, the county spreads to the west and borders the state line to the north. Bergen County has dozens and dozens of small and large towns... but only one city: **Hackensack**...the county seat.

During the early years of the twentieth century, Englewood Cliffs and **Englewood** were the sites of the original film studios. Most exterior scenes were shot along the *Palisades* (the giant sheer rock cliffs that run along the Jersey side of the Hudson River, from Weehawken up into New York). The term *cliffhanger* was coined from *The Perils Of Pauline* serials filmed there.

Then came the '30s, and the county's new claim to fame was the town of Fort Lee when construction was completed on the **George Washington Bridge**, spanning the Hudson River and connecting New Jersey with uptown Manhattan's West Side.

Just south of the bridge in **Cliffside Park** was **Palisades Amusement Park**, which drew millions of people throughout the '50s and '60s (and was the impetus for Chuck Barris to write Freddie Cannon's 1962 hit, *Palisades Park*). It closed in the early '70s...leaving behind millions of teenage memories.

Bergen County was where Hudson County residents strived to move once they earned enough to leave the blue collar environment behind...no more apartment-building-lined streets, pollution from the factories and smokestacks, traffic, mediocre and over-crowded school systems and the constant sound of population and progress.

From the '30s onward, with the mobsters having substantial amounts of excess cash available, Bergen County became dotted with the large homes of *la famiglia's* mid-level soldiers and the palatial estates of the upper-echelon lieutenants and capos. Bergen County was where *da guys* lived. Hudson County and New York City were where they worked and played.

Oh...and if some of the names become a little confusing for you, I've put a *Cast of Characters* at the end of the story (and it's in alphabetical order...just in case you need to reference it once in a while).

Now you know a few of the things you needed to know

Huh?

Like all children, I was influenced by the things around me during *the formative years.* Some children grow up in a family of doctors, lawyers, investment bankers, owners of small and large businesses, police chiefs, insurance salesmen, stockbrokers, corporate executives, or small town and big city politicians. If something went wrong in *their* family they usually blamed it on families like mine...*or* they came to families like mine for help.

In *my* immediate family there were no doctors, lawyers, investment bankers and so on.

This is my story, based on actual events, of living on the fringe of what *some* people call "the Mafia."

You see, several members of my immediate family were *connected. Connected* simply means that through blood, honor or business...you have a direct connection to the Cosa Nostra, the Mafia, Our Thing, La Famiglia, the Mob. And *those* members of my family made a very comfortable living for many, many years through this affiliation.

I thought about becoming more involved when I was in my early 20s, but at the time it was the mid-1970s. I was a professional musician and having too much fun living the *rock 'n' roll* lifestyle. I was living every dream of most of my high school and college buddies (and at the time... that mattered!), so why would I want to cut my hair, wear dark suits and ties...and take the chance of getting whacked?

Instead, I decided to watch *da guys* from the sidelines.

I was able to enjoy the best of *a few* worlds. I was having my little slice of rock 'n' roll success, I had a great social and family life, I got to play with my connected relatives...and I *also* got to hang with *The Boys From Hudson County.* I got to be a part of the games, the hustles, the respect, the scams, the Federal investigations, the women, the stories, the parties...and the cash.

I got to do some wild things...and I got to meet some *very* interesting and unique people. A lot of them aren't with us anymore. Most of them are dead. A couple of them had to leave the area and can't/shouldn't/don't want to come back. Some are in State and Federal penitentiaries...and will be for years.

A few of them were able to survive. I run across a couple of the survivors from time to time. And then there's my family...

Round 1

Christ, I hate flying!

Especially after all the time I spent in the air since the early 1970s.

It was Friday, October 9, 1998. It would have been John Lennon's fifty-eighth birthday.

There I was, sitting alone in the back of a nine passenger stretch, clad in jeans, a pair of sneakers and a knitted sweater that I picked up in Laguna Beach a few weeks earlier.

I opened a rear window, slid on my sunglasses, looked outside and lit a joint as the limo headed down New Jersey's Garden State Parkway to get me to Newark International Airport for my 9:35AM flight.

I was never very good with alcohol, so an occasional joint always took off the edge when I was on my way to an airport.

Besides, it was only eight in the morning.

Much too early for a martini.

And as part of my job, I had to fly.

A lot.

At the time, I was working for a very large New York insurance company. When I was hired, they wanted someone to work with a market that most corporations and conglomerates have problems relating to: Unions.

This particular trip was to oversee the company's presence at the largest Public Employee Benefits convention in the country. Over 6,000 representatives were attending, and I, as one of the guest speakers, would be spouting about the *need* that ultimately would be filled by using my company's program.

I was very good in front of large groups.

I had lots of practice at that.

My other function on this trip was to host an extravagant hospitality bash in my hotel suite for several officials from large national unions.

I had lots of practice with that, too.

By the time the limo arrived at the airport and the driver opened my door, I was buzzed.

I handed the redcap ten bucks as he took my bags from the trunk.

Even stoned, I had the robotics down.

He asked to see my ticket and picture ID, and then he hit me with the standard security questions, to which I gave the standard passenger responses.

"Yes, I packed my own bags," "No, no one known or unknown to me gave me anything to carry," and "Yes, they've been in my possession since I packed them."

Then I headed into Terminal C.

It made me recall a time before America worried about terrorists, when we could show up twenty minutes before a flight and not have to show ID or pass through metal detectors in order to board a plane.

I was good for more than twenty trips a year, but this particular one had me thinking.

It had me thinking *a lot*.

As I took my first class seat aboard Continental's flight 1679, it really began to sink in that it had been twenty-one years since I was in Las Vegas.

Vegas.

Twenty-one years.

Right down to the month.

Throughout the nearly five hour flight I opened my laptop and did some work, read a couple of magazines, drank three Bloody Marys and socialized with the flight attendants...who used to be called stewardesses. I did anything to avoid thinking about Vegas.

As the pilot brought the plane down low so we could see the Grand Canyon, it all started to come back to me.

When we passed over Lake Mead and the Hoover Dam I knew it was less than a half hour before I'd be hearing those high-pitched bells of the slot machines in the airport.

Business would only keep me here for three days. So why did I make plans for six?

Because of *family*.

My cousin and Godfather, Gerald, better known as Jerry, along with his wife and mother, moved here about three years ago after almost 20 years in Palm Springs, and I wanted to spend some time with them.

If there was *anyone* that I'd want to be with in Vegas...it would be with *Jerry*.

As the plane circled, I looked out the window and saw a skyline and landscape that was dramatically different from the first time I was here on my own in late August of 1975.

Back then...there was nothing. There were small patches of civilization here and there, but it was desolate until you actually got within a mile of The Strip.

Now, there are miles of hotels, casinos, homes, highways, shopping centers, golf courses and housing developments. There doesn't seem to be one square foot of unused property in this old desert oasis.

Over the years I had read the articles and seen the TV specials about how Las Vegas had grown and how it now resembled a family theme park with rides and circus acts for the kids, shops and pools for the wives, and casinos and hookers for the dads.

But the allure of the decadence; of the wild nights with Frank, Dean and Sammy; the rare Elvis and Howard Hughes sightings; the coolness; the glitz; the excitement...that was all gone.

Inside, I never really cared about what the town had become because as far as I was concerned I was *never* coming back here anyway.

When the plane touched down, everyone applauded.

I slowly shook my head and smiled.

The applause triggered a flood of memories as the plane taxied to the terminal and the canopy approached us.

This surely wasn't the same McCarran Airport I had flown into 22 times over twenty-six months during the mid '70s.

It used to take 10 minutes to get through this airport. Now it took more than thirty. But eventually, I found my luggage and was in the Hertz van headed to my rented Lincoln.

I checked into a $1,900-a-night penthouse suite at The Mirage, and as soon as the bellman left the room I picked up a phone to make the call.

"Jerry. I'm here."

"Whatcha think, Juan?" After all these years, he still called me Juan. "It's changed since the last time you saw it, huh?" he asked as I opened the remote-controlled curtains to look out over The Strip.

I let out a small nervous laugh.

Only Jerry knew what that laugh meant.

Vegas, for me, existed in a previous lifetime.

It was October of 1977.

My last memory of this town was the morning two towering, well-dressed muscle-men and their equally well-dressed boss, introduced to me simply as "Mr. Smith," escorted me into a waiting limousine.

As I slid into the rear seat I saw another guy sitting there. He looked nervous and appeared to have been punched around a bit. He didn't speak when I nodded to him. He just turned and looked out the side window.

Mr. Smith sat in the front with the driver. His men sat facing me and the other guy. No one was smiling.

We only drove for about fifteen or twenty minutes before we were surrounded by sand and brush. The car pulled off the paved road and continued on the sand for about a half mile before stopping. The odd part was that the low skyline of The Strip wasn't that far away.

Mr. Smith got out and opened the passenger side rear door. The driver stayed in the car as Mr. Smith, his guys, the quiet passenger and I stood in the morning sun.

Mr. Smith looked directly at me and asked, "Any idea why I brought the two of you here?"

I looked at the other guy. He started to weep.

I looked at Mr. Smith and replied, "Nope. No idea."

Mr. Smith pointed to the guy and said, "See this piece of shit? *He* tried scamming one of the casinos, too."

With that, one of Smith's men pulled out a pistol and shot the guy in the head. I jumped at the sound, then froze at the sight of the guy falling to the ground...motionless, with blood spurting from the hole in his skull. It all happened within a second.

Mr. Smith, now flanked by the steroid twins, came close to me and pushed his finger deeper into my chest with each word as he told me to "... get your fucking ass out of Vegas and go back to Jersey on the next fuckin' plane! 'Cause if you're not outta your room and outta Vegas by noon, your body'll be in a fuckin' hole in this desert by tonight, and they'll *never* find you! And tell Casiano to keep Tommy Dolan, that Irish cocksucker, outta this town! How long did he think we were gonna let ya's take our money? Now walk your guinea-ass back to the hotel, pack your shit and *disappear!*"

Then he signaled his men. One grabbed me from behind. The other punched me in the stomach. I collapsed against the limo and slid to the ground as Mr. Smith turned and slid into the back seat. His boys stared at me as if they were taking a mental picture…and then one at a time they followed their boss.

The limo pulled away leaving me in a cloud of dust…and next to a dead guy.

Now…Vegas is a place to bring your family.

In front of my hotel there was a man-made volcano with scheduled eruptions.

Bugsy Siegel *never* would have believed this.

Round 2

It all started on Friday evening, August 28, 1953, around 6:30.

In a third floor apartment at 727 25th Street in Union City, New Jersey, my twenty-seven-year-old father-to-be, Carmine '*Rocky*' D'Amore, was putting on his gold watch, diamond pinky ring and a new suit, as he prepared for his usual weekend job; handling security and collections at one of the numerous backroom casinos in Hudson and Bergen County that were run by Charlie '*Lucky*' Luciano's *family*.

By day he was a recently elected shop steward for the Textile Worker's Union of America's Local 2052, with its headquarters on Hudson Boulevard.

His oldest brother, Dominic, better known as *Geil* (pronounced: *Geel*), a business agent for the Pipefitter's Union, got Rocky *both jobs* through his brother-in-law, Frank DeNike. Frank was the president of the Pipefitter's Union, Godfather to Geil's teenage son, Gerald...*and* head of Luciano's northern New Jersey region.

At the time, Frank was in his mid-forties and was the stereotypical connected Italian of the fifties and sixties. He stood no more than 5'6, weighed at least 250 pounds, usually had a cigar in his mouth, and was *always* impeccably dressed. Sometimes the cigar was lit, most of the time it wasn't. Frank never got his hands dirty, literally and figuratively. And he was always happy to do anything not just for *the family*, but for *our* family.

A little after Rocky finished dressing and was preparing to leave, his pregnant wife, Ann, felt something that she thought he'd like to know about.

"Rocky! I think it's time!"

Now, Rocky had no problem breaking a guy's arm or leg when it was required. He probably had no problem putting a gun to someone's head and pulling the trigger if the situation called for that, either. After all, by the time he was twenty-one he was a combat-hardened World War II Sergeant. He even stayed in Germany as an MP for two years after the war. But the moment his wife was ready to give birth to me, his son, he froze.

He immediately telephoned his brother's house a few blocks away.

"Geil! She's ready to have the baby! What should I do?"

"Take her to the hospital."

"I can't! I'm too nervous to drive. What if it happens in the car? Get over here and drive us! We'll meet you downstairs."

He hung up, gathered Ann's things and began to walk her down the three flights of stairs.

As they stepped out onto the sidewalk, a big shiny black Cadillac Fleetwood pulled up to the apartment house. Geil got out of the passenger door, laughing at his brother's fear. Rocky looked at the driver's seat to see the boss, Frank DeNike.

Ann was escorted into the back seat and her husband slid in next to her.

During the ride, the conversation consisted of Rocky giving the directions to Margaret Hague Hospital in Jersey City, and asking Frank to avoid the potholes and sharp turns.

Geil was still laughing at his brother as he kept telling Ann to relax and that everything would be fine.

Frank, on the other hand, kept telling Ann, "Don't you dare have that baby on my new leather seats!"

I wasn't born until 11:59 the following morning; one minute before noon, on August 29.

As Rocky was pacing the floor of the waiting room, the doctor informed him of the birth of his son. My father said to Geil, who he had forced to stay throughout the night, "I'm naming him John, after Pop."

As my bassinet was rolled into the nursery, the first sets of eyes to see me through the glass belonged to my dad, Uncle Geil, Frank DeNike, my uncle's 16-year-old son Gerald, who a month later would be holding me over the baptismal as my Godfather, and a face that I wouldn't be formally introduced to for another 23 years, yet hear the name many times, Rocco Casiano.

Rocco was around 21 years old and a former boxer from Bayonne who found a more profitable career as Frank DeNike's right hand man. I think *Enforcer* would be a more appropriate title.

He stood no taller than 5'7, with the typical face and body of a boxer, and a voice that sounded like his larynx had taken a few good hits from 1950s two-time world boxing champion Carmen Basilio.

He spoke very softly and had a jovial laugh.

When Rocco was smiling or laughing, that was a good sign...because when he wasn't, people would start to disappear.

It was Monday, September 7, Labor Day, 1959. My mother was dressing me in a custom made tuxedo. Jerry was getting married, and as his 6-year-old Godson I was given the honor to be the ring-bearer.

The reason it was taking place on a Monday was because Jerry and the rest of *da guys*, including my father, were busy making money over the Labor Day weekend. It was that simple.

You can say and think what you want about people connected with the Mafia, but above all, they're simply men doing business just like those who make their way to the train station and eventually to the office. The fact that these guys usually drove to work around two in the afternoon in Caddies and Lincolns and ran their businesses from the backroom of a local tavern or garage instead of a corporate tower on Madison Avenue didn't mean the business was run any differently. No matter which way you look at it, it all comes down to the bottom line. Business is business. And a wedding takes second place to business.

Jerry's wedding was a big day for the D'Amore family, and it was the biggest day in my life...up to *that* point, anyway.

When you're only six and dressed like all the *big people* as your favorite cousin is taking you around to tables where the ladies...*and the men*...are kissing the both of you, and you're the center of attention...you remember that kind of stuff. And I did.

What I was too young to realize at the time was that I didn't *look* like I belonged with these people...much less be part of their family.

All of these guys...my father, my uncle, my Godfather and nearly every other male there...looked like your typical bunch of Italians. Dark skin, jet black or very dark brown hair and eyes. They were all impeccably dressed in suits and sporting their best jewelry.

It wasn't hard to pick *me* out of this group. I had inherited my mother's looks. Her family came from northern Italy, so until I turned nine I had blonde hair, then it turned to a very light brown. My eyes were baby blue and my skin was much lighter than everyone on my father's side.

And I *hated* being dressed in that tuxedo!

But on that day, Jerry and I formed a bond that many years later I would understand as *family*.

Being in the wedding party was my official introduction to *a different kind of life*. One that I would be a part of during the next three-and-a-half decades.

Except for a couple of our cousins, the wedding party was made up of Jerry's closest, uhm...associates.

There were two guys in particular that I always remembered seeing around Uncle Geil's house. When I was very young I'm sure I even thought they were *also* cousins because I never saw Jerry without them.

Mike Caruso was one.

He stood about six feet and always had a smile on his big rubbery face. Mike was fun to be around. He was *constantly* working on a scam or hustle, and could sweet talk his way through any confrontation or situation.

And of course, he could break any limb on your body within a second's notice, *especially* if Jerry told him to do so.

And then there was *Taz*.

Tony Costa.

To a seven or a seventy-year-old, Taz was a mountain in a man's body. Easily more than six feet tall, Taz was at least 240 pounds of pure muscle. He was, like the rest of the men there, a dark skinned, dark haired, well dressed Italian, and was to Jerry what Rocco was to Frank DeNike. Even Sinatra's bodyguards stepped aside when Taz wanted to say hello to Ol' Blue Eyes.

Taz couldn't go anywhere without being noticed.

Taz and Mike were good guys to have on your side.

Individually, Mike and Taz were intimidating.

Together...their appearance and reputation were enough to get the job done.

One of Jerry's favorite stories took place in the late '60s when he sent his guys to collect money that was owed by a dockworker in Hoboken.

Cosmo Manzi was more than a month behind on his loan payments, and after a few friendly attempts by Jerry to collect, Mike and Taz went to see him.

The dockworker was waiting in the back of a parking garage expecting Jerry, and he planned to confront him with a large metal mallet. But as the two large bodies appeared, Manzi realized this was a fight he didn't have a chance of winning.

The closer they got, the more he feared he was about to die.

They stopped several feet away and Mike asked, "You have Jerry's money, Cosmo?"

He slowly shook his head and answered, "No."

"Then we gotta hurt you," Taz said.

Fear flooded the dockworker's face and a pool of urine began forming at his feet.

Taz approached from the left and Mike from the right.

Manzi raised his hand and yelled, "Wait! Don't! Please! Let me do it! You guys'll get carried away."

Taz and Mike looked at one another. They didn't know what to expect.

Manzi raised the mallet in his right hand, put his left hand against the wall and smashed it.

As all three men heard the bones crumble, Manzi fell to the ground and let out a piercing scream that echoed off the garage's concrete walls.

"It ain't enough," Taz said as they took a step closer.

Shocked, Manzi looked up and with his good hand he again signaled them to wait.

He took the mallet, raised it and brought it down on his right knee.

Again his scream echoed as his kneecap shattered.

He looked at Mike and Taz as tears ran down his face. They appeared temporarily appeased.

Mike grinned and said, "A week from today me and my friend are gonna come to your house with a fruit basket. You'll give us an envelope with *all* the money you owe Jerry, plus *all* the vig. Okay Cosmo?"

Manzi couldn't muster a sound. He just nodded.

"You won't let Jerry down again, will you?" Taz asked as he took another step closer.

"No! No! Please, stop...please. No more, no more," he whimpered.

Taz looked down at him and said, "You beat the shit outta yourself, and you're telling *me* to stop?" then shook his head. "You dumb fuck."

Mike and Taz turned and walked away, leaving Cosmo on the ground in pain, lying in his urine and crying.

As they climbed into Mike's Buick, Taz turned to Mike and said, "Jeez, I was just gonna slap him around a little."

"The dumb fuck," Mike added.

And they drove away.

At Jerry's wedding reception, which took place at the Chateau Renaissance in North Bergen, the media and FBI were taking pictures of everyone who walked through the front doors. Why they needed a shot of my grandmother, I'll never know.

Sitting at Frank DeNike's table were the faces the FBI *really* wanted to see, but their attempts were futile. The reason they never saw these men was because they were driven to the kitchen entrance in the back of a customized delivery truck that had all the comforts of a living room assembled and bolted into it.

The truck, painted with the logo *Trojan Horse Catering*, was kept in one of Brother Moscoto's many garages throughout Bayonne and Jersey City. It was used by Frank and his crew whenever they wanted to go somewhere without having their picture taken or their whereabouts known. The truck was backed up to the service entrance, the rear door would open, steps would come down and the discreet occupants simply walked into the affair through the kitchen.

Their wives arrived at the reception by limo.

By the spring of 1966, my father was a business agent for the union and making more money from both his day and weekend jobs, so we moved to a better community.

Secaucus is a little town in the meadowlands of north Jersey, no more than three miles from Union City and still in Hudson County. It was unique in that it was only 10 minutes from the Lincoln Tunnel and midtown Manhattan. Secaucus was the last refuge of the white middle and upper-middle class in Hudson County, and was increasingly becoming surrounded by progress and population. But for *da boys from Hudson County*, Secaucus was still considered the suburbs.

It's September of 1967. I was fourteen, a freshman at Weehawken High School and had just started my first band after taking guitar lessons since I was seven.

For the past nine years music had consumed my life.

From the time I sat in front of a small round-screened black and white television in 1958, and watched as my 9-to-13-year-old girl cousins went out of their minds for Elvis on The Ed Sullivan Show, I knew this *music thing* was something I should be interested in. A few years later The Beatles and the rest of The British Invasion added rocket fuel to the fire. By the time I heard The Rascals, Hendrix and Vanilla Fudge, I was hooked.

Sure, I still played baseball and football with my friends, and I somehow managed to maintain a B average in school, but the rest of my time was made up with guitar lessons, practicing charts and copying chords and riffs from every possible 45 and album I could buy.

Something personally important happened in my life when, in 1968, I bought Deep Purple's first album, *Shades Of Deep Purple*. I was so impressed with the keyboardist, Jon Lord, that I immediately dropped the H from my first name.

I also flipped at the picture of his long thick hair and mustache. But not yet being *able* to grow a mustache, nor allowed to grow my hair over my collar, I opted for the spelling change, much to my father's anger in that I was showing disrespect toward *his* father.

After practicing in my drummer's basement for several months, the band was ready to audition for our first gig.

Besides the local church-run CYO dances, the only other place in town to perform was The Plaza Arena. The Arena was a boxing ring during the week and a dance hall for the local kids on the weekends. The bands would actually set up and perform from the center of the ring to the three hundred or so paying customers.

I found out that the Arena's owner was Al Nucci...a former boxer who owned a tailor shop in the center of Secaucus. What I didn't know was that eight years earlier he was the tailor who made the tuxedo I wore at Jerry's wedding, and he was a long-time friend of my father...and Rocco Casiano.

It was Saturday afternoon, March 23, 1968. The band was rehearsing and we thought the time was right. I called information and got the number of Al Nucci's Custom Tailor.

The phone rang twice before a gruff male voice answered, "Hello, Nucci's!"

"I'd like to speak to Al Nucci please."

"Yeah, this is Al. Who's this?"

I tried to make my fourteen-and-a-half-year-old voice sound older.

"My name is Jon D'Amore, and I have a band called The Mixed Expressions. We'd like to play at The Plaza Arena."

"Oh yeah?" I heard him laugh, "Where have you played before, kid?"
Silence.

"We haven't. We're a new group. All of us are from Secaucus and Weehawken." I used a sales pitch, "And we're sure we can fill the place up with our friends."

"Oh yeah?" he laughed again. "What kind of music do you play?"

"Everything they want to hear!"

"Not for nothin', but if ya's never played anywhere before, how do I know you're any good?"

"Why don't you come down to where we rehearse? You can listen to us."

"I don't have time. I'm busy. I gotta--"

I cut him off.

"Then listen to us right now!"

I placed the phone on the table, ran to my amp, counted to four and the band ran through The Temptation's *My Girl*, and The Young Rascals version of Wilson Pickett's *In The Midnight Hour*.

When I returned to the phone I was sure I'd be listening to a dial tone, but instead the voice on the other end said, "Listen, I gotta go measure Frank Sinatra for a suit. I ain't got time for this right now."

I thought, "Sinatra? Yeah, sure." Little did I know how wrong I was.

"What did you say your name was?" he asked.

"The Mixed Expressions."

"No, not the band's name. What's *your* name?"

"Jon. Jon D'Amore."

"D'Amore? You know a guy named Jerry?"

"Jerry D'Amore? From Union City?"

"Yeah."

"Yeah. He's my cousin. Why?"

"Then Rocky's your *father?*"

"Yeah," I answered innocently.

"Why didn't you tell me that? Yeah, all right. I need a band for the Arena in three weeks." He paused to look at a calendar. "Saturday, April thirteenth. Can you make it?"

Not having any other bookings, the answer was easy.

"Yes!"

"Okay. Be there at four o'clock to set up. You start at twenty after eight. Play three forty-minute sets and be finished at eleven."

"Sure, no problem. Oh, uhm...how much are we getting paid?"

"Ninety bucks. And what's the name of the band?"

"The Mixed Expressions. Ninety bucks? But there's six of us!"

"Ninety bucks, that's it." He wrote down the name of the group. "See you in three weeks. If I have to get hold of you...I'll tell your cousin."

Then he hung up.

That was my first encounter with Al Nucci. There would be many more over the next five decades.

Round 3

By the time I was twenty, I was working as a session musician and flying between New York and California. The music business had become a very exciting and profitable career for me. I had graduated from Weehawken High in June of 1971, and turned 18 at the end of the summer. Right after my birthday I signed a management contract and started playing with a few touring acts.

When I was in San Francisco, I'd stay with an old high school friend, Bill Zitane, who had relocated to attend college.

When I was in L.A., I stayed with my father's cousin, Pasquale '*Patsy*' D'Amore, his wife Rose, and their two children, Phyllis and Joey.

Patsy had become famous for introducing pizza to southern California in the late 1930s, then made an even bigger name for himself with two Hollywood restaurants.

In 1939, Patsy's brother Franklyn opened *The Casa D'Amore* at 1644 North Cahuenga Boulevard, just south of Hollywood Boulevard. Patsy, 37 at the time, was the chef. Then in 1949, Patsy opened *The Villa Capri*, located at 1735 North McCadden Place.

On May 21, 1957, with its grand opening shown live on KTTV, and with Frank Sinatra as the Master of Ceremonies, the new *Patsy D'Amore's Villa Capri* opened its doors at 6735 Yucca Street.

But besides his Italian food, it was Patsy's outgoing and personable manner that led him into friendships with Sinatra, Dean Martin, Sammy Davis Jr., Joey Bishop, Joe DiMaggio and Marilyn, Bogie and Bacall, James Dean, Bobby Darin, Jimmy Durante, Natalie Wood and Robert Wagner, Milton Berle, Jackie Gleason and many, many other celebrities.

It was at Humphrey Bogart's 1957 memorial dinner at The Villa Capri that Lauren Bacall passed the title of The Rat Pack along to Sinatra and his boys. Before that, it was used for years by Bogie and his poker buddies.

Before going out there in 1974, I had only met Patsy and his family three times.

The first time was in July of 1955. I wasn't even two years old when my parents took me across the country in a TWA DC3 prop job, specifically for July 17, the Opening Day of Disneyland.

One of my father's favorite stories happened during that trip.

My father was holding me in his arms while standing with Patsy in the kitchen of the original Villa Capri, when the rear door opened and in walked James Dean with a young starlet that he was dating at the time... Ursula Andress. My father said she was the most beautiful woman he had ever met. The actor loved Patsy's Italian food, but he hated coming in through the front door only to be the object of the tourists, gossip columnists and photographers' attention, so Patsy happily allowed him to come in through the back and have a table in the private dining room whenever he needed it.

Upon being introduced to my father, James Dean took me from Rocky's arms.

As he held me, he asked Rocky, "What's the kid's name?"

"John D'Amore," was my dad's proud reply.

"Oh yeah? Well what do you know, John," he said to me. "We've got the same initials."

After a short while the D'Amores said goodbye and left the two actors to their meal. At the time, no one would have imagined that about two-and-a-half months later the 24-year-old man with whom I shared initials would be killed as he sped along a mountainous Paso Robles road in his Porsche.

Though I was too young to recall any of it, I grew up watching the 8mm films of the trip. And that was when California first put the hook in me.

My second encounter with the West Coast D'Amores was in 1964 when Patsy and his family were stopping in New Jersey on their way home from a visit to Italy. There was a small *family* gathering at Uncle Geil's new home in Ridgefield.

The third time was the most memorable.

My father thought it would be fun to drive across the country during the summer of 1968. It was only one year after the *Summer of Love*. He couldn't have picked a better time to expose me to Hollywood. I was just short of 15 years old and had already determined I wanted to be a rock 'n' roll star. For me…it was a *great* time to be in Hollywood.

We visited Patsy's spacious Studio City home, complete with a pool, maid, Cadillacs, my 18-year-old cousin Joey's two Jaguar XK-E's and what seemed like his never-ending stream of Hollywood girlfriends.

It was May of 1974 when I arrived in L.A. for some recording sessions… six years since that first gig for Al Nucci, and since I had seen or spoken to Patsy. He was now 72 years old.

My manager had made arrangements for me to stay at a hotel near the studio I'd be working in. Before I went to the airport baggage carousel, I stopped at a payphone. I figured I'd make dinner reservations at The Villa Capri for that evening and see the California D'Amores.

"Hello, this is The Villa Capri," the woman's voice said.

"I'd like to speak to Patsy D'Amore, please."

"Who's calling?" the voice pleasantly asked.

"This is Jon D'Amore, his cousin from New Jersey."

A moment later he was on the phone.

"Hallo! Who'sa dis?"

"Patsy! It's Jon! Jon D'Amore. Rocky and Ann's son."

"Hey Giovanni, paisan. How are you?"

"Fine, Patsy, just fine!"

"What's the mada? You father, is he okay?"

"Yes. Everyone's fine. I just called to tell you I'm out here in L.A.!"

"Where?"

"I'm out at the airport. I wanted to make--"

"What airline? I'll send the car. It'll be there in a half hour."

I laughed, "No, thanks. That's okay. I just called to let you know I'll be in town for about a week. I was gonna make a reservation for dinner tonight and to see if you and your family would be around. I'm taking a cab to the hotel."

"No! You wait outside. I'll send a car for you. No D'Amore is gonna stay at no hotel! Where are you? What airline?"

"I'm at United."

"Whatta you wearing? How'sa my driver gonna know you?"

"What am I wearing?" I shrugged my shoulders. I didn't know what to tell him. "Jeans, glasses, I'm carrying two guitar cases--"

"Never mind. You just wait outside. He'll be there in a half hour. United? I'll see you when he bringsa you here. Ciao!"

He hung up.

Should I have told him my hair was halfway down my back?

I collected my suitcase and guitars and went out to the curb.

I had no idea what kind of car was coming. And I'm sure the driver had no idea who to look for.

It must have been more than an hour before a black Cadillac pulled up to the curb and the rear electric window went down. A face I never saw before looked at me.

"You Patsy's nephew?"

"You mean cousin?"

"Whatever."

"Yeah."

He said something to someone inside the car.

The driver got out and loaded my gear into the trunk without saying a word, then he opened the passenger door and motioned for me to get in.

As I slid into the back seat, I was kissed on the cheek by Patsy's older brother, Dominic Francesco D'Amore, who was better known as *Franklyn*. I barely remembered him from our 1968 trip. Good thing my father occasionally spoke about him.

Franklyn was 13 when he came to America with his Uncle Salvatore in 1906. Salvatore went to Boston and Franklyn found his way to Manhattan, and then to Little Italy's Mulberry Street. Though he wasn't very impressed with it when he got there, he spent the next decade working an assortment of jobs and going to a local boxing gym to work out. This caused his body to become very fit. During those years, Franklyn also made it a point to become an American citizen.

When the United States entered World War I, he signed up. In 1918, his battalion was nearly wiped out during a mustard gas attack. Franklyn was one of only a few survivors and spent time in a military hospital recovering from the assault and its effects. He was honorably discharged in 1919, and he returned to New York City.

It was then that he used his good looks and strong body to successfully break into vaudeville.

There were two other men in the car, but I wasn't introduced to them.

Franklyn immediately asked me about the East Coast D'Amores, and for the rest of the ride he proceeded to tell me stories about how he brought Patsy over from Italy in 1922. At the time, Patsy was 20 and Franklyn was 30. He spoke of how my grandfather, Giovanni D'Amore, picked Patsy up after he passed through the immigration process on Ellis Island and took him to the family's apartment in Union City.

"You father, *Carmenuche*, he wasn't even born yet," he laughed.

Franklyn continued performing in vaudeville and Patsy went to work in one of the hundreds of pizzerias scattered throughout Brooklyn and Manhattan's Little Italy.

By the early 1930s, Franklyn was successfully touring the vaudeville and burlesque circuit, making great money *and* a name for himself in the industry. During a tour on the west coast, he found happiness in the movie industry and the warmer, sunnier, more profitable climate of the orange groves and farms of Los Angeles and the San Fernando Valley.

In 1939, as one of Franklyn's tours brought him back to Jersey, he collected his younger brother, who by now had his own pizzeria on Avenue U in Brooklyn. They kissed my grandparents and 11 of the 12 children my grandmother would eventually have, and just like Horace Greeley advised...they went *west!*

As the Cadillac cruised up La Cienega Boulevard to Sunset Boulevard, I told the driver the name and address of my hotel and that I'd like to check in and drop off my guitars and luggage.

"Patsy wants you to stay at his house," Franklyn said.

"That's very nice, but the hotel is part of my contract. It's not costing me anything and it's within walking distance of the studio I'll be working at."

"*Hey!* We said '*No!*'" he barked. "If you gotta go someplace, you let me or Patsy know and a car will take you there. Now, how'sa you father? Is he still with the union?"

I guess that was about as far as I was taking *that* conversation.

"He's fine. Everyone is fine. And yeah, he's still with the union. But he's the vice president now."

When the car pulled up to the corner of Yucca and McCadden and then into the driveway of The Villa Capri, the two unnamed passengers got out first, I followed and Franklyn followed me. One of them opened the restaurant door, the second went in. As Franklyn and I entered, Patsy, who was 72 at the time, rose from the table I would come to know as "*Patsy's Table*," and sauntered over to give me a hug and a kiss.

"Giovanni! How are you? You hungry?"

From that moment on, Patsy and his wife, Rose, were my west coast parents, and Joey and Phyllis were the older brother and sister I never had. They made it so that whenever I returned to Los Angeles, it was like coming home.

Over the next 15 months Patsy, Franklyn and one of their old buddies, Antonio, would take me along for walks around the neighborhood in Studio City and Hollywood and reminisce about *the old days* while throwing around names like Ben Siegel, Jack Dragna, Mickey Cohen, Dominic Brooklier, Johnny Stompanato, Sam Giancana and Johnny Roselli.

In his broken English, Patsy would tell me, "...we useta go ta Santa Monica. Tony Canero hada gambla boat called *The Rex*. Lotsa fun. Lotsa fun."

He always smiled as he recalled his nearly four decades in Los Angeles.

"*Madone!*" he'd say as he waved his hands in the air, "Whata fun we use-ta have-a-here."

They'd talk about nights at The Villa Capri in the '50s and '60s, like when a bunch of wise guys would be sitting at a table and one of them would get called to the phone. The mobster would come over to Patsy and ask if a certain person had an unpaid tab. Patsy would go into the office, check his records and come back to say either yes or no. If the answer was yes, the wise guy would slide a couple of hundreds off of a roll, hand it to Patsy and say, "This should take care of it. He won't be back no more."

Patsy's stories would *always* end with a shrug and a laugh.

Every day in California was a beautiful day for me...until one Friday night in August of 1975 when I was working on a session in San Francisco. I returned to my friend Bill's apartment to see a message he had taken from my father. It simply said, "Call right away."

Something had to be wrong. He *never* called me when I was away.

It was around one in the morning New Jersey time when I called and woke him.

He picked up the phone, but didn't say anything.

The first words out of my mouth were, "What's the matter, Pop?"

"Where are you?" he asked.

"San Francisco. Why? What's the matter?"

"Can you get down to Los Angeles tomorrow?"

"I don't know. I'm working here. *What's the matter?*" I asked with more urgency.

"Rose called. Patsy died. He had a heart attack."

I went silent.

"Can you go there tomorrow? We'd like you to represent the family."

"Yeah," I said, barely audibly. "Yeah, of course. I'll leave first thing in the morning."

"Call me when you get there."

"Yeah," I said as I hung up.

I turned to Bill, who had no idea what was going on, and said, "I don't even have a suit with me." I spent the rest of the night sitting in his living room talking about the great times I spent with Patsy, a man fifty-one years my senior.

I called Hughes Airwest and made a reservation to fly into Burbank on the first morning flight.

When I got to Patsy's house around ten-thirty on Saturday, the place was already filled with flowers and people to comfort the family. I was told his body wasn't going to be laid out until later that evening and then buried on Monday morning.

During the afternoon, Phyllis took me shopping for a few suits. While they were being altered, we drove to Beverly Hills for a haircut, after which my waist-length hair was now slightly below my ears.

I called my father when we returned to the house.

"Your cousin Jerry wants you to call him," he said.

"Huh?"

"Take this number. Call around noon your time on Tuesday. That's when he'll be there."

I grabbed a pen and wrote it down as he rattled it off.

201-865-8066.

My father continued, "And he said to *come around* sometime."

I knew what he meant. To *come around* meant to reverse the last four digits to 6608. It was one of the ways Jerry, my father and the other guys would keep the numbers secret just in case anyone else was listening in on the line.

By the area code and prefix I knew it was a Hudson County number.

"I'll call you when I get back to San Francisco. I have to finish the session I left," I said while wondering why Jerry wanted me to call him.

"Okay, just make sure you call him on Tuesday."

After attending the wake that evening we went to The Villa Capri, where a continuous stream of people came by to pay their respects to Patsy's wife and children.

When I woke up at the Studio City home on Sunday morning the caterers were setting up a brunch buffet in the living room and dining room like I'd never seen before.

By 10 o'clock people started coming by. We spent Sunday afternoon and evening at the funeral parlor and repeated the previous night's gathering later at the restaurant.

Little did I know that when I woke up on Monday, the day of Patsy's funeral, it would be *another* one of those days I'd never forget.

A limo pulled into the driveway to take us to the funeral mass at Saint Charles Church on the corner of Moorpark Street and Lankershim Boulevard in North Hollywood, which would be followed by the cemetery. As we were heading for the car, Rose asked me to wait at the house as she was still expecting a few people who were flying in, and a phone call or two. She gave me the keys to the house and to Patsy's Caddie, and told me to meet them at the church.

As the limo pulled away I heard the phone ring. I ran to the living room and picked it up.

"Hello?"

"Hello. Joey?" the caller asked.

"No, this is Joey's cousin, Jon."

"Jon, I'd like to speak to Rose."

This voice sounded *very* familiar.

"I'm sorry, but they just left for the funeral. I'll be seeing her in about a half hour. Can I take a message?"

"Yeah. Just tell her Frank called."

Now I knew whose voice it was!

"Hello...Mr. Sinatra," I stuttered into the phone. "It's nice to speak with you. *I'm from New Jersey, too!*"

Christ, how I hated when people would come up to me and say stuff like that.

"Yeah? I'm here playing the Garden State Arts Center for a couple of days."

"Down on the Parkway? Yeah, I know it. I'm a musician."

More stupid banter.

"That's nice, kid. Listen, tell Rose I can't get to L.A. for the funeral because of this gig. But if there's anything she needs, or if there's anything I can do, she knows who to call in Palm Springs. Okay?"

"Yes sir. Absolutely."

"Okay. Bye."

I tried to get in, "*My mother was born and raised in Hoboken,*" but he had already hung up. Good thing.

I just spoke to Frank Sinatra!

Now to *anybody*...that would be exciting enough. But to an Italian from Hudson County, which also happens to contain his hometown of Hoboken, speaking to Sinatra was an *honor.*

Just then the doorbell rang. It was the out-of-towners.

As I drove up to the front of the church there was a line of limousines, at least 30 of them behind the hearse and three flower cars. Behind the limos was a continuous line of Caddies, Benzes', Bentleys, Lincolns and Rolls-Royces.

I dropped off the visitors and found a parking space three blocks away. Once I got to the church I was quickly led to the front pew and seated with Franklyn, Rose, Phyllis and Joey.

As we followed the casket out, I got my first good look at the attendees. It seemed like every mover-and-shaker-du-jour was there.

Outside, I started the three block walk to Patsy's Cadillac.

"Where are you going?" Phyllis asked.

"To the car. It's down this way. I'll follow the procession to the cemetery."

"No! You're riding with us in the limo. We'll send someone for the Caddie later."

I really *was* a part of this family.

There was a motorcade of fifty to sixty cars and limos going to the cemetery, and about a dozen motorcycle cops stopping traffic along the route. As we rode, I told Rose about the call from Sinatra.

The ceremony at the cemetery was short. I did my best to comfort Rose and Phyllis while Franklyn and Joey met with the scores who came to pay their final respects to Patsy.

As the line of people passed before us, I found myself deep in thought about Patsy, and how he took me into his heart...simply because we were family. He and his wife made me feel as if I always had a place in their home...and at the restaurant...whenever I came to town.

In the time that I had spent with him I had grown to love and admire the man.

I *also* realized that with Patsy's death came the end of an era. It was the end of a special time in my life...and in the lives of many of Hollywood's elite.

We spent the rest of the day at the house and went back to The Villa Capri for dinner.

I didn't wake up until 11:30 on Tuesday morning.

I washed my face, had a cup of coffee and waited for noon. Then I dialed 201-865-6608.

It only rang once.

"Yeah?"

I recognized Taz's voice, but it was best not to mention names during these calls.

"Hi. It's me. Is he there?"

"Yeah, kid. Hold on."

I was just shy of 22 and they were still calling me "*kid.*" I hated that.

I heard Taz say, "Your cousin," as he handed the phone to Jerry.

"Hey, *Juan!*"

That was the first time Jerry called me Juan...and from then on, he almost *always* did...especially when we spoke on the phone.

"Yeah," I laughed at hearing it. "How you doin'?"

"Good, thanks."

"What's the matter?" I asked.

"Nothing. Why?"

"My father said you wanted me to call."

In typical Jerry-fashion and with just the right amount of Jersey attitude and humor, he said, "What's the matter? I can't have my cousin call?"

"But I'm out in L.A.! I thought there was a reason...?"

"You're out there for Patsy's funeral, right?"

"Well, yeah. I was in Frisco when I found out, but I'm flying back up tonight to finish the session I was doing."

"We, you know, the family, think it was a nice thing you did. You know, goin' there and representing us and all," he said.

"Well...they're very nice to me, and we've all gotten very close over the last year. And *I got to talk to Sinatra on the phone yesterday!*"

"No shit? We went to see him last night at the Arts Center."

"Yeah. He told me he was playin' there."

"Don't you have a birthday comin' up?" he asked from out of the blue.

Seeing as we saw each other or spoke on the phone on that one day a year for as long as I could remember, I thought it was odd that he asked.

"Yeah, in eleven days. On the twenty-ninth. You know that."

"How old are you gonna be?"

"Twenty-two. You know *that*, too."

"Where you gonna be? That's a Friday, right?"

"I don't know. I guess I'll be back in Jersey."

"Why don't you stay in California, then meet me in Vegas on your birthday. I'll take you to dinner. Stay with me for a few days," he said.

It sounded good to me. I knew I didn't have any sessions booked for another three weeks.

"Okay. I'll finish my work up north by the weekend, then I'll come down to L.A. and stay here until the twenty-ninth."

"I'll have my travel agent send you a ticket from L.A. to Vegas for the afternoon of the twenty-ninth."

"Thanks, that's great. But...make the flights through Burbank. It's closer and easier."

"Twenty-two, huh? I'll make this one special for you. Oh, by the way, what kind of clothes do you have with you? That rock 'n' roll hippie stuff?"

"Well, yeah...except for the three suits I just bought the other day. You're gonna love this...I cut my hair, too."

"*This I gotta see!*" he laughed. "Do me a favor, be wearing a suit when you get to Vegas. I'll be with some people I want you to meet."

I shrugged, "Yeah. Sure."

"When your plane lands, take a cab to The Frontier. When you get there, go to the desk and tell them who you are and they'll know to put your stuff in my room."

I gave him the Studio City address and told him I was looking forward to seeing him.

Later that afternoon I took Rose, Phyllis and Joey out for lunch before they dropped me off at Burbank Airport for my trip up to Frisco. Actually, I never wanted to leave L.A.

After Bill picked me up in San Francisco, I dropped my gear off at the apartment and we took a walk along the Embarcadero. I told him of Patsy's funeral, my short but memorable conversation with Sinatra, and my upcoming birthday trip to Vegas with my cousin and Godfather, Jerry.

As we were able to do back then, it wasn't long before we'd run into a couple of attractive ladies that we would wind up wining and dining, and usually end up in an apartment smoking killer weed and having a foursome or swapping partners at some point during the early hours of the morning. Hey, it was the mid '70s, and in San Francisco it was like the '60s were still hanging on.

I spent the rest of the week working in the studio finishing the job I left behind. The last thing I needed was to get lectures from my manager and agent about not being reliable. They usually started with, "Do you have *any* idea how many young punks are out there just waiting to take your job? If it weren't for me..." Blah, blah, blah.

But, they *did* keep me working. And it wasn't that long ago that *I* was one of those young punks that took somebody's place because he decided to spend more time with a vial of coke, a spoon or straw up his nose and a tall blonde trophy-wife.

As anticipated, by Friday afternoon I finished my recording responsibilities, so Bill and I hung around the city until he took me to the airport on Sunday afternoon.

When the plane touched down in Burbank I was happy to see Phyllis waiting at the gate. We threw my luggage and guitars into the back of her Mustang convertible and headed for Studio City.

I was feeling more and more at home in Los Angeles.

On Monday, Phyllis took the day off from her job at the CBS Television

City studios to take me shopping. Vegas would require more *hip* and less *hippie* attire.

It was 1975...remember leisure suits?

When she asked me what I was looking for, I told her, "Since I'm gonna be hanging with the boys from Hudson County, I guess I'm gonna need some black silk shirts, Italian loafers...is there anywhere I can pick up some extra chest hair?"

She didn't get it.

Tuesday came and everyone went to work. It was the first time I had ever been in the Studio City house alone for the day. Rose left me the keys to Patsy's Caddie, but instead I decided to go for a walk around the neighborhood using the same path Patsy, Franklyn, Antonio and I had taken many times before.

I walked for a couple of hours before realizing that the early afternoon sun was directly overhead, and decided to spend the rest of the day back at the house in the pool.

I found a rock station on the radio and turned on the outside speakers, then took a pitcher of vodka and orange juice and a bowl of fruit to the backyard, stripped and made myself comfortable on one of the chaise lounges that were scattered around the pool.

Somewhere around 3:30 I lit a joint, and as Hendrix played *May This Be Love* in the background I realized that this was where I wanted to spend the rest of my life.

The temperature was easily in the mid-80s as the sun started to go behind the tall spiked Cypress trees and the Hollywood Hills.

The phone next to the lounge chair rang. It was Phyllis. I was drunk, stoned, naked and dripping in Hawaiian Tropic Coconut Oil. This was not the time for me to converse.

"What are you up to?" she asked.

"Laying by the pool...listening to some music," I figured there was no need to go into *too much* detail, "...and watching the sun go behind those trees."

"This is the time of day for it," she said.

"You know, I can actually *feel* the sun going down. Can *you* feel the sun go down?" I asked.

But before she could answer, I sat up and actually thought a light bulb went on above my head.

"Can you feel the sun go down!" I repeated, but not asking it as a question. "That's a great title!" I said to a confused Phyllis as she listened to my vodka-and-pot induced rambling. "Isn't that a great name for a song?"

"I guess," was her only response. "Listen, I was wondering if you wanted to come to dinner with me tonight. I'm meeting my friend Linda from work, and I thought you'd like to meet her."

I knew I'd soon be hungry, and I always liked hanging out with Phyllis anyway. It didn't matter to me that one of her friends was going to be there.

"Okay. What time?"

"Around seven-thirty. Meet us at Viva Fettuccini on LaBrea."

"Cool. Later."

As soon as we hung up I walked to the baby grand that was in the front living room, wiped the coconut oil off my hands and laid a towel on the piano bench. Then I found one of Patsy's memo pads, wrote *Can You Feel The Sun Go Down* along the top and spent the next hour sitting naked at the piano and writing the chord structure, melody and lyrics. Of all the songs I had previously called original, this was the first that I really believed *had* something.

I was right. A year later it was used as the theme song in a screenplay written by the international journalist, Tom Sullivan.

By six-thirty I had straightened out and sobered up.

I admired my lineless tan as I stepped out of the shower and stood in front of the mirror. I dressed, went out to the backyard and took a few hits on a joint, then walked into the front living room to run through *Can You Feel The Sun Go Down* again and again and again.

I left the house by 7:15 and pulled Patsy's Cadillac out of the driveway onto Canton.

I decided to take the scenic trip, so I made a left on Laurel Canyon and went over the mountain just to pass Frank Zappa's log cabin. Though I was in the music business and working with "names" in the industry, there were times when I was still just a fan.

It wasn't long before I was on LaBrea and in front of Viva Fettuccini. As the valet pulled the car away, I could see Phyllis and her friend sitting under the awning with a bottle of wine in an ice bucket.

"Jon, I'd like you to meet Linda Rossi."

I took her hand and said, "Hello, Linda. It's very nice to meet you."

She was 24 years old with shoulder-length brown hair and blue eyes. Since she was sitting, I had no idea what the rest of her looked like.

"It's nice to meet you," she replied. "Phyllis told me a lot about you."

I looked over to Phyllis. "All good! It was all good! I promise!" she protested.

I was starving, so after a few minutes of small talk I asked them if we were ready to order.

Linda reached for the bottle. I stopped her and slid it out of the ice bucket to fill their glasses.

"And he's a gentleman too?" she asked Phyllis with a smile, then continued, "Well, we've been sitting here for about an hour, and this is our second bottle. So you've got some catching up to do."

I decided not to mention that I had already been wasted earlier in the day.

We proceeded to knock off another two bottles of Chablis and laughed through dinner and whatever the topic of conversation turned to.

At one point Linda laughed so hard I saw something fly from her face and land right in her glass of wine.

"Hey! I can't see!" she nervously said. "Something's wrong with my eye!"

"Do you wear tinted contacts?" I asked.

"Yes! Why?" she answered.

"One of them just popped out and landed in your wine."

There was Linda, pleasantly drunk...one brown eye and one blue eye, poking her finger in her wine glass. Of course, the lens was quite easy to find, since those were the days of *hard* contacts. It wasn't difficult to see the small blue disk at the bottom of her Chablis.

"I can't put it back in until I clean it, and I didn't bring my glasses with me," she said as she popped out the remaining one from her other eye and put them in a lens canister.

"No problem. I'll drive you home," Phyllis said.

"Where's your car, Linda?" I asked.

"I left it at CBS and came here with Phyllis."

"Oh," I said, thinking nothing of it.

Then she looked at me and said, "But I'd like *you* to drive me home. Is that possible?"

I looked at Phyllis. She just shrugged her shoulders and smiled.

"If that's what you'd like," I answered.

"I'll pick you up in the morning on my way to work," Phyllis assured Linda.

When the bill came, I grabbed it. There was no way I was going to let Phyllis pay for a meal. Not after the countless gourmet lunches and dinners I had at The Villa Capri, or the slices of pizza at their stand at The Farmer's Market that her parents never let me pay for.

As we walked to the curb to wait for our cars I noticed Linda was a few inches taller than me...and had a body I found hard not to stare at. After more laughing, Phyllis kissed us both on the cheek, got in her Mustang and drove away.

While we waited for the valet to bring the Caddie, I asked Linda where she lived.

"I have an apartment in Hollywood, on Flores. Not very far. Are you busy? Do you have someplace else to go tonight?"

"No. Actually, I don't have anything to do until Friday."

"What's Friday?"

"It's my birthday, and I'm meeting another one of my cousins in Vegas for a few days."

"Your birthday? Well then, let me give you a birthday kiss!"

Before I could say anything, she pressed up against me and planted a delicious kiss on my lips while grinding her body, which I had noticed to be quite attractive once she rose from the table, against mine.

Just then the car pulled up. The valet opened my door, but I stayed at the curb and opened the passenger door.

"You *are* a gentleman, aren't you?"

I just smiled, shut the door after she slid in and walked to the other side. I handed the valet a couple of bucks and put the car in drive.

We continued to talk and laugh during the ride. She was right, it wasn't far. We were there within ten minutes.

I parked in front of the apartment house and walked her to the door.

"It was very nice to meet you. Maybe we can get together when I get back from Vegas," I said.

"Aren't you going to come in?"

"It's around ten. Don't you have to get up for work?"

"What's *that* have to do with anything? I'd like you to come in and see my place."

You don't have to tell a nearly-22-year-old-musician *that* twice.

As we walked into the living room she turned on some music and told me she'd be right back.

"I'm going to clean these contacts. I won't be long."

"Take your time. I'll be right here," I answered.

She disappeared into her bedroom as I scanned her sparse record collection.

As promised, she reappeared several minutes later. But I wasn't ready for her entrance.

She slithered into the living room in a white, see-through nightgown and panties.

I sat down on the sofa as she leaned across me to turn out the lamp and then went around the room lighting strategically placed candles.

Of course, I was sitting there...*smiling*.

She then went over to the stereo, turned off the music, faced me and began to do a rendition, and quite well I might add, of Marilyn Monroe's "*Happy Birthday*" to JFK.

Ahhhh...Hollywood.

Needless to say, when Phyllis called Linda in the morning to say she was on her way, Linda told her not to bother stopping by as she wasn't going to work that day. Nor did she go to work the rest of that week. The only time we left the apartment was to find a restaurant...and buy more candles.

Thursday evening I took Linda, Rose, Joey and Phyllis back to Viva Fettuccini to thank them *all* for their hospitality.

On Friday, Linda and I celebrated my one-minute-before-noon birth in her jacuzzi with a shot of tequila and a joint. At the precise moment, she sat up, raised her breasts above the water, looked at me and winked. She reached over, grabbed the salt shaker and sprinkled some on her left nipple...then squeezed a lime on the right one.

"Here you go, birthday boy," she seductively cooed.

I immediately reacted by filling my shot glass, sliding in between her legs, licking the salted nipple, downing my shot and running my tongue all over her lime covered breast.

Around 1:15, we threw my bags in her car and left for Burbank Airport. I was on my way to meet Jerry.

"You look very nice in that suit," she said as we turned off Hollywood

Way into the entrance of the airport.

"Well, it's for my cousin Jerry. He said he wants me to meet some people he's doing business with, and that I should be in a suit when I get there."

"Oh? What does your cousin do?" she asked.

Hmmmm. Interesting question. How was I going to answer that one?

"He's a consultant," I replied.

"For what?"

"I'm not really sure."

"Will I see you again?"

"After Vegas, I'll be back for a day or two before headin' to Jersey." Then I smiled at her and said, "I have another L.A. session booked in a few weeks, so one way or the other, we'll get together."

She smiled back.

When she pulled the car to the curb, I took my two pieces of luggage from the trunk and kissed her.

"Happy birthday...and call me," she sighed as she put the car in gear and drove away.

I smiled, handed the bags and five dollars to the bell cap and said, "I'm goin' to Vegas!"

Round 4

The flight from Burbank to Vegas took less than an hour.

As the plane passed through the mountains all I could see was desert on both sides with the odd tract of homes here and there. But when we banked to get lined up with the runway, The Strip came into view.

I'd been to Vegas once before. During the cross-country drive with my parents in 1968, we stopped here for a couple of nights. At some point we even went to The Frontier Hotel & Casino to see Diana Ross and The Supremes.

Now, seven years later, I was going back to the same hotel to meet Jerry and celebrate my twenty-second birthday.

As the plane touched down, everyone applauded.

Now, I had seen that happen whenever a flight was bumpy or had problems, but there was none of that during this one. I asked the stewardess what the applause was for.

"They *always* do that when they get to Vegas," she answered.

"You're kidding. Why?"

"Have you ever been here before?" she asked.

"Not really. Once as a kid."

"Are you a gambler?"

"Not really."

"Are you here on business?"

I laughed, "No. Not really."

"Well, if the gambling bug gets you, and if you ever fly out this way again, believe me, you'll be applauding when you land in Las Vegas."

I still didn't get it.

The plane came to a halt and I looked out the window. I was surprised at the relatively small size of McCarran International Airport. As they rolled the steps up to the plane, I remember laughing and commenting to whomever was sitting next to me that this airport still didn't have the motorized ramps that come out to the plane from the terminal.

The hatch opened and the cool interior air was sucked out as the hot, dry desert air filled the cabin.

It was around three in the afternoon and the sun wasn't just hot, it was scorching. It must have been at least 100 degrees on that late August day. By the time I reached the tarmac I was sweating under my suit jacket and had to loosen my tie and undo the top button.

The baggage was unloaded and I was in an air-conditioned cab on my way to The Frontier in record time.

The first big-name hotel as we hit The Strip was The Hacienda. Then came The Tropicana, The Aladdin and The Dunes. As we approached Caesars Palace I remembered it was the newest of the hotels when we were here in '68. But now, diagonally across the street from it was the largest hotel I had *ever* seen.

It was the new MGM Grand.

It was the tallest structure in Vegas, and so massive that besides the 100 yard long casino filled with blackjack, craps, roulette, poker and baccarat tables, it had its own underground mall, a movie theater, a spa, a jai-alai fronton *and* an arena used for championship boxing matches and rock concerts.

As we drove past it I said to the cab driver, who appeared to be an old local, that I would come back here someday soon and stay at the Grand.

Just once.

Just to say I did it.

He looked at me in the rear view mirror and said, "Not unless you book it six months in advance, pal. That place has been sold-out and jammed since the day they opened!"

"Oh well," I shrugged and sighed.

Little did I know that less than a year later, Jerry, Mike, Taz and a few of the other people I was about to meet would be calling me '*The Phantom Of The Grand.*'

As the cab pulled into the driveway of The Frontier, the doorman opened my door and a bellman took my two pieces of luggage from the trunk.

"Do you have a reservation, sir?"

"Yeah…I think."

He led me to a specific registration counter where I was greeted with a friendly smile from the attractive girl standing behind it.

"Good afternoon, sir. Do you have a reservation?"

"Not under my name, but I'm here to meet someone and check into his room."

"And his name is...?"

"Jerry...er...Gerald D'Amore."

After a moment of going through a list, she looked at me and said, "Well, it looks like Mr. D'Amore is expecting more than just *you* this weekend, sir."

"What do you mean?" I asked.

"Mr. D'Amore has five rooms under his name."

"Five?"

"And you are...?"

"Jon D'Amore."

"Yes, you're on the list."

"Well, which room is *he* in? That's where I'll put my bags," I told her.

"It appears that when he registered, he signed for all of the rooms and took the keys for each of them. I'm afraid all I can do is give you the room numbers. You can call him from a house phone and then tell the Bell Captain which room you would like your bags sent to. Mr. D'Amore will have your room key for you."

"That works for me. Thank you," I responded.

She wrote down the room numbers.

I thought it was odd that none of them were near one another. They were scattered throughout the hotel on several floors.

I went to a house phone and called each of the rooms. No one answered in any of them.

I randomly picked one of the room numbers and gave the bellman five dollars to deposit my bags there.

Now I had to find Jerry.

It was the first time I was actually in a casino and of age to do something about it. The downside was that I didn't know *anything* about gambling. My father was very cool about that. He didn't gamble. He didn't even bet on football games. From years of working in those backroom casinos, my father always knew that the odds are with the house. Even the best gamblers lose.

It only took me a few minutes to find him. He came walking through the lobby with a five-man entourage in tow. This is how I'll always remember my Godfather, Jerry.

At the time he was 38 years old, 5'10, with a medium build, black hair and a van dyke with a little gray in it. It was when he had the van dyke that he was often referred to as '*The Beard.*'

He was wearing light beige loafers of supple leather, silk socks, tailored beige slacks, a silk shirt with the top three or four buttons opened and the standard yet tasteful array of gold chains, rings, watch and bracelet. But what set Jerry apart from the crowd were his canes. He owned an assortment of canes...and when the weather and occasion permitted, he would also wear a cape. He owned an entire collection of them.

I didn't recognize any of the other men that followed him. But it was obvious *he* was in charge.

I knew not to call his name from thirty yards away, so I headed in his direction. It took him a little longer than usual, but his eyes lit up when he recognized me. It must have been the shorter hair and suit.

"Juan!"

"Hi, Jer!"

We hugged and kissed. Typical Italian male stuff.

"Where are your bags?" he asked.

"I checked them into one of your rooms."

"Which one?"

I told him the number.

He pulled a list out of his pocket, looked at it and then turned to the guys behind him. "Who's got the extra key to Dolan's room?"

One of them came forward and replied, "I do."

"Where is he?" Jerry asked.

"He went over to The Trop and said he'd be back by four-thirty."

We all looked at our watches. It was 4:15.

"Did you unpack yet, Juan?"

"No. I just had the bellman put them in there. I haven't even been *in* the room yet. Why? What's wrong? Who's Dolan?"

"Nothing's wrong. It's just that...that's Tommy Dolan's room, and he don't like roommates. I've made arrangements for you in another hotel anyway. A room under your own name. I'll take you over there and get you set up."

He went to the bell captain's desk, slipped him a few bucks and within ten minutes my two bags were being thrown into the trunk of another cab.

Before we got in, Jerry turned to one of the guys and said, "Tell Taz I'm with my cousin. Have him get Dolan and meet us around six in the lounge. He'll know where."

We got into the back of the cab and he told the driver to make a right as we pulled out of the driveway.

"Is Tommy Dolan the guy I'm wearing this suit for?" I asked.

"One of them. While you're here...dress up a bit. Can you do that for me?"

"Anything for you, Jer."

After a short distance, Jerry told the driver to make a left into the driveway. My eyes lit up. We were going to The MGM Grand. *Happy-fuckin'-birthday to me!*

"I hope you don't mind. I figured you wouldn't want to be around The Frontier with me and those guys. You'll have a better time here anyway. I'm gonna be tied up with business. Besides, Mike is staying here...to look after you."

"I heard this place is booked solid six months in advance. When did you make the reservation?" I asked.

"Yesterday."

I smiled, shook my head, then asked, "So...what kind of business?"

"Later."

"Where's Taz?" I asked.

"Where I need him. In the room right next to mine."

"But I saw a list of all of the rooms that were registered under your name. And none of them were next to one another."

"What makes you think I'm staying in a room under *my* name?"

"Oh," I said, matter-of-factly.

The cab pulled under the giant marquee. Jerry threw the driver a ten for a three dollar trip, and the bellman grabbed my luggage as we headed inside. I headed for the registration counter, but Jerry grabbed my arm and led me to the roped off VIP desk as he said, "Don't say anything. Just smile and go along."

The pretty Asian girl behind the counter greeted me with the same smile I received at The Frontier.

"Good afternoon, gentlemen. Can I help you?"

"Yes," Jerry said to her, "You have a reservation in the name of Jon D'Amore."

She looked at her list then looked at Jerry and said, "Yes Mr. D'Amore, here you--"

He cut her off.

"I'm not Mr. D'Amore. *This* is Mr. D'Amore," he said as he pointed to me.

She changed her focus to me and said, "The casino has been expecting you. I hope you had a good flight from New Jersey? At the request of the Casino Manager we've prepared a special suite for you. We hope you enjoy it. If there are any problems, or if there is anything I can do for you, please call me. My extension is here on my card."

She continued to smile as I signed the registration card. Then she handed me her card and two keys for room 2536.

"I'll have your bags taken to your room, and if you'll give me a moment I'll have a hostess show you around the hotel."

"Thank you," I said.

"That won't be necessary," Jerry interjected. "I'll show him around."

We both looked at him.

"Have you stayed here before, sir?" she asked.

He just smiled, thanked her for her help and led me away.

I nonchalantly gave him the second key to the room.

"Thanks," Jerry said. "I was gonna ask you for it anyway."

"Yeah, I sorta knew you would."

As we walked the length of the one hundred yard long casino and settled into a lounge at the farthest end overlooking the monstrous gaming field, something magical began to happen. It started when the cocktail waitress approached our table.

Jerry said, "I'll have a Chivas on the rocks, hon," before she asked what we wanted.

They both looked at me. I wasn't a drinker and my experience up to that point was primarily Bud, Bolla Soave, shots of tequila and the occasional vodka mixture. But I really wanted to do it right.

"Same for me, please," I responded.

As she walked away, we looked down at the people gambling at the tables.

"Ever been to a casino, Jon?"

"No. It never interested me."

"Ever play craps or blackjack?"

"When I was touring. We'd play twenty-one backstage and in the hotel rooms. Nothing big. Probably not even the right rules."

"Your father never taught you how to play craps?"

"Nope."

Jerry smiled and said, "I think you're gonna have a good time while you're here."

"Well, that's the plan, isn't it?"

"Hey! That's right! It's your birthday!"

He put a hand on each side of my head and pulled me to him. He kissed me on both cheeks and began reminiscing about seeing me in the hospital nursery the day I was born, and becoming my Godfather a month later.

"It's funny, isn't it?" he said as he sat back and looked at me.

"What do you mean?" I asked.

"How you wound up with opposite ends of the spectrum for Godparents."

I sat back and laughed, "Yeah, that *is* funny."

Though *he'd* never admit it, it was clear he was referring to the different sides of the law between himself and our Aunt Pat...my God*mother*, my father's youngest sister, and only a few months older than Jerry.

In the late 1950s, Aunt Pat married a Newark Police Officer named David Toma. He became a detective and made a name for himself during the '60s as a big organized crime fighter.

In 1973 there was a TV movie made about his life, aptly titled "Toma," which led to a series. Tony Musante played Uncle Dave, and Susan Strasberg was Aunt Pat. After a couple of seasons Musante walked, claiming he was being typecast as an Italian detective, so the remaining "Toma" scripts were changed a bit and resold as "Baretta" for the actor, Robert Blake.

Obviously it was a bad career move for Musante. Though he continued to work, his star never seemed to shine as bright as it did during that period.

At the time Jerry and I were having this conversation, Uncle Dave was at the pinnacle of his popularity.

The waitress approached with our drinks.

"No! No! Get those out of here! It's my cousin's birthday. Bring us a bottle of Dom Perignon!" he said as he reached into his pocket, slipped a ten out of a roll covered with hundred dollar bills and sent her on her way.

"Whoa! Jerry! That's very nice, but you don't have to do that," I said.

He lowered his voice, leaned close to me and said, "Don't worry, Juan. It's free."

"What do you mean, '*It's free*?" I asked in an equally quiet tone.

"When she comes back with the bottle, show her your room key and sign your name on the tab. And put on a nice tip. *Always* leave a nice tip while you're here. Just write what you want to leave on the tab."

"Yeah, so...when I check out, who's gonna pay this bill?" I asked.

"The hotel is picking everything up," he answered.

"Huh?"

"I had the Casino Manager make your reservation. They think you're a high roller in from Jersey. So when--"

I cut him off and said, "*That's* why the girl at the desk asked if I had a good flight from Jersey?"

"Yep."

"But what happens when they see that I don't gamble? They're gonna charge me for everything!"

"Don't worry about it."

"What do you mean, don't--"

"I said don't worry about it. I'll take care of it." A sly smile came across his face. "By the time you leave here, you'll be a gambler...or at least they'll *think* you're a gambler!"

That was my cousin Jerry.

We then spent the next half hour speaking on a level at which we had never communicated before. We discussed my music career and the success I was achieving in the "session" community. He realized that while we hadn't seen each other very often over the last few years, he was no longer seeing me as this long haired, pot smoking, rock 'n' roll guitar playin' hippie that happened to be related to him.

And I was talking to him about a lot more than just his wife and two kids.

It seemed that because we had always related to each other on an older-cousin-younger-cousin basis, and we had never been outside of Hudson and

Bergen Counties together, our conversations were always family related.

The affiliation between Jerry, our fathers and Frank DeNike was never discussed. It was just accepted and dealt with quietly.

While we were sitting in the lounge of The MGM Grand on my twenty-second birthday, drinking my first bottle of Dom Perignon, I realized I was about to experience something that could possibly change the direction of my life…if I wanted it to.

A couple of years earlier Frank DeNike, Jerry's Godfather, had passed away of natural causes, which is saying something about the man's reputation and good standing in the underworld community. He had a heart attack and died in the arms of his beautiful, younger and dedicated wife May, as they were dancing at one of his union celebrations. The next day, Frank's torch of power was passed to Rocco Casiano.

Due to the relationship between Jerry and Frank DeNike, Jerry began stepping up the ladder as one of Rocco's closest associates and biggest money-makers.

And don't think Jerry didn't seize the opportunity.

"Come on, Jon. It's time to get you into your room, and we still gotta make dinner reservations. The guy I want you to meet should be here in about a half hour."

It was around 5:30 as we rose from our little table.

By now the ringing of the slot machines and the constant sound of the crowd, punctuated by the occasional roar of victory at one of the dozens of crap tables, was nothing more than background noise. I was happy to be a part of whatever Jerry had in store for me.

We walked over to one of the handful of gourmet restaurants that bordered the rear of the casino and approached the maître d's podium.

"You don't mind an Italian birthday dinner, do you?" he asked.

"What a surprise, huh?" I laughed.

The maître d' immediately shook Jerry's hand.

"Ciao, Mr. D'Amore!" he said with an Italian flair, "It's nice to see you again."

"Ciao, Stefano. Grazie. That's very nice of you to say." Jerry moved closer to him. "Stefano, can you give us a private table tonight for five, around seven o'clock?"

Stefano looked at the reservation book, then without raising his head he apologetically said, "I am very sorry, but we are completely filled...from six until nine-thirty. *Especially* the private tables." Then he raised his head with a smile. "But for you, Mr. D'Amore, I can make the exception."

Jerry took out his roll, handed me a fifty dollar bill and told me to go to a roulette table and put it on 22.

"I got a hunch. For your birthday," he said as he slyly smiled again. "I've got to take care of something. I'll meet you at the roulette table and then we'll go to your room."

It was obvious Jerry wanted to be alone for a couple of minutes, so I looked across the casino and spotted the closest roulette table. As I walked toward it I got caught up in the idea of putting fifty bucks down on one number just for the fun of doing it. I had *never* done anything like that before.

When I reached the table the ball had just fallen onto the wheel. I found an open spot and watched.

"Twenty-nine. Black twenty-nine. There is no winner on twenty-nine," the croupier said.

Twenty-nine. Today's date. My birthday!

I laid the fifty on twenty-two. Then something happened to me that had never happened before. My hands were sweaty. Is this what gambling does to you?

"All on twenty-two, sir?" the croupier asked.

"Yes."

He changed the bill into chips and slid them right onto the number.

"Good luck, sir."

More bets were being placed as the croupier spun the wheel and dropped the ball. I watched the ball begin to spin in a circle as I wiped my damp palms together.

I felt a hand on my shoulder. I turned around. It was Jerry.

"How we doin'?" he asked.

"Don't know yet."

The croupier slowly waved his hand over the table signaling that no more bets could be placed.

We waited for gravity to bring the ball down to the wheel.

Suddenly I noticed that my hands were dry. It was as if they were never wet to begin with. It was as if once Jerry stood next to me, it made everything all right.

My hands never got sweaty again after that…and I never questioned it. It's funny, some things you remember from the minute they happen… and don't know why.

"Twenty-two! Black twenty-two!" the croupier announced. "Pay the winner on the inside bet!"

We heard the words and looked down.

Jerry laughed and said, "That's *you*, Juan."

"Holy shit!" was my only response.

The croupier slid stacks of chips toward the center of the table, looked at me and asked, "Would you like to place another bet, sir?"

I looked at Jerry.

He said, "Put it all on twenty-nine!"

"Whoa! No!" I yelled. "That came out just before you got here. Don't do it!" I looked at the croupier and said, "No, thank you. I'll just take what you have there."

"And what about your original bet, sir?" the croupier asked.

"Yeah. I'll take that too!"

Jerry started laughing, "You're right! You're *not* a gambler…yet."

The croupier took back the roulette chips and gave me three gray $500 chips, two black $100 chips and two green $25 chips, plus another two $25 chips from the original bet.

"How much did we win, Jer?"

"Let's see? What did they give you?" He looked at the chips and counted. "There you go. Seventeen hundred and fifty dollars."

"What?" I gasped.

He said, "Thirty-five-to-one. Good odds, huh?"

"Good hunch," I laughed.

"I'm a gambler. And gamblers go with their hunches. Now tip the table. When you win that big, you tip the table."

"How much?" I whispered.

"Whatever you want."

I took one of the green chips and tossed it to the croupier as he spun the wheel and dropped the ball.

"Thank you," I said.

"Thank *you*, sir!" he responded.

As we walked away, I heard ball hit the wheel and the croupier yell, "Twenty-nine. Black twenty-nine. There is no winner."

I cringed as I handed Jerry the chips.

"What are you doing, Juan?"

"That's your money Jer. *You* told me what to bet. *You* won!"

He started laughing at me as we neared the elevators.

"No. Don't worry about this. This is nothing." He handed the chips back to me. "Use it to enjoy yourself around town for the next couple of days."

"I've got my own money. I don't want to take yours," I answered.

"Okay," he said with a laugh, "Give me back my fifty."

There was no arguing. I looked at him.

"Okay, you stubborn guinea bastard…here's a hundred." I handed him a black chip. "That's your fifty and a hundred percent *vig*."

We both broke out laughing.

The elevator doors opened and we got inside.

"Hit twenty-five, Juan."

It only took a few seconds before the doors opened and we were there. We stepped out of the elevator and turned right, reading the room numbers until we reached 2536.

I unlocked the door and swung it open.

"This is *my* room?" I asked with audible astonishment.

"Yep."

"This is un-fucking-believable!"

"Happy birthday, Juan."

We walked into the enormous sunken living room with its cathedral ceiling. The entire exterior wall was a window with a panoramic view of The Strip. The late afternoon sun bathed the walls with a warm and breathtaking array of colors. The room was decorated with two gigantic plush sofas and six chairs, a formal dining table, a bar with a sink and refrigerator, and the best of all…a baby grand piano in front of the window.

"I told them to give you a suite with a piano, just in case you got bored."

"Nice touch," I answered, thinking about how great *Can You Feel The Sun Go Down* would sound on it.

The bedroom was a hedonist's paradise. The bed was reminiscent of the one Dean Martin had in those Matt Helm movies. It was huge and round with all of the controls for the lights, television, radio, cassette deck and electric curtains all built into the curved headboard. The only thing it didn't do was vibrate or slip me into a pool-sized bathtub.

Jerry called my name and pointed to the circular mirror over the bed.

There were two bathrooms in the suite, but the one adjacent to the bedroom was enormous. It had a separate bathtub, jacuzzi and shower, each large enough for four people. And here I was in Vegas...with a place like this...on my birthday...with no female companionship.

Sure...I know how easy it is to get one, *especially* in Vegas. But I had a rule: Never pay for sex.

We walked onto the terrace and looked down at The Strip.

"So Jer...you gonna tell me what's going on?"

"Sure, but you've got a few days here. We'll spend some time together and talk."

"I haven't unpacked yet. Do I have time to put my stuff away?" I asked.

"Yeah. I've got to make a couple of calls. Go freshen up and we'll head back down to the casino in about twenty minutes."

He walked over to the telephone and sank into one of the sofas. His fingers tapped four digits. When someone answered he simply and softly said, "Twenty-five thirty-six," and then hung up.

I went into the bedroom and began to unpack the luggage that was delivered earlier.

When I was nearly finished getting myself together someone rang the doorbell. Jerry was still on another call in the living room, so I went to the door and opened it.

Standing in the doorway was a big familiar body with a friendly rubbery face. It was Mike Caruso.

"Happy Birthday, kid! How ya doin'?"

"Hey Mike! It's good to see you! I'm doin' fine."

"Wow! Look at you. You look great! I can't remember the last time I saw you in a suit with your hair this short."

"Ha ha. Very funny. Get in here," I said as I pulled him in.

Once inside we did the standard Italian hug and kiss.

"Nice place you got here," he said as he gave it the once-over.

"Yeah! Pretty wild, ain't it?"

"Well, this is where they put the big rollers. I'm down on fourteen with the regular folk."

I looked surprised and asked, "How come?"

"Well, normally I stay at The Trop. So I usually get a suite there. But I'm not here under my name, so..."

"Oh," I said.

I knew that wasn't unusual for these guys. There was no reason to ask him why.

"I guess you haven't spoken with your cousin about anything yet, huh, kid?"

"No. Not yet."

I knew not to ask Mike about it. I also knew that something was up... and *I* was going to be a part of it.

He went over to the pad next to the phone and wrote his room number.

"Here. I'm in fourteen-thirty. If you need me for anything, just dial that."

"Write down the name you're using too. Just in case I have to page you in the casino," I said.

"I don't think I need to write it down, I'm sure you'll remember it." Then he laughed and looked at Jerry. "I'm registered under Dave Toma."

I looked at him with a half-serious and half-comical expression.

"You're joking."

"No," he replied. "It was Jerry's idea. Obviously, there's more than one Dave Toma in the world. I don't have to be the famous one, right? Jerry just gets a kick out of using it from time to time."

"Yeah," I laughed, "I'm sure he does!"

In their *business*, Jerry was known for coming up with clever names, or *covers*, to use when they were pulling off one scam or another.

After a few minutes of socializing with Mike, Jerry finally hung up the phone and said, "Let's go. Tommy and Taz are on their way over."

As we were all prone to do, each of us walked to a separate mirror in the suite to check our appearance before we walked out the door.

Typical.

When we reached the casino I headed over to the cashier's cage to cash in my roulette winnings.

Within moments we were sitting in the same lounge Jerry and I had visited earlier.

As I would see over the next two years, this was to become one of our regular meeting places.

From our strategic perch overlooking the casino Mike spotted the two men we were waiting for. He motioned to Jerry.

As they made their way through the throng of Friday night gamblers,

Jerry leaned toward me and softly said, "This is the guy I'm doing things with out here."

"The guy with Taz?"

"Yeah," he answered.

"Who is he?" I asked.

"Tommy Dolan."

"Dolan doesn't sound very Italian to me," I said in a whisper.

"He's a friend of Casiano's. Tommy makes Rocco a shitload of money."

"Where's he from?" I asked.

"Bayonne."

"Trust him?"

Jerry paused and thought for only a second.

"No. The only people I want you to trust out here are me, Mike and Taz. But learn everything you can from the rest of these guys."

"Learn what?" I asked.

"Just watch."

They approached the table.

I stood up to greet Taz.

I reached out to shake his hand, but he grabbed me and crushed me against his massive and muscular body.

"Jesus! I didn't even recognize you! You look great, kid!" he said while I was still crushed against him.

"Jon," Jerry said while still sitting in the chair, "Meet Tommy Dolan."

After Taz let go of me and I was able to catch my breath, I said, "Nice to meet you, Mr. Dolan."

"Nice to meet you, kid. Call me Tommy," he said as he shook my hand.

The first thing anyone noticed about Tommy Dolan was his height and weight. He stood over six feet tall and had to weigh nearly 300 pounds. He reminded me of a light bulb...with the large bulbous end at the bottom.

After that, there were the obvious physical Irish traits. Except for a slight Vegas tan, he was very light skinned and had freckles that were fading into a dry wrinkled face that looked older than the 46 years it really was. He had blue eyes and reddish-brown unkempt hair that was starting to thin, with wisps of gray.

His voice was *very* deep and gruff, as if he took a piece of sandpaper to his voice box from time to time. But then, the fact that he chain-smoked could have had something to do with it.

I remember his hands. They didn't go along with this tall, obese Irish gangster from Hudson County. They were thin and soft, and his fingers were exceptionally long.

Unlike Jerry and *his* guys, Tommy wasn't concerned about his appearance. His slacks and sport jacket could have used a pressing months ago, and the polo shirt was too tight, which only accentuated his large stomach.

Within seconds a waitress came over and we ordered drinks. As before, I ordered whatever Jerry did.

Tommy and Jerry were speaking ear to ear as I told Mike and Taz about my short phone conversation with Sinatra.

The waitress was setting down our second round when Tommy leaned toward me and said, "Jerry tells me today's your birthday."

"Yep."

He leaned closer and asked, "Ever gamble?"

"No."

"Would you like to?" he asked with a big smile on his face.

I looked at Jerry. He nodded back to me.

"If I knew what I was doing? Sure," I answered as I returned my focus to Tommy.

"Don'tcha worry kid. I'll teach you."

"And he's one of the best," Jerry interjected.

I stood up and put my hand in my pants pocket. I felt the sixteen-hundred-and seventy-five dollars from my hit at the roulette table, plus the five hundred I brought with me.

"I've got some cash on me. Let's go!" I said.

They all started laughing.

"What's so funny?" I asked.

"Sit down!" they all said.

Tommy leaned toward me and quietly said, "Sure, we'll play. But we don't use *our* money. Rule Number One…Never use your money to gamble. *Always* use someone else's."

I didn't get it, and the look on my face showed it.

Tommy reached into his jacket pocket, took out a form and a pen and placed them in front of me. It was for a credit line at The MGM casino.

"Fill this out," he said as he handed me a pen.

I looked it over.

I looked at Jerry and said, "What name do you want me to use?"

"Your own," he said.

Whoa! I had to know more.

"Can I talk to you for a minute, Jer?"

We both stood up and went to a dark corner of the lounge.

"Jerry, that form wants my name, Social Security number, employer, bank account numbers, salary--"

He cut me off and said, "Don't worry about any of that. I'll fill it out with you."

"Mind telling me what's goin' on?" I asked.

"After dinner."

"Jerry, I--"

"What did I tell you before? Don't worry about it."

We went back to the table and Jerry sat next to me as I put only my name, address, date of birth and phone number on the form.

"That's all? They'll never give me a credit line with just that," I said as I signed my name at the bottom.

They all quietly laughed and told me not to worry about it. I handed the form and pen back to Tommy.

He finished his drink, stood up and said, "You guys go to the restaurant. I'll go take care of this and meet you there."

He folded the form, put it back into his jacket and walked away.

"Come on, Juan. It's time for your birthday dinner," Jerry said as I watched the big Irishman disappear into the crowd.

As we got up to leave, Jerry moved into position. This simply meant Taz was first, Jerry was in the middle and Mike would cover the rear.

I got to walk next to Jerry.

The maître d' was dealing with several couples at the podium when he saw Taz approaching. He stopped his conversation and walked toward the velvet rope with a, "Yes gentlemen, right this way."

He left the people at the podium and ushered us through the restaurant to one of several large private alcoves behind thick curtains.

As he held the chair for Jerry, he said, "I hope you'll find this table satisfactory. I've made all of the arrangements for your dinner, and if there's anything you need…just let me know."

"Yes, Stefano. We're expecting one more person. He should be here in a few minutes. Please show him where we are," Jerry said as he slid him a twenty.

"Of course."

"Oh! And Stefano, before you leave. This is my cousin Jon. He's staying at the hotel for a few days and he's new in town. If he--"

"Say no more." Stefano handed me his card and said, "If you need reservations at any of the restaurants here or at any of the other hotels, just call my extension and I'll take care of it for you."

Jerry smiled.

As Stefano walked through the curtains, a waiter entered through a door in the rear of the alcove to tell us about the evening's menu.

Ten minutes later, Stefano returned to the alcove with Tommy Dolan, who entered laughing.

"It's all taken care of," Tommy said as soon as Stefano left.

"How much?" Jerry asked.

"Twenty-five," said The Irishman.

"Good," Jerry replied…somewhat seriously.

I didn't know exactly what they were talking or laughing about, but I figured I'd be finding out soon enough.

For the next hour-and-a-half we ate a specially prepared gourmet meal, drank two bottles of Dom Perignon and a couple of bottles of wine that went for $100 each, and I listened to these guys talk about who hit for what at which casino.

The maître d' entered through the rear door and asked, "Gentlemen, are you ready for dessert?"

After getting nods from around the table, the door swung open and out came four showgirls, complete in their glittering, though very skimpy outfits, singing "*Happy Birthday.*" Stefano and the waiter carried a cake and placed it in the center of the table. Extra chairs were brought in and the girls sat next to me until we were finished eating our dessert. Then they each kissed me on the cheek, leaving their lip prints, and disappeared through the door.

"Was this why you sent me to the roulette table? Is this what you had to take care of when you were making the reservations?" I asked Jerry.

He just smiled.

"What about the hunch to play twenty-two?"

"The number was a hunch. *When* to play it? I had no idea."

I leaned over and kissed him on both cheeks.

When Stefano brought the nearly $1,500 bill, Jerry slid it to me and said, "Add a four hundred dollar tip to it and sign your name."

He saw me get nervous.

"Trust me," he calmly said, then put his hand on mine.

And I did…because for your Godfather, you'll do *anything*.

I shook my head, smiled and signed.

It was around 9:30 when we left the restaurant and found ourselves back at the lounge. Tommy went to a house phone and made a call to The Frontier. He was going to have a couple of *his* guys come over.

In the interim, Jerry started my education in gambling.

"You're gonna be playing craps tonight, Juan."

"You gonna be standing next to me?"

"Yep." He looked at me and smiled. "In about twenty minutes we're gonna go over to one of those tables. You're gonna look at the pit boss and say--"

I interrupted him and asked, "The pit boss?"

"You see the guys in the suits standing in the pits watching the crap tables?"

I looked over as he pointed them out.

"Yeah."

"When we get to the table, just tell one of 'em you want three thousand dollars from your line."

My eyes widened as I looked at Jerry.

"Don't worry." He smiled again. "He'll ask you your name and room number, and a couple of minutes later he'll come back with a marker."

"A marker?"

"It's an IOU. Just sign it."

"And then what?"

"Then they'll slide three grand in front of you."

"*Then* what?"

"That's when I'll tell you what to do. Just do whatever I say and I'll teach you as we go along. All you've got to worry about is the *pass line*."

"The pass line?" I asked.

"You'll see."

I just sat there and smiled.

Tommy returned to the table and said, "Bobby and Louie will be here in a few minutes." He turned to me and said, "Okay, here's what you've got to know before you get to the tables."

I leaned closer to him as he explained the basic rules of craps.

"You're gonna bet the pass line," he said.

"Yeah, so I hear," I answered as I looked at Jerry.

Tommy continued, "When the shooter takes his first roll and it's either a two, three or a twelve, you lose. If the first roll is a seven or an eleven, you win. If he rolls a four, five, six, eight, nine or ten on the first roll, that's the shooter's *point*, and he'll continue to roll until he either *hits* his point, and then you'll win, or if he rolls a seven *before* he hits his point, you'll lose."

"That's it?" I asked.

"That's it, kid."

"What about all the other numbers that he rolls before he wins or loses?"

"Those are *side bets*. Don't worry about side bets, *come bets, hardways, field bets, Big Six and Eights*, nothing. Just bet the pass line and back it up the way Jerry tells you to, and you'll do fine."

It seemed like a lot to remember…not to mention having to remember it fast and correctly. I knew I had to give these guys my undivided attention and listen to everything they were saying.

A few moments went by before Tommy turned to Jerry and said, "You'd better get to a table and start getting the kid's money before they get here."

A rush of adrenaline hit me as we stepped down into the casino. I was really going to be gambling for the first time in my life.

We walked around to at least a dozen tables before he picked one out.

"Is this the one you got *a feeling* for?" I asked.

He quietly laughed and said, "Nope. It's got the right minimum and the ends are open."

"Minimum?"

"Yeah. The size of the bet. Some tables have a five dollar minimum, some are ten, some are twenty-five."

"What's this one?" I innocently asked.

"A hundred."

I stopped in my tracks.

"A hundred bucks a *bet?*"

"Yep," was his simple response.

"And what do you mean about *the ends* being open?"

"That's where I like to stand. I can see everything that's happening around the table without moving my head," he said quietly.

The table was very active, but not too crowded. Jerry steered me to a spot at one of the ends. I called the pit boss over and did what Jerry told me to do. In less than five minutes there was $3,000 in black and green chips in front of me.

"Good luck, Mr. D," he said before he walked back into the pit.

"Mr. D. That's funny," I said as I laughed and turned to Jerry. "See! He didn't call me *kid*."

Jerry just smiled. He knew it bothered me, but it was a stigma I was stuck with, and there were more important issues to deal with at the moment. He had to teach me how to gamble.

The shooter was in the middle of a good roll. He eventually hit his point and I watched as chips were distributed to the winners and wiped away from the losers. I was quick to see that even when the shooter wins, *somebody* loses.

The stickman yelled, "They're comin' out!"

More people came to the table. It wasn't long before all of the spaces were filled.

"Okay, Juan…it's time to get to work."

"Cool. What should I do?"

"Put two hundred on the pass line," he ordered.

"Two hundred?"

I placed two black chips in the section in front of me marked *Pass Line*. The shooter rolled.

"Eleven. A winner! Pay the pass line."

The people at the table cheered.

I turned to Jerry and said, "We just won two hundred dollars!"

He smiled, looked down at the other end of the table and said, "Beginner's luck."

I went to pick up my winnings.

"Leave it," he said.

"Four hundred?"

"Yeah," he answered without looking at me. His eyes were fixed on all the action that was going on around the table.

"Coming out!" the stickman yelled again.

The shooter rolled.

"Six! An easy six. The point is six."

Apparently once a point is made, that's when the action *really* starts on a crap table. The dealers began placing bets as chips were tossed to them from all sides. I watched, but didn't understand *any* of the side bets.

"Okay," Jerry said, "Put another five hundred behind it."

"Huh?"

"That's called backing up the bet. You're laying odds that he'll roll the six."

"Nine hundred dollars?" I nervously asked.

Again…Jerry smiled.

With each roll of the dice I became more and more anxious. Jerry just watched the table.

After five or six passes, or rolls of the dice, the shooter rolled a seven.

"Seven. Craps. Take down the pass line," the stickman yelled.

As the dealer took away the chips, my mouth opened and I looked shocked.

"Shit!" I said.

Jerry just smiled and said, "Put another four hundred down."

I assumed Jerry had a system, or at least knew the odds. So I placed another four black chips on the pass line.

"New shooter coming out! Place your bets," the stickman announced.

Five new dice to pick from were placed in front of the next shooter as people called their bets while their chips were still in the air. It was all very exciting.

I looked over the table to determine the amount of money that was being bet. There was over five grand on the pass line alone. There were also a few people betting heavy on the *Don't-Pass Line*.

Don't-pass bets are the opposite of the pass line, except for the 12.

If the shooter crapped out on the come out roll by rolling a 2 or a 3, I lost and the don't-pass won. If the shooter rolled a 12 on the first roll, I lost but the don't-pass line didn't win *or* lose.

If the shooter rolled a 7 or 11 on the first roll, I'd win and the don't-pass would lose. If the shooter hit his point, I'd win and the don't-pass would lose, and if the shooter rolled a 7 instead of his point, I'd lose and don't-pass would win.

I saw betting the don't-pass line as betting *with* the house, because it would seem logical that more rolls would lose than win. It seemed to be a safe bet.

A little old lady picked up two of the five dice and laid another $100 chip down on her $200 pass line bet just before she rolled. Then she flung the dice into the air toward my end of the table.

"Seven! Pay the pass line," the stickman yelled as the table applauded for her.

Another $400 was put in front of me. I went to pick it up.

"Leave it," Jerry whispered in my ear.

It wasn't easy, but I obeyed his order.

I had $800 on the pass line.

The dice left her wrinkled hands and they rolled to a 9.

"Back the nine with a thousand," he told me.

"Eighteen hundred bucks on a roll?" I whispered back to him.

He just smiled.

I noticed that I was now the biggest bettor at the table. The pit boss was watching me. The other gamblers at the table were watching me. A small crowd began gathering around the table.

Jerry leaned toward my ear and said, "The pit bosses are watching how you bet. It wouldn't be a bad idea to make a couple of side bets just to make it look like you know your way around a crap table."

"But Tommy said--"

"Don't worry. We've got to have the casino think you know how to gamble."

During the next several rolls he had me put chips on hardways, big 6 and 8's, field and come bets, and *buy bets*. Once the point is determined, a buy bet allows the gambler to bet on the numbers 4, 5, 6, 8, 9 and 10. If the shooter rolls any of the buy numbers before he hits his point or craps out, the gambler's side bet, assuming he was on that particular number, wins.

It wasn't long before I lost the three grand, so I signed another marker. This time for $2,000.

For the next forty minutes I continued to bet according to Jerry's orders, along with learning the rules of the game.

By now there was a lot of excitement at the table. There were at least four or five people betting similar amounts to mine on the pass line. With each roll the excitement grew, and little by little I was losing my chips.

"Christ, Jerry! What am I doing wrong? We're losing a bundle here. I thought you knew how to *win* at this game?"

"Actually, Juan, you're doing fine," he whispered as he continued to smile.

"You've *got* to be shitting me?" I whispered back.

The stickman yelled, "Seven. Craps. All pass line bets come down."

"Shit!" I said again as the dealer took my $400 pass line bet, my $600 odds and another $400 I had scattered around the table on side bets.

I turned to Jerry with a look of frustration. It didn't faze him. He was still looking at the table.

He leaned close and whispered, "From time to time I want you to nonchalantly take a few black chips and slip them into your pocket without letting anyone see it."

I looked at him.

"I'll explain later," he said.

It wasn't long before I didn't have any black chips left in front of me. In all, I lost more than $4,400, and had slipped another $600 into my pockets.

Jerry said it was time to go, so I picked up the remaining $400 in $25 and $5 chips that I made from hitting several side bets.

The pit boss came up to me and asked, "Would you like another marker, Mr. D?"

"No thanks. I'll try again tomorrow."

"Would you like to go to the midnight show in the Main Room as a guest of the casino? I'll personally see to it you get good seats. It's David Brenner!"

"No thanks. I'd like to get up to my room and outta these clothes."

"No problem then. See you tomorrow, Mr. D."

I nodded as we walked away.

I headed toward the lounge to meet up with Taz, Mike and Tommy, but Jerry said, "I've got to get to a payphone. Go straight to your room. Don't talk to *anybody*. Not even people you know. We'll meet you there in ten minutes."

I didn't question him and obediently walked to the elevators.

I entered the room and was immediately taken by the night view of

Vegas from my twenty-fifth floor perch.

Apparently, the maid had come in and opened the curtains, turned down the bed covers and placed some chocolate mints, shaped like casino chips, on the pillow.

I sat at the piano and began to play *Can You Feel The Sun Go Down*.

It was only a few moments before I heard a key open the door to the suite. In walked Jerry, Mike and Taz, so I stopped playing.

"I hope you don't mind I used this, Juan," Jerry said as he held up the key.

"That's why I gave it to you, Jer," I reassured him.

"We hear you did pretty good for your first time out!" Taz said to my look of confusion.

"Did *good?* I lost more than *four thousand dollars!* That's *good?*"

"Don't worry, Juan," Jerry said. "Let's see what happened on the other side when Tommy gets here."

"What do you mean 'the other side'?"

Just as I asked, the doorbell rang.

Mike opened it and in walked Tommy with two other men.

"Nice job, Jon. You did just fine," Tommy said in his gruff voice and Bayonne accent. "I saw how the pit bosses were watching you, so it was a good idea to start laying some side bets."

Yeah…like I *knew* to do that.

I looked at Jerry. He just smiled.

As Tommy walked into the living room he lit a cigarette and said, "I want you to meet a couple of my guys from Bayonne. You'll be working with them over the next few days."

I recognized them as two of the gamblers down at the crap table. They were betting the don't-pass line.

"Tommy," I said, "I just lost over *four grand.* How do you figure I did fine?"

All six men started laughing.

Tommy introduced the two strangers as they put out their hands to shake mine.

The first guy was a little shorter than my five-foot-six height and somewhere in his mid-thirties. It seemed like the lines of life were etched into his face and covered with a coat of nicotine that came from his constant cigarette smoking.

He looked at me with distrust in his eyes. There was something scary about him, but then...look at the company he was keeping.

"Jon, this is Bobby Grant," Tommy said.

"Nice to meet you, Bob," I said while noticing that not everyone we'd be dealing with was going to be Italian. I thought the Mafia was a *private* club?

"It's Bobby. Not Bob," he said, coldly.

I just nodded and made a mental note not to fuck *that* up again.

The next person I met had an air of style and sophistication. He was dressed in a very expensive Italian suit and smiled as he shook my hand.

"Jon, this is Louie Calderone. Louie's my main guy here. Any problems at a casino, if you can't find me or Jerry, look for Louie."

"Hello, Louie. Nice to meet you."

"Nice to meet you, Jon. Jerry's told us about you. I'm sure you'll have a good time while you're here. How was your birthday dinner?"

"Great," I said, gratefully looking at my Godfather, Mike and Taz.

Louie had a pleasant smile and a calm voice. But as time went on, I'd learn that this man could calculate bets and odds faster than anyone. He had a brain for numbers. He could also make you disappear into a four-foot hole about 10 miles outside of Vegas or into an oil drum in a landfill in the Jersey swamps if you pissed him off.

"Okay! So let's see how ya's did," Tommy said as Louie and Bobby placed thousands of dollars in black and green chips on the cocktail table in the middle of the living room.

I put the six black chips that I slipped into my pocket on the table, along with another four hundred in green and red chips.

"Very good!" they *all* said.

"Would someone please tell me what's so good about me *losing* four grand?"

Louie decided to explain it to me.

"Let me make this as simple as possible. When you came to the table, how much of your own cash did you lay down?" he asked.

"None," I answered.

"And when Bobby and I went to the table, we each had a thousand dollars in chips. So that accounts for two grand that we brought to the table. Right?"

"Okay, right."

"Now if you recall, Bobby and I didn't approach the table together, we didn't stand next to one another and we didn't associate with you, right?"

"Right."

"So as far as the casino and the pit bosses are concerned, we're not together. There's no affiliation between the three of us. Right?"

"Right."

"And that's important. Got that?"

"Yep."

"So over the next hour or so you take a couple of markers for a total of five grand. *Now* how much do we have at the table?"

"Seven grand all together," I quickly answered.

"That's right. Seven grand. Of which five is *their* money."

"Well, that's one way to look at it," I said. "The other is that since I signed for it, the five grand is actually money that they expect *me* to pay *back*."

All the men looked at Jerry.

He looked at me, took a drag on his cigarette and said, "Don't worry about that, Jon. I'll explain that end to you later."

Louie continued with my education into the scam.

"You see, while you were betting the pass line, Bobby and I were making bets equal to yours on the don't-pass line. But in order not to draw attention from the pit bosses, we were splitting your amounts. When you were betting four hundred, Bobby and I were each betting two hundred, or I'd bet a hundred and he'd bet three. When you were backing up your bet, we'd split it and back up ours. If you bet an odd amount, say five hundred, we'd alternate. One of us would bet two and the other would bet three. We had to make sure the pit bosses didn't see we were matching your bets. We were watching you the whole time. And the fact that you didn't know us and didn't do anything to call attention to us had the pit bosses at a loss."

"Okay, I understand that. But can you tell me how we're *ahead* here?" I asked with a respectful smile.

"Sure. All you've got to do is remember that whenever you *lose*, we *win*, except when someone throws a twelve on the come out roll. Fortunately, that didn't happen too often tonight. So barring the twelves, if you *lost* a thousand, theoretically, we should have--"

I interjected, "*Won* a thousand."

He continued, "So if you *lost* more than four grand, then we--"

I jumped in again, but with excitement, "Should have *won more than four grand!*"

"That's right, kid," he said as he looked over to Bobby and Mike who were counting the chips, and asked, "What do we have there?"

Bobby answered, "Sixty-eight hundred, *after* we took out the original two thousand we went to the table with."

"The extra was due to the side bets," Louie said. "Good move, Jerry."

I looked at Jerry as he rose from the sofa. He walked over to me and said, "The pit bosses record your *play.*"

"My *play?* What's that mean?" I asked.

"They grade you. The kinds of bets you make, the amount you bet, how you act at the table, if you're a drinker or not, that kind of stuff," Jerry answered.

"No shit?"

"So, Juan, after a couple of days of gambling just like you did tonight you'll have a high grade and they'll have no problem picking up your tab. You're gonna drop around twenty-five grand in about five or six days. What's the most you could cost them? Even with the airfare, the most is three, maybe four grand. So as far as they're concerned, once the money's paid back they just made more than twenty grand and you're a pacified customer. They figure you'll come back at some point to win the twenty-five grand you *lost.* And the odds say you'll lose again."

"Ahh! Again we get back to that point about paying them back," I said.

"Don't worry about it. I'll take care of it," he answered as he looked down at his watch. "It's eleven-thirty. We've still got things to do over at The Frontier."

He ground out his cigarette, then put his arm around my shoulders, walked me toward the bedroom and said, "Why don't you get outta that suit and relax. Get a good night's sleep. I'll have Mike get you around ten-thirty tomorrow morning. Come over to The Frontier and I'll explain what's going on while we have breakfast. Okay?"

"Okay. But...are you sure I did all right?" I asked as we entered the bedroom.

"You did great. You turned five grand into sixty-eight hundred on your first night! I got guys that take two days to do that." He lowered his voice to a whisper and continued, "When I explain it to you tomorrow you'll understand *everything.* But no matter what I tell you, you can't tell anyone.

Not even the people in the other room."

"Mike and Taz?" I asked.

"Mike and Taz are the *only* people in that room I want you to trust."

He shut the bedroom door and came close to my ear, "Jon, you're my family. The relationship between our fathers and you and I, and *this thing* we do, that we're *a part of,* is something you're not used to. As long as you trust me...I'll take care of you out here. Just do what me, Mike and Taz tell you, and don't tell *anyone anything* and everything'll be fine. There's things that I'll tell you because..."

He went silent.

I looked at him, awaiting his words.

"Just because," he whispered. Then he backed away from me.

I knew it was because we were family, and no matter how close he was with anyone else, Jerry would trust me because of the bond we had as cousins, he as my Godfather, and the relationship between our fathers. So I understood why he said, "Just because."

He sat on the edge of the bed and continued, "We're not high-profile to the casinos with these credit lines. They're more worried about the fuckin' Sheiks and their quarter-million dollar lines. To the casino, your twenty-five K is nothin'. They're not gonna be watchin' us as long as we don't gamble too big, or *stand out* and draw attention to ourselves...nothing to raise any red flags. As long as we do that...everything runs just fine. Now... you never heard me say that. Got that?"

Before I could answer, he stood up and led me to the door.

As we walked into the living room, Jerry said, "Mike, hang out with the kid for awhile. Let him relax. He's got a long day tomorrow."

I watched as Bobby, Dolan, Louie, Jerry and Taz slipped out of the room one at a time over a ten-minute period. Only Jerry, Taz and Louie... *the Italians*...stopped to look in a mirror before they left.

Once they were gone I turned the air-conditioning up and opened the sliding glass door to the terrace.

"It's beautiful, isn't it, kid?" Mike asked.

"Yes. Yes it is. But I gotta get this friggin' cigarette smoke outta the room." I turned to him and said, "You wanna go downstairs and get a drink?"

"Nah. We don't need to go downstairs. We'll get a *set-up* sent up here."

"A set-up?"

"I'll tell you what. Go take a shower and get comfortable. I'll call Room Service and take care of it. By the time you get out of the shower, you'll have your nightcap."

I laughed, and as I headed in the direction of the bedroom I heard Mike pick up the phone and say, "Hi, honey, this is Jon D'Amore in twenty-five thirty-six. Can you get a set-up to my room right away?" There was a pause as she asked him something, and then he continued, "Chivas, Cuervo Gold, Dewar's, Tangueray Gin, Crown Royal, Smirnoff Vodka and a bottle of dry vermouth. A bunch of mixers and some olives in a jar. Lots of glasses and some ice. Oh yeah, and four Buds."

He hung up and yelled, "It'll be here in fifteen minutes. Whatcha want? I'll have it ready."

I yelled back, "Chivas, rocks!"

"Just like your cousin," he laughed.

I heard the sounds of the television as Mike settled onto one of the sofas and flipped through the channels.

Just before I stepped into the shower I looked at my watch. It was just about midnight.

As the water ran over my body I thought to myself, "I woke up this morning in Linda's apartment in Hollywood where we celebrated the moment of my birth in a jacuzzi with a joint and a shot of tequila. Then I hopped a plane to Las Vegas, was given a suite at The MGM Grand, drank Dom Perignon with my Godfather and won seventeen-hundred-and-fifty dollars at a roulette table the first time I ever gambled in a casino. It was all followed by a gourmet dinner with four knockout showgirls for dessert, and then I get told I did '*real good*' for losing more than four grand at a hundred dollar crap table. *This* is gonna be a trip to remember!"

That was my twenty-second birthday. You don't forget stuff like that.

Round 5

It was Saturday, August 30.

My eyes noticed it was daylight as I staggered through the suite to answer the bell.

When I opened the door, there was a waiter with a tray.

"Your coffee and juice for two, sir."

"I didn't order this," I said as he walked into the living room to place it on the dining table.

He looked at the tab.

"Yes sir, that's correct. This was ordered by a David Toma in room fourteen-thirty. He said to tell you that he'll be joining you."

As I heard the name, especially when I least expected it, I burst out laughing.

He handed me the bill and a pen. I kept laughing as I signed my name and tip on the receipt.

The phone rang as the waiter walked out.

"Hello?"

"Coffee get there yet?"

"Yes it has, Uncle Dave," I managed to say, still laughing.

"I'll be there in five."

"What time is it? It's not ten-thirty yet, is it?"

"It's only nine. I figured you'd need time to get ready, and maybe we'll play a little before we go over."

I was surprised.

"Play a little?"

"Sure. Maybe we can take them for another couple of grand before breakfast."

"Don't we need to bring a friend?" I asked, referring to having two guys bet the don't-pass line.

"Not always. It depends on the action and how big you bet."

"See you in five," I said before I hung up.

I took a glass of orange juice and walked out onto the terrace. Though it was only nine in the morning it already felt like the temperature was tapping ninety.

Like clockwork, Mike rang the bell.

While he watched the news and drank his coffee, I showered and shaved. Taking a cue from Mike's appearance, there was no reason to wear a suit for breakfast, so I broke out some of the new apparel I acquired in Beverly Hills.

"You look great, kid," Mike's deep voice boomed as I walked out of the bedroom. "Maybe a little *too* slick...too *flashy* for some of those guys from Bayonne."

"Hey Mike, you know if it was up to me I'd be wearing jeans, a tank top and sneakers. But I wanna look good for Jerry. Besides, this shit's comfortable, it looks good and it cost a fuckin' bundle...so fuck it, I'm wearin' it."

We sat around for a few minutes while Mike reminded me of the process of getting chips at the table and how to bet. He would go to the casino first and find the right table. I'd go to the opposite end of the table and begin to play. We'd gamble until twenty after ten, at which point I'd pick up my chips, go to the cashier, cash them in and then head toward the door.

As if on cue we each checked ourselves in the mirror. Mike walked out of the suite. I waited about three or four minutes...and then left.

For ten o'clock on a Saturday morning The MGM Grand crap tables were already crowded. It didn't take long to find Mike and the chosen location. I grabbed a spot in the opposite corner and called the pit boss over.

Just like the night before, I signed a marker and $2,000 was placed in front of me.

I started with $100 bets and backed them up with another $100. There was no need to attract attention to myself with larger bets. Besides, Mike had to cover whatever bets I made by himself, so we didn't want to be conspicuous.

I thought that it was a little odd that I didn't feel nervous or scared while I stood there gambling, still unsure as to *why* losing another two grand was something that would make my cousin happy.

Apparently Mike picked a good table because there were a lot of people betting big on the don't-pass line, so the pit bosses never noticed us.

I saw Mike laugh as I started making a few side bets and picked up twenty-five and fifty dollar winnings here and there.

It wasn't long before I lost over a thousand dollars on pass line bets, but I noticed I was making money on the side bets. I was also sliding a couple of black chips into my pockets without the pit bosses or dealers seeing.

By the time we were ready to leave I had two black chips and several green and red ones in front of me. It appeared to the pit boss that I had just blown around $1,600 in twenty minutes and he marked it on his clipboard.

He leaned toward my ear and said, "Maybe you'll have better luck after lunch, Mr. D."

"Yeah, hope so," I said as I picked up my chips and walked away smiling.

As we both hopped into the back of a cab, Mike said, "Your cousin's gonna be proud of you, kid. You did real good."

I put my hand up to shield my eyes as the cab pulled into the bright sunlight, and replied, "I can't wait to find out how losing money is doing *real good*."

It only took a few minutes before the cab dropped us off and we were walking through The Frontier's casino. Mike led me directly to the restaurant where Jerry and Taz were sitting.

All true connected guys are either *part* of a crew, or *have* a crew. Rocco Casiano was a '*made* member' of the Genovese family, and his closest guys, like Jerry and Tommy Dolan, were a part of his crew. As a matter of fact, the two of them were a part of Rocco's *inner* crew. Some of Rocco's guys had their own crews. Tommy had about twenty in his. Jerry had about a dozen, and where I was sitting at that moment was within his inner crew.

As coffee, juice and breakfast were served, Jerry began to tell me how I was going to lose $25,000 over the next few days, and how happy I was going to make him, Tommy Dolan, and ultimately, Rocco Casiano.

I'm sure Vincente 'The Chin' Gigante was *also* going to be happy, since he was the one Rocco reported to. Gigante was *The Boss* of the Genovese family.

But since The Chin wasn't at the hospital to see me wheeled into the nursery the day I was born, I wasn't too concerned about his happiness at that moment.

On the other hand, it's not like I wanted to piss Gigante off either.

Legend has it that Gigante, *another* former boxer, made his early bones on May 2 of 1957, when he failed a hit on crime boss Frank Costello.

At the time, the story goes, Vito Genovese was an underboss of Lucky Luciano's family. Lucky was in semi-retirement in Sicily, and Vito wanted the title of *capo di tutti capi*, but feared that Costello, another Luciano underboss and a long-time friend of Lucky's, would cast his Commission vote against him. So under direct orders from Genovese, Gigante was to take Costello *out*.

It can never be said that the old-timers were cowards or disrespectful, because around midnight on that spring evening as Costello returned home to The Majestic Apartments on Central Park West and waited in the lobby for the elevator, Gigante came up behind Costello and spoke to him in order for both men to be face-to-face. A boss deserves the respect of seeing who his assassin is, a coward kills a man from behind. The Chin was playing by the rules.

"This is for you, Frank," he supposedly said as he put a pistol to Costello's head and looked him in the eyes. But Costello flinched a split second before the trigger was pulled and only suffered a superficial wound.

Gigante, seeing a fallen Costello with blood running from his head, assumed the job was done and left the apartment building for a long trip out of town.

When Gigante showed up several months later, he walked into a Manhattan police station and said, "I hear you guys are looking for me. For what?"

He was arrested, tried and acquitted for the attempted murder of Frank Costello.

He was acquitted because Costello refused to identify him.

Costello, everyone assumed, wanted to get *his own* justice. And besides, these guys didn't deal with each other in a State or Federal Courthouse. They took care of their laundry...as clean or as dirty as it may have been... their own way.

After the failed hit, Vito Genovese was suddenly *very* concerned about his health.

Genovese realized that he either had to set things straight with Costello or face a war with the rest of the families for the unsanctioned hit.

A secret meeting between Frank Costello and Vito Genovese was set up and a deal was to be cut.

But when the meeting took place, instead of Genovese seeking forgiveness, it was a fearful Costello who wanted to retire and settle in quiet solitude on his estate in Sands Point on New York's Long Island.

Costello agreed not to go to The Commission seeking revenge against Genovese, and in return, Genovese, with Costello's approval, could take over Lucky Luciano's family and the title of *capo di tutti capi*...as long as Vito no longer took hits at Frank.

It sounded like a fair deal to Vito.

Apparently no reprisal was taken against Vincente Gigante, since Genovese owed his new position as boss of all bosses to Vincente's poor marksmanship. Had Gigante actually killed Costello that night, surely a war would have ensued as a result of the unsanctioned hit against someone so high in The Commission. Vito Genovese and Vincente '*The Chin*' Gigante would have been quickly eliminated.

Genovese eventually died in prison in 1969. The baton as head of the *Genovese family*, as Luciano's family was now called, passed for a short time to Fat Tony Salerno. But Fat Tony didn't get the *capo di tutti capi* title from The Commission. *That* honor went to Carlo Gambino, whose family was making a bigger name and place for themselves in New York during the '60s and '70s.

It wasn't long before Salerno also wanted to retire, so he quietly passed the reins of *la famiglia* over to Gigante. Out of respect for their old boss, they kept the family name *Genovese*.

It was under the name of the Genovese family that Casiano, Jerry, Dolan...even my father, did their business.

I leaned toward Jerry as he spoke. I didn't want to miss anything he had to say.

"You see Juan, the casinos fly big gamblers in. They pick up the airfares for their wives and girlfriends, too. They give them rooms. The bigger the credit line, the nicer the room."

"Yeah. I noticed," I threw in.

"They'll give you all your meals, your drinks, the tips, shows, *whatever*," Taz jumped in with an adolescent's excitement. "Everything and anything. If you lose enough, they'll give you women."

"So far it still sounds pretty profitable for the casino," I said. "These people are brought into town and agree to gamble anywhere from tens of thousands to hundreds of thousands, which the odds say they'll lose. It's a winning situation for the casinos, isn't it?"

"Well, it was until Tommy Dolan started comin' out here and came up with the scam," Jerry answered.

I leaned closer.

"You see, here's where it's a winning situation for *us*," Jerry began explaining…again, with that recurring sly smile appearing on his face.

I looked at Taz and Mike. They were smiling because they knew the outcome of what I was about to be told.

"Remember last night when Louie asked you how much money we went to the table with, and how much we, as a team of three guys, *left* the table with?"

"Yeah."

"Okay. *We* make out because the casinos are giving you up to six months to repay that twenty-five grand. Interest free. Okay?"

"Yep."

"So assuming you didn't fly in from Los Angeles but came in from Jersey with one of our guys on your guest ticket, the two of you get out here on free airline tickets. You get a room, food, whatever. So what has it cost us?"

"Nothing."

"Now, while you're here you go to the tables and call for your line. In your case, you take out all twenty-five grand. That means that with the help of the other guys working the table with you and barring the twelves that get rolled, they *win* the twenty-five that you *lose*. But the fact is, we now have the casino's twenty-five grand in *our* hands. Let's just say, after expenses and salaries, we bring back--"

"Salaries?"

"Sure. Whatdya think? These guys are comin' out here from Jersey for a tan?"

I just shook my head and smiled.

"So let's say that after expenses we bring twenty-two of your twenty-five thousand back home. Right?"

"Yeah. But they want it back within six months," I say.

"Now think for a second. We're getting twenty-two grand. We *invest* that money…"

It suddenly hit me. Jerry was quick to see he didn't have to go any further.

I took over for him.

"So you guys take the money and put it out on the street. What's the current vig?"

Mike quickly answered.

"We wholesale it out to our guys at twenty percent for ten weeks. *They* put it on the street for forty to fifty percent."

"And you guys get a piece of that too, right?" I asked.

"Smart kid," Taz responded.

"So, let's see," I said, "On the low side your end is two hundred bucks on every thousand every ten weeks. How many weeks in six months? Twenty-six, right?"

I grabbed a Keno card and pencil. They all sat back and watched me calculate the numbers.

"That's enough time to make two turns on the money and then collect it," I said as I multiplied and divided the numbers. "So if you're making four hundred on every thousand...that makes four grand for every ten grand. For twenty grand you're making eight. And for twenty-two grand you're making eighty-eight hundred. But, you've lost three grand of your profit to bring the twenty-two that you started with back up to the twenty-five that you've got to repay the casino. So your profit is only fifty-eight hundred."

They all sat there quietly while I continued to think it through.

A few seconds later I asked, "Is fifty-eight hundred worth it? Considering you've got to take your slice, or salary as you call it, then pay your people. Then there's Tommy and *his* crew. Where's the profit for Casiano?"

"We're not out here alone," Taz said with a smile.

I was momentarily confused.

"And besides," Mike cut in, "Your cousin is one of the best handicappers I've ever seen."

"You're losing me," I said.

"We don't just put the money out on the street. Jerry can pick baseball, football and basketball games better than *anyone*," he said.

"And *that* money turns over within days instead of weeks," Taz added.

"So you guys place bets with bookies from other families and *they* take a loss, while you're betting with the money that you hit the Vegas casinos for!" I said.

"You catch on very quick, Juan," Jerry proudly whispered.

Taz lightly grabbed my arm.

"Remember what Dolan said about gambling with your own money?"

"So you're using the casino's, even back in Jersey! Very cool," I laughed as I sat back in my seat.

Then I asked Taz, "What did you mean when you said, 'We're not out here alone'?"

Jerry leaned forward. "Me and Dolan have eighteen guys in town this weekend, and they all have lines. We're split up in eight casinos. Here at The Frontier, The Trop, Caesars, The MGM, The Sahara, The Riv, The Dunes and The Aladdin. Each one of those guys have *at least* a ten thousand dollar line in at least one of those casinos. Some have fifteen, some twenty, and some, like you, have a twenty-five."

Once again I did some quick calculating.

"So if you have eighteen guys with an average of seventeen-five at each hotel...eighteen times seventeen-five. That's a little over three hundred grand."

"Three-fifteen to be exact," Jerry said. "But don't forget, some of 'em have a line at two or three casinos. So the number is higher."

"Out of three-fifteen, how much will you take back to Jersey?" I asked as I ripped up the Keno card.

"About two hundred and seventy-five after expenses. Maybe more."

"Tax free, interest free, clean cash. With six months to pay it back," I said and smiled.

"And when we're not working back in Jersey, we're out here having the time of our life," Mike added.

I ripped up the pieces even smaller.

As we ate breakfast, they told me the places and shows to see while I was in town, so I asked, "How long do I stay here? How long did you get my room for, Jer?"

"You can stay as long as you're gambling, maybe a day or two longer if you're losing big, which you will. We'll go through your twenty-five grand in about four or five days. We don't want to arouse any suspicions by doing it any faster. They don't know you yet. So maybe in a year you'll be able to go through that much in a couple of days without anyone noticing." Jerry looked around the restaurant and continued, "These fucking oil and cattle cowboys drop that...and more...in a day."

"In a year? Jer, I'm not gonna do this for the next year. I've got my music. I'm just here for my birthday. *Remember?*"

They all laughed.

I looked at them.

"What's so funny?"

Mike answered, "You don't have to come here anymore if you don't want to, but let me tell you something--"

Jerry cut him off and continued, "After you get treated like *King Shit* for the next few days with people kissin' your ass and jumpin' whenever you want them to do something for you, let us know if you don't wanna come back again."

Taz leaned across the table and whispered, "How about when you've got nothing to do for a few days? You come out here and pick up an extra grand of pocket cash, eat some great food, see some great shows."

A big grin crossed his face as he looked me in the eyes and kept going, "And a guy like you? Any idea what kind of women you could have when they see you droppin' five grand a night? And I'm not talkin' hookers. *No fuckin' way*. That's bullshit."

Jerry and Mike shook their heads in unison as Taz took a mouthful of orange juice.

Once he swallowed, he continued, "We're talkin' women with money, and they're lookin' for a young fuck...just...like...*you*. There's daughters of rich gamblers looking for a guy to hang out with while mom sits at the blackjack table and dad's blowin' his wad at a crap table or with some hooker."

He stopped to take a breath and then went on, "There's stewardesses, entertainers and dancers. You name it, it's here."

He leaned back into his seat and started laughing, "Once you come back a *second time* and you're more comfortable with what we're doin', and once you know your way around the hotels and see all the pamperin' you'll get, just let me know if you don't wanna do this anymore."

It only took a second for Jerry and Mike to nod and join in on the laughter.

It all *sounded* good.

But what was different about the life that I was currently leading and the one *they* were offering?

I was traveling quite regularly. At 22, I was already making around

$78,000 a year from the sessions, and there was never a concern about the quality *or* quantity of female companionship.

And besides, I loved what I was doing. It was *music*.

Why would I want to incorporate Vegas into a life that was already heading in the direction I always wanted? And...it was legitimate.

Why would I want to enter a world of cryptic phone calls consisting of one and two word responses usually ending in a question?

For me, the answers were simple.

It was because of the *adventure*.

It was because of *these guys*.

It was because somewhere inside of me, I always wanted to do *something* with them.

It was because I had watched them since I was a kid. I saw the way they acted, the way they dressed, the way other people showed them respect, and the respect they showed to those who deserved it. I also saw the way they straightened out those who *didn't* show it.

Was it inherent? Was it genetic? Was it that I felt living on the fringe of The Mafia was acceptable and safe? Or was it that I didn't have the balls to actually be a full-fledged Mafioso?

If something went wrong and I had to pay back some or all of the twenty-five grand, I'd be able to do it.

Reluctantly.

But I'd do it.

Besides, I was sure if something went wrong, Jerry would straighten it out or cover my loss...and my ass.

It didn't seem like I was actually doing anything that would get me tossed into the Hackensack River with blood and air bubbles coming out of the bullet holes in the back of my head. I certainly wasn't gonna cheat my cousin. And I definitely wasn't going to try to cheat Rocco Casiano.

I figured that as long as Jerry, Mike and Taz were looking out for me, and as long as I never called Bobby Grant '*Bob*'...I was safe.

Round 6

They were *right*.

During the remainder of my 6-night/7-day stay I was pampered beyond anything I had experienced in my life.

I had always known that I was *very* fortunate when it came to the decadent side of life. Certainly it was the music business that put me in that position. It was the mid '70s and the last strands of the sexual revolution were still holding on. The fact that I was 22, single and making a healthy income as a studio musician allowed me to enjoy the best of a *very* comfortable and hedonistic lifestyle.

By Sunday, August 31, I had realized I'd be at the crap tables with the guys from around four in the afternoon to midnight. That meant my days would start with breakfast on the terrace, followed by a few hours at the pool before I would shower, shave and dress to Jerry's specifications for that evening's gambling.

At some point that day, Mike and Taz came out to the pool and shuttled me into the MGM's spa. It was the first time I had ever gotten a real massage…and from a big German guy named Otto. That was followed by my first manicure, pedicure and facial. And like the rest of the guys, I had my fingernails coated in clear polish. This must have been that '*King Shit*' thing Jerry was talking about.

By Monday, September 1, I had already gone through nearly $15,000 of my credit line. The pit bosses were calling me '*Mr. D*' and a few of The MGM Grand cocktail waitresses called me '*Jonny*'…not one of my favorite names, but I tolerated it when it came from a pretty woman.

It was on that Monday, around 1:30 in the afternoon, that Taz's words over breakfast at The Frontier started to come true.

I was lying face down on a chaise lounge that was reserved for me at poolside.

A second Bloody Mary was in front of me as I eyed the females that surrounded the huge pool, while trying to keep my tan even on both sides.

A woman's voice behind me said, "This sun is vicious. You should put some lotion on your back to keep from burning."

I turned around to see an attractive, tanned woman in her early forties smiling at me from about 15 feet away. She wore a black one-piece bathing suit and had several pieces of gold jewelry around her neck, wrists, ankle and fingers. Most striking was the large diamond solitaire on her left hand. She was sitting on a lounge chair, surrounded by what appeared to be her husband and two other couples. The women were all similar in their gold accessories, age, marital status and appearance. The men were in their late forties or early fifties, wore short pants and flowered short-sleeved shirts, and each had a similar amount of gold dangling from their necks, wrists and fingers. Except for the glitter of their jewelry, there were no obvious traits to make me think that any these men were Italian.

Her husband was in a conversation with his friends about horse racing and didn't even notice my response when I told her I couldn't reach certain parts of my back and that I was going to my room shortly. I thanked her for her concern, smiled and went back to my Bloody Mary and female gazing.

Less than five minutes had passed before I heard all three men complaining that they "...*didn't come to Vegas to sit by the god damn pool!*" They decided they were going to Caesars Palace for the remainder of the afternoon and that their wives were to be ready for dinner by seven.

There was no goodbye kiss or "I'll see you later, honey!" as the men finished their beers and left their wives behind.

"What schmucks," I said to myself as I continued with my mindless relaxation in the sun.

They were *definitely* not Italian.

A couple of minutes passed before a shadow came over me and I felt someone sit along the edge of my lounge chair. Seeing as Jerry, Mike and Taz were the only ones who knew where I was, I assumed it was one of them coming to tell me it was time to lose another couple of thousand dollars.

I turned my head to see my concerned female friend pouring suntan lotion into her hands as she said, "I hope you don't mind, but I wouldn't want to see you get burned. It would be impossible for you to sleep that way, or do anything *else* on your back. I'll get those spots you can't reach."

We both smiled and I thanked her as she began to spread the lotion around, while at the same time giving me a fairly decent back and shoulder massage.

"You don't feel tense at all," she said, somewhat surprised.

"Life is good," I answered with a smile.

"You're very lucky."

She quickly changed the subject.

"My name is Michele. And you are...?"

"Jon. Jon D'Amore."

"D'Amore. That's a very nice name," she said as she continued to rub the lotion into my back and shoulders.

"Thank you."

Then she stopped rubbing but kept her hands on my back as she turned to her friends and said with almost Italian-perfection, "His last name is...*D'Amore*."

I was forced to smile as each had something to say about its English translation...something I've had to hear for more years than I care to recall.

I eventually asked her about the men who had left them behind. Her hands quickly tightened on my back. It was obvious this was a subject she didn't want to discuss, but she made it clear that her companions all felt the same about the way they were treated by their husbands "...*every time we come to this friggin' desert.*"

Then Michele introduced me to her friends, Sharon and Jeanette.

I pulled my chair around to face them, called over a poolside cocktail waitress and ordered a bottle of Dom Perignon and four glasses.

The ladies were appreciative and impressed with my choice.

I, on the other hand, was laughing to myself as it became more apparent that being comped can certainly make one appear to be something different from what one is. But, I *was* enjoying myself...just like Jerry, Mike and Taz said I would.

The conversation then turned to where we all came from.

Though they all originated from different parts of the country, they now resided in a suburb of Atlanta where their husbands were partners in an automotive supply company.

Eventually, they wanted to know what I did for a living and what brought me to Vegas. Obviously, I wasn't going to tell them what I was doing at the hotel, so I simply told them I was a musician and that my stay at the hotel was a birthday gift from my cousin.

"*Your* birthday?" they all happily giggled. "That's why we're here, too!"

Sharon, a tall blonde with a wonderful smile and larger-than-normal breasts that she was self-conscious about, said, "It was Michele's birthday the other day and our husbands decided *this* was where we wanted to come to celebrate."

The cocktail waitress returned with the champagne. All three women cheered and applauded as the cork popped high into the air and landed in the pool.

Michele said her birthday was on the Friday that had just passed, which was August 29, so, of course, I had to tell her the good news.

"That was my birthday, too."

She leaned over from her chair, put her arms around my neck, pulled me close and said, "Happy birthday, baby."

She kissed me on the lips and I quickly felt her tongue slip into my mouth.

It was at least 15 seconds before the other women said to her, "That's enough, Michele. People are watching. And besides...it's *our* turn."

Each one of them took a turn giving me the same birthday kiss as the champagne was being poured. I looked up at the cocktail waitress and ordered another bottle.

"Though I'll never tell you *my* age, how old are you, Jon?" Michele asked.

I quickly thought that I should lie and tell them that I was a few years older, but just as quickly decided against it.

"I just turned twenty-two."

"*Twenty-two*," they each sighed as if remembering a time when they were so much happier.

We spoke, laughed and drank for another 20 minutes before I looked at my watch and realized that I should be getting ready to meet with *da guys*.

"I'd love to hang out with you," I said, "But I've got to get up to my room and get ready to meet my cousin. Please enjoy the rest of the champagne. It was great meeting you. Maybe we can meet here again tomorrow?"

They each pouted a bit, but were very understanding. I told them I'd come out to the pool around noon the next day and that they should look for the lounge chair with my personalized "*Reserved*" sign on it.

They assured me that since they were staying at the hotel until Wednesday they would look for me.

When I got up from my chair all three of them noticed something that had slipped my mind. The semi-erection I had since the three of them kissed me was quite evident in my bathing suit. As I looked at them, I noticed three pairs of eyes aimed at my crotch.

"*D'Amore*, eh?" Jeanette, the quietest of them, said, with an Italian flair.

I smiled, finished the champagne that was still in my glass, put on my shirt and sneakers and reluctantly walked away.

Before I reached the door to the hotel I felt an arm around my waist.

It was Michele.

"Hey, birthday boy!"

I stopped before I entered the building.

"What can I do for you, birthday girl?" I asked as I noticed that she had slipped into a pair of high heels, a shirt and a pair of shorts, with a small purse hanging from her side. It was clear that she no longer wanted to sit by the pool.

"It sure would be nice to smoke a joint with someone. Do you have the time?" she asked.

"That's assuming I smoke. Isn't it?" I answered slyly.

"You did say you were a musician, didn't you? I took a shot."

I laughed at being stereotyped, looked at my watch and asked, "Your room or mine?"

"Am I going to run into a girlfriend or a wife waiting for you?"

"Nope."

I asked her if Sharon and Jeanette weren't going to wonder where she was.

"I'm a big girl. They know I can take care of myself," she said. "Besides, they've got a bottle of champagne to keep them occupied."

She put her arm through mine as we entered the hotel and made our way to the elevators.

As I scanned her body from head to toe, I asked, "What floor are you on?"

"My husband comes here a lot, so the casino comps him based on his line. We're on the sixteenth floor."

As we entered the elevator she asked, "Where are you?"

I hit the button marked 25 and said, "I hope you like the view."

She grabbed my arm tighter and moved closer to me.

For a fleeting moment I resented that this woman was attaching herself to me simply because she believed I was a young, semi-successful, pot smokin' musician lounging poolside at some world-class hotel, who cavalierly ordered bottles of Dom Perignon and had a penthouse suite.

But just as quickly as that moment of resentment came, it left and I put it behind me.

Way behind me.

Apparently there's a different mindset in Las Vegas when it comes to fun and pleasure. The guys were right. I was beginning to see this town as a Disneyland for adults. And I was holding an "E" ticket for *all* the rides.

The doors slid open as the elevator reached the twenty-fifth floor and we made pleasant conversation while we walked down the hall to 2536.

I could hear the phone ringing as I slid the key into the lock.

I rushed into the living room to answer it as Michele slowly stepped in behind me.

"Hello?" I said.

"Hello, Juan."

"Hey, Jer. What's up?"

"How was the pool?"

"I just came up. It was *very* nice. You're right. I'm really enjoying this."

"Good. I'm glad. It's about two-thirty," he said, causing me to look at my watch. "Will you be ready by three-thirty or so?"

"Yeah," I answered somewhat hesitantly as I looked at Michele leaning against the piano in her tight shorts and high heels while she surveyed The Strip through the panoramic windows. "If you...uh...if you need me to be there, I'm there."

"You all right?" he asked.

I diverted my eyes to something else.

"Uh, yeah," I said as my concentration returned to the man that was making all of this possible.

"Okay, I'll send Mike for you around three-thirty."

I wanted just a little more time.

"Can you make it around four instead?" I asked as Michele came closer to me.

"Yeah, if that's better for you. But no later," he answered.

"Do I wear a suit tonight?"

But before he could answer, Michele was nodding her head and whispering, "*I'd* like to see you in a suit," into my other ear.

"No," he said. "That's all right. No jeans though. Something nice."

"That's okay. I think I'll wear a suit."

"Good. I'll see you later."

We hung up.

I took Michele's hand and led her onto the terrace. She leaned against me as we looked across the street to Caesars.

She took a joint from her purse, lit it and took a few long hits before she put it to my lips. As I inhaled, she exhaled.

She suddenly seemed distant as she said, "Sometimes...when I speak to him, it's like I'm talking to a wall."

"Been married long?" I asked.

"Twelve years," she answered with a deep sigh. "And I do everything I can to stay attractive for him. I diet. I exercise. But nothing matters. He couldn't care less."

She wasn't lying. She was in fantastic shape.

"Do you have any fantasies, Michele?" I asked, while discreetly trying to keep her from pouring her guts out.

She faced me and responded, "Fantasies? No one's ever asked me that."

She laughed and ran a hand through her dark hair as she thought about the question and how to answer it.

"When I was younger I used to think that having fantasies wasn't normal. Well, except, of course, for the one that every girl has. You know, the gallant knight in shining armor, the white charger, being whisked off of my feet and carried away to a castle somewhere...where he'd go off to slay dragons and we'd live happily-ever-after."

She smiled and took another hit off the joint as she thought more about my question.

As she handed it back to me, she continued, "A few years after we were married the fantasy changed. I guess it started with what I always assumed was the common one. A deserted island, I'm lying on the beach, an unknown person walks by, then...well, I'm sure nothing different than the fantasy *every* person has at some point."

She shook her head and decided she wanted to go back into the suite. As we entered the living room she asked, "What about you? Any fantasies?"

I ground the roach into an ashtray and thought about my answer.

"I've been lucky," I said with a smile, "My music career's made most of my fantasies come true. I realize I'm never going to be *the star*, but I'm very happy working in the studio. I make a good buck. I get to travel. I get to hang out with talented and famous people." I pulled her closer…"And I got to meet you."

And then we kissed.

After we came up for air, she put her lips next to my ear and asked, "Would you be my fantasy? Would you be my stranger on the beach?"

I smiled and nodded. What *else* would you expect a 22-year-old to do when asked such a question?

She slowly took off her shirt and shorts as she walked to the center of the living room. Less than a minute later she had stripped the bathing suit from her body and was wearing nothing but high heels, some jewelry, a tan and a smile.

We spent the rest of our time together having sex in the shower, in the living room and eventually in the bedroom.

We didn't realize what time it was when we heard a voice coming from the living room.

"Hey kid? You here?"

I looked at Michele and then at the clock next to the bed. It was five to four.

"Fuck!" I whispered, "It's Mike. Shit!"

"Who's Mike?" she whispered back.

Just then he appeared in the open doorway to find Michele straddled atop my body.

"*That's* Mike."

He just stood there and smiled.

"Hey, kid. Jerry told me to come and getcha. Sorry about the interruption."

Michele hopped off of me and covered herself under the sheet.

I looked at him and said, "I didn't realize what time it was. I'm gonna need another twenty minutes. How'd you get in?"

"Jerry gave me the key. Sorry about that. I didn't call 'cause I thought you'd be ready to go. I'll, uh, I'll wait down in the lounge," he said, half apologetically and half humorously. "But you'd better hurry, they're waiting for us at The Trop."

Just before he turned to leave, he said, "See you downstairs, kid, and nice to meet you, sweetheart."

After we heard the door close we laid there for a few seconds before I said, "I *hate* when they call me *kid*."

She rolled on top of me and said, "Take my word for it, Jon. You're no *kid!*"

Then she gently kissed me before we got out of bed and went back into the shower to clean up.

It wasn't long before I was standing in front of the mirror knotting my silk tie.

Michele walked over, kissed me and said, "Thank you for being my fantasy. I hope..." She paused to think and then continued. "I hope we can do this again before I leave?"

I didn't answer. The look in my eyes was all she needed to see.

"Thank you," she whispered as she ran her hands over my suit jacket.

We walked out of the room and went to the elevator. When we descended to the sixteenth floor I held the doors open and watched her walk down the hall. She turned and blew me a kiss.

When the elevator reached the lobby the sound of slot machines bombarded me with their incessant ringing and relentless dispersing of coins from their bellies.

I found Mike nursing a scotch.

"Do I have time for a drink?" I asked.

"Not really. They wanted us over there about ten minutes ago. But apparently you were busy, huh?"

I smiled and said, "I'm sorry about that."

He smiled back. He was just busting my balls.

When the waitress approached, I asked for his tab and signed it. I was learning fast.

It only took the cab five minutes to get us to The Tropicana. It was my first time there, and I noticed that the casino was small compared to The MGM. But then back in the day, *all* the casinos were small compared to The MGM.

We quickly made our way to the fourth floor and knocked on a door. Bobby Grant opened it. The room was filled with cigarette smoke and at least ten guys from Jerry's and Tommy's crews. Most of the time it was best not to be introduced to them.

As I walked in, they all said the same thing.

"Hiya, kid!"

This time I smiled as I recalled Michele's words.

Only Jerry said, "Hi, Jon."

Chips were everywhere. At least eight grand was stacked on the cocktail table. Another fifteen grand was on the dresser. Taz and Louie were sitting on the bed counting an even larger pile that lay between them.

Bobby, Louie and a couple of other guys from Dolan's crew had rooms and lines at The Trop. They were going to draw markers and bet the pass line. Jerry's guys were here to play the don't-pass line.

After Jerry and Dolan gave me a lesson in watching the table and splitting my don't-pass bets with Taz, it was only moments before I was in the casino standing at a crap table betting a couple of hundred dollars on each roll.

As I gambled, I couldn't help but notice the attractive blonde dealer across from me. Her name tag read "Sandy." She raised her head and noticed me staring at her as I laid my bet. I smiled. She smiled back and said, "Good luck."

I had to remember where I was, what I was doing...and who I was doing it for. To even *think* of fooling around with a dealer would be the most stupid thing I could do.

I made it a point not to look at her and turned my attention back to the action on the table.

Less than four hours had passed since Mike found Michele riding me and we had already hit the casino for over $12,000.

Dolan decided it was time for Jerry, Taz, Louie and me to go back to The MGM. It was this kind of hit-and-run tactic that made it hard for the casinos to see what these guys were doing. They'd never stay at the same casino for more than four hours. They'd just go from one hotel to the next, picking up anywhere from five to twenty-five grand at each stop.

The four of us arrived at The MGM in separate cabs about three to four minutes apart, and then met in my room. It was nearly eight o'clock and we were hungry, so I called Room Service and ordered dinner.

Around 9:30, Jerry made a quick call to Dolan at The Frontier. As soon as he hung up we were on our way downstairs to the casino.

I called the pit boss over, asked for $3,000 and started betting the pass line while Taz and Louie covered me.

1. Giovanni D'Amore, circa 1922
Jon's grandfather.

2. Dominic and Jean D'Amore, Union City, NJ, circa 1937
Jon's uncle and aunt…and Jerry's parents. Jean was pregnant with Jerry at the time.

3. Carmine "Rocky" D'Amore, 1945

Jon's father. Twenty year old Rocky (aka "Me-nu," short for Carmenuche) stayed in Germany for two years after WWII as a Sergeant in the Military Police.

4. Carmine "Rocky" D'Amore's Military Police ID card, Germany, 1946.

**5. Cousin Jerry, Uncle Dominic and Rocky D'Amore,
North Hudson County Park, North Bergen, NJ, 1947**
Shortly after Rocky returned from the Army.
Three men Jon grew up loving. Jerry would become Jon's Godfather.

6. Jon's parents, Carmine ("Rocky") and Ann D'Amore's Wedding Day, April 15, 1950: Married at City Hall in Union City where there was an election taking place the next day. Hence, the polling sign to "Vote Bottom Row G."

7. Infant Jon and Ann D'Amore 1953
Jon inherited his mother's looks.

**8. Frank Sinatra (center), Patsy (far left) and Rose D'Amore
(standing behind Sinatra), Las Vegas, NV, circa 1957**

Patsy was a famous Hollywood restaurateur from the late 1930s to 1975 with *The Villa Capri*, one of Tinsletown's most favorite and star-studded eateries. Frank was one of their closest friends.

9. Jon and Rocky D'Amore, North Bergen, NJ, Easter 1957
Like father…like son.

10. D'Amores at *The Villa Capri*, Hollywood, CA, circa 1960
Patsy D'Amore (far right) celebrates his birthday with his wife Rose (3rd from right), his brother Franklyn (far left) and other family and friends. Note the wine bottles along the top of the wall. Franklyn D'Amore was a famous vaudevillian and became an equally reknowned Hollywood restaurateur from the late 1930s to 1950s with *The Casa D'Amore*.

11. Textile Union Officials and Senator John F. Kennedy, June 1, 1960: Union Business Agent Rocky D'Amore (top right) supporting the future president.

12. Jon's First Electric Guitar and Amp, 1962: The start of Jon's first career. Check out the Danelectro amp, the sharkskin suit (custom made by Al "The Tailor" Certo) and diamond ring.

13. Frank and May DeNike (center) with Patsy and Rose D'Amore (on the ends), circa 1967: North Jersey Mob Boss Frank DeNike's Las Vegas wedding picture. Patsy and Rose were the Best Man and Maid Of Honor. May was Jean D'Amore's sister.

14. **Rocky D'Amore, Las Vegas, NV, July, 1968:** With his wife Ann and son Jon, Rocky drove across the country and stopped in Las Vegas to see *Diana Ross & The Supremes* at The Frontier Hotel & Casino. A couple of days later they were in Hollywood, CA, and it changed Jon's plans as to where he wanted to spend the rest of his life.

15. **Joey Giardello, Al "The Tailor" Certo, Jack Dempsey and Willie Pep, Secaucus, NJ, circa 1968:** Famous boxers at the tailor shop (note the photos along the top of the wall).

16. Rocky and Ann D'Amore, circa 1969
Jon's favorite picture of his parents.

17. Jon D'Amore, 1974
If he wasn't on stage, he was in a studio somewhere.

18. **Two Friends with Rocky Graziano and Al Certo (on the right), 1975**
Al liked to hang around with boxers.

19. **John Phillip Law, November, 1975**
The famous actor met Jon D'Amore a month earlier at *The Villa Capri*. It was the beginning of a life long friendship.

20. **Jon D'Amore, Las Vegas, 1976:** On the balcony of his 25th floor suite of the original MGM Grand on the Vegas Strip.

21. **Jon D'Amore, Fort Lee, NJ, November, 1977:** A favorite photo of Jon's, this was taken in Palisades Interstate Park directly under The George Washington Bridge.

22. **Jon D'Amore, Belmar, NJ, Summer, 1979:** With Las Vegas just a memory and his music career doing very well...Jon took a break down at the Jersey shore to see some friends.

23. **Jon D'Amore, 1980:** In the studio doing what he enjoyed the most.

24. Jon (holding the machine gun) and Friends, May 1, 1982
It was a day to party and dress up. The car was used in The Godfather.

25. Jon and Rocky D'Amore, 1987
Like father…like son.

26. At a D'Amore Family Reunion, circa 1993: Left to right - Jon's Cousin Carmine Flora (named after his Uncle 'Rocky'), Rocky's brother-in-law, the famous Newark cop David Toma (remember the mid-1970s ABC-TV show "Toma"?), and Rocky.

27. Jon D'Amore, July, 1993
During the corporate days. Rock & Roll and Vegas were long behind him, yet the pinky ring remained.

28. Jon and Aunt Jean D'Amore, 2006
Still Jon's favorite aunt. At 93 years old, she passed away on Sunday, January 16, 2011, to finally be with her husband Dominic, and son Gerald (better known as "Jerry," Jon's cousin and Godfather).

29. Jon D'Amore and Al Certo, Secaucus, NJ, 2006: Friends since 1968. Al "The Tailor" gave Jon's band their first paying gig at The Plaza Arena, starting Jon on his first (and favorite) career. Note the photos along the top of the wall (some things never change).

By now Jerry felt confident that I knew what to do at the table, so he sat in the lounge to get an overview of the casino action, and to see if we were being watched by hotel security...other than by the constant overhead eyes and cameras above the casino's ceiling.

If he felt that I had been there long enough, or if too many players were leaving the table, he would wander over and throw a hundred dollar bill down to place a bet. That would be our cue. Louie would be the first to pick up his chips and walk away after the shooter won or lost. I was next, but first I had to smile at the pit boss and then head back to my room. Taz would lower his next bet and then walk away after the outcome. Jerry would then leave the table a roll or two after we were all gone.

For a Monday night the casino was very active, so it wasn't long before I started making some side bets. I could see Louie and Taz smiling to themselves as they watched me.

It was around 11:15, and I was hunched over the edge of the table watching the dice as they rolled my way from a shooter down at the other end.

I felt a hand on my back slide up to my shoulder. I stood straight up and turned around to see Michele standing behind me. I made sure I looked around to see that her husband wasn't close by.

There was no sign of him.

Her appearance was much different from when I originally met her that afternoon. She was now wearing a fantastic blue satin dress that did everything to form-fit her body, and her impeccable hair and make-up enhanced her tanned, beautiful face. I was happy to have her standing next to me.

She leaned against me and whispered, "He went to The Riviera with his partners."

"How was dinner?" I asked as the action continued on the table.

"Fine," she answered in a normal voice, but lowered it as she again came close and whispered, "But nowhere near as good as this afternoon was."

I smiled and looked at my cohorts. Louie was watching my bets and the action on the table. Taz, on the other hand, was looking at Michele, and then at me...with that "*I told you so!*" look on his face.

"So, are you winning?" she asked.

I looked down at the rack and did some quick calculations.

"Not really. I started with three grand and I'm down to about eleven hundred," I said as I shrugged my shoulders as if to appear that it didn't matter.

Of course, she had no idea that the concept was for me to lose it all.

I continued to bet the pass line and lay down some side bets. Every once in a while I'd feel her hand glide up and down my back as she moved closer to me.

"So, where are your partners?" I asked as the shooter rolled his point and the dealer pushed eight hundred dollars in front of my pass line bet.

Michele looked down at my winnings, smiled and said, "Sharon went to her room to freshen up. Jeanette is pissed off at her husband because he ignored her at dinner, so she made him take out a five hundred dollar marker. She's over there playing." She pointed in the direction of the blackjack tables. "Sharon said she'll be down in about fifteen minutes. Jeanette will have blown her husband's money by then. I'm sure they'll find me."

"What did you tell them you'd be doing?" I asked as I laid five black chips on the pass line.

"Looking for you," she whispered.

I smiled...until the shooter's come out roll stopped in front of me.

"Eleven. A winner!" the stickman yelled, "Pay the pass line."

"*Shit!*" I said to myself.

"Look at that! Maybe I'm your good luck charm!" she said as she kissed me on the cheek.

I don't think Louie and Taz were looking at it that way. *Their* function was to reap my losses.

But she may have been right.

While she stood there I began picking up winnings from most of my side bets, and the shooters were hitting their points more often than usual. It wasn't long before I had recouped my original $3,000 just from the pass line bets, and more than a thousand from side bets.

Jeanette and Sharon came up behind us, each appearing as stunning as Michele. They huddled around me as I gathered up more winnings.

It was also apparent that I was becoming the center of attention at the table.

Here was this 22-year-old novice, gambling thousands of dollars and surrounded by three attractive older women.

I was very lost in that thought...so I didn't notice that because I was winning so much, it wasn't logical for Taz and Louie to be betting the don't-pass line and losing their money. So one at a time, they left.

Once I realized they were gone I figured I'd stay for one or two more passes before I'd pick everything up and walk away...and to beg their forgiveness.

As the roller tossed the dice, I felt another set of hands on my shoulders. Before I could turn to see who it was, I heard, "Hello, Juan."

Shit. I fucked up...and now I was gonna pay for it.

I slowly turned and whispered in Jerry's ear so that the girls couldn't hear, "I'm sorry, Jer. If it means anything, I'm ahead. I'll be in my room in five minutes. I hope I didn't fuck anything up?"

"I came to tell you *not* to leave." He came closer and whispered even softer, "As long as you don't go below the three grand, whatever you're ahead is yours. Do whatever you want with it. Just don't lose any of the three."

"What time you want me in the room?"

"Don't worry about it. Looks like you made some friends here," he said as he looked at my three companions. "I'll catch up with you tomorrow. Bring it over then."

"You sure?"

"What are ya gonna do? Fuck *me* outta money? Have a good time."

I smiled and we kissed each other on the cheek before he slipped into the crowd to catch a cab to The Frontier.

The ladies and I stayed at the table for another 15 minutes or so, and when I saw that I had over $6,000 in my rack, I decided it was time to walk away.

As I gathered up the chips the pit boss came over and asked if I wanted to cover the $3,000 marker that I had taken when I came to the table, but my mission was to keep the chips and turn it into cash for Jerry.

"No, thanks. I'm coming back down later," I said as I made eyes toward the three women surrounding me.

He took the hint, smiled and said, "See you then, Mr. D. Have a good evening."

We walked over to the lounge and the three ladies sat around me as the cocktail waitress came over.

"Good evening, Jonny. Any luck tonight?"

"Been lucky all day," I answered, knowing that only Michele would get it.

I ordered a bottle of Dom Perignon, and as we drank, Jeanette told us how she did at the blackjack table with her husband's money.

As the bottle quickly emptied, Michele decided that she wanted to smoke a joint. It was unanimous, so I quickly offered my suite. After the last drop of champagne was consumed, we were in an elevator on our way to the penthouse.

Only Michele didn't "oooh" and "ahhh" when we entered.

I walked over to the living room phone, called Room Service and ordered two more bottles of Dom and lots of ice for the buckets.

It was after midnight and the temperature outside could not have been less than eighty, so we immediately headed for the terrace to admire the light show on The Strip. We smoked a joint before the champagne arrived, and it was only a matter of time before one of them asked me to play a song on the piano.

I took off my suit jacket and loosened my tie as I sat down and started striking some chords, just to get the feel of the keyboard. I explained to them that I was a guitarist and that my piano skills were limited to three and four finger chords with my right hand and bass notes with my left. And above all, I *was not* a vocalist.

Fortunately, I had found that a joint and some champagne in the listener is *always* an advantage to the performer.

As they leaned against the piano, I told them that I had recently written a song about the setting sun over the Hollywood Hills, then went right into my latest composition. When it was over, they stood there for a few seconds before they applauded and whispered "*Beautiful*," and "*That was great.*"

That was the reason I wanted to be a musician. That reaction from people after you perform something you've created. *That* was the reason I loved to perform. Whether it was thousands of fans at a concert, a recording engineer sitting in another room listening through monitors, or three women in a Vegas hotel room...that was the life I *really* wanted. And at that moment, and for the next few hours, I was living it. I *really was* living it.

Jeanette walked over to the bar and brought back one of the bottles to fill our empty glasses. Then she sat next to me and pulled my face to hers. She slowly ran her hands through my hair and pressed her lips against mine.

When she eventually pulled away I heard Michele's voice from behind me.

"Well Jon, it looks like you've made another friend."

I didn't know what to say. It was an awkward situation. I didn't know how these women would react to what I was thinking I'd *like* to have happen.

Michele and Jeanette looked at Sharon, then Michele asked her, "What do you think, Sharon? Do you want to be Jon's friend, too?"

Sharon emptied her champagne flute with one long swallow, then looked at her two friends and asked. "Will he sing for us again later?"

They all turned their heads toward me.

"*Any* time," I answered.

Michele and Jeanette each took me by an arm and led me away from the piano. Sharon collected our champagnes glasses and bottles, and I was led into the bedroom.

Apparently, these women were either mind-readers...or Michele "kissed and told."

Room service was called for another two bottles of champagne and over the next few hours the ladies and I became more than friends.

It was nearly 3:30 in the morning before they left, one at a time.

Michele was the last to leave. As we were kissing each other goodbye, she asked if I was surprised by what had just happened. I told her it wasn't the first time I'd had a ménage, but that I didn't expect this evening to turn into one.

I asked if she had mentioned our afternoon session to her friends.

"I didn't *have* to. They knew I went with you after I left the pool. They could tell what happened just by the look on my face throughout dinner. And like I said, they knew I was going to look for you after our husbands took off." She leaned back into my arms and continued, "I told them we spoke about fantasies and that I asked you to fulfill one of mine. It seems they had some of their own. The fact that the three of us took you to bed was just something that happened. It wasn't planned. But for us, it was a fantasy you made come true."

We gently kissed again, and then she left.

I couldn't go to bed yet. I had work to do.

I threw on some clothes, grabbed Jerry's three grand in chips and went down to the casino to cash them in.

When I came back to the suite I poured the remaining champagne into my glass, sat at the piano, took a few hits on a joint and played a bit more before I went to sleep.

I slept a little later than expected, but when I arrived at my reserved chaise lounge around noon, I saw that sitting right behind me, again, were the same six people from the day before. Each of the women smiled as I approached...and I returned their look with a smile and a wink.

Their husbands didn't notice a thing.

Not even 15 minutes later, as if on cue, the men decided once again that the pool was no place for a gambler to languish. They wanted to go to one of the casinos downtown "...*where the odds are better!*"

Before he walked away, Michele's husband turned to her and said, "And don't forget to be ready for dinner. We'll be back by seven. Dinner's at eight-thirty."

"What a schmuck," I said to myself, *again,* and shook my head.

As soon as they left, I called over a cocktail waitress and told her, loud enough for my new friends to hear, "Send two bottles of Dom Perignon up to twenty-five thirty-six in fifteen minutes."

I slipped her a twenty, put on my sneakers and shirt, turned, winked at the ladies and went to my room.

One at a time they arrived. Michele was first, then Sharon and, finally, Jeanette. Once the champagne arrived and we burned a joint, they asked me to sing for them.

I obliged...and played John Lennon's *Imagine.*

We spent the rest of the afternoon as we had twelve hours earlier.

At some point during the festivities, Jerry called and told me he was going to be very busy and that they wouldn't need me until "...at least eight or nine tonight."

From the bedroom phone I assured him that I'd be ready and that I had *that thing* from the night before put aside.

"So, Juan, enjoying yourself here in Vegas?" he asked.

I looked up at the mirrored ceiling to see the reflection of three beautiful, naked women lying on my large circular bed, then I took a deep breath, smiled and said, "Yes, Jerry. Yes I am."

Round 7

It was around 2:45 on Thursday afternoon. Mike and I had checked out of The MGM a couple of hours earlier and were eating lunch at The Frontier with Jerry and Taz. The four of us were killing time until their 4:15 flight left for Newark. My flight to Burbank was scheduled to leave ten minutes later.

I told the California D'Amores I'd be arriving by 5:30, and Joey said he'd meet me at the airport. It may sound odd, but after a week of Vegas I was looking forward to Hollywood and my guitars.

The rest of Jerry's crew, along with Tommy Dolan and his guys, checked out of their rooms and left earlier that day.

Jerry said Dolan returned to Jersey with over $275,000. On top of that, Jerry, Mike and Taz were carrying another $175,000 because Dolan had no room left in his suitcase.

Rocco Casiano was going to be very happy.

"*Shit!*" Taz suddenly roared as his hands tapped the pockets of his jacket.

Our eyes shot to him with puzzled looks on our faces.

"I forgot all about these," he said as he pulled out two gray one-thousand dollar chips from The Tropicana and tossed them on the table. "I slipped them off the rack and forgot to cash them in. *Shit!*" he roared again in anger.

"No problem," said Jerry, "We've got time, and we gotta pass The Trop on the way to the airport anyway. What'll it take...five minutes?"

Mike and Taz gave a knowing laugh. I didn't get it.

Jerry signed the tab for lunch and within ten minutes the four of us and our luggage were in the back of one of The Frontier's comped limos.

As the car pulled up to The Trop, I assumed Jerry, Mike and I would wait while Taz cashed in the chips.

But as usual, it didn't turn out that way.

"Come on, Juan. Time to play a hunch," Jerry quipped as Mike and Taz exited the limo.

Over the past week I had learned never to question him...especially about his hunches. And besides, considering I had gone through twenty-five grand over the past few days, the 'casino bug' was getting to me. I wanted to see what they were going to do with this money.

It was nearly 3:15 when we walked into the casino. As usual, the ringing slot machines were the first sounds I heard, but they were also the first to disappear as I listened for a table calling my name.

And as usual...Jerry heard it...and found it.

The four of us walked over to a $100 minimum blackjack table with two women and a man sitting at it. It was apparent they were all together. The man and the older woman appeared to be married and in their fifties. But the young woman, who I thought was attractive even though I had never been partial to redheads, was in her early 20s and didn't resemble the people she was with. I couldn't figure out the relationship, but I didn't give it much thought once Jerry told me to sit down and Taz placed the two gray chips in front of me.

"I'm not very good at blackjack, Jer," I whispered.

"Don't worry. We're right behind you. All you gotta do is use the basic strategy of the game," he said.

To which I responded, "Huh?"

Mike leaned toward me and said, "Just listen to your cousin and do what he tells ya."

I looked at Jerry.

He smiled and pushed one of the chips into the circle in front of me.

The dealer slid the cards from the shoe and gave each player and himself two. One of his was turned face-up.

It was a two.

I had ten in the hole.

The gentleman busted when he motioned for a card and his fourteen turned to twenty-two with the flip of an eight. The dealer quickly scooped up the four $25 chips.

His wife was standing with whatever she had in her hand, and the girl I was sitting next to smiled as she pulled a nine to go with her twelve.

"G'head," my cousin whispered. "Let's see what you pull."

I scratched the cards to the felt and the dealer tossed an ace in front of me. I turned to Jerry and smiled.

"Beginner's luck," he laughed.

The dealer flipped over his other card to show a ten. He now had a 12. If he pulled a nine then I'd have a *push*, otherwise known as a tie, and would neither win nor lose.

He slid a card from the shoe and flipped it over. It was an eight. He had twenty.

The wife threw down her cards to show an eighteen. The dealer scooped up her hundred.

Both the girl and I laid our cards down to show him our twenty-ones. The dealer slid a black chip in front of her, and a gray chip in front of me.

"Good hunch, Jer!" I said as I picked up my winnings and the two chips I started with. I stood up and prepared to walk away.

But then I heard the same words I had come to hear time and time again.

"Where you goin'? Put those chips back down and let it ride."

I also heard Mike and Taz laughing as I smiled and did what Jerry told me to do.

I put the two chips into the circle and waited for the dealer to determine their fate.

The girl saw that I doubled my bet, so she followed suit and slid her winnings from the last hand on top of her single black chip.

The cards were dealt with the dealer showing an eight. The gentleman played it safe by not taking another card. His wife busted quickly and the girl sat with her hand.

I picked up my cards and showed Jerry my two kings.

He turned and said something to Mike and Taz, causing them to laugh...again.

The dealer flipped over his card to show an ace. He had nineteen.

The husband cursed and tossed his ten and seven to the dealer.

The girl and I laid down our twenties.

Two hundred dollars was placed in front of her, and two more gray chips were placed in front of me.

Jerry said, "Let it ride."

I told him he was crazy and pulled back two of the four grand.

"Come on. It's found money," he said with a laugh. "Take the risk and gamble."

"Let me just play it safe...just this once," I said.

After the dealer put our cards in front of us, I looked at his *face-up* card. It was a two.

Once again the gentleman at the end busted when he called for a card that put him over. His wife also lost when she tried to turn a fourteen into a winner. The girl was dealt a Blackjack and was immediately paid one-and-a-half times her bet.

She smiled and thanked me, as if I actually had something to do with it!

I noticed that she had a very proper British accent, unlike her companions who sounded as if they were from the midwest.

I picked up my cards and saw two sevens. Jerry quickly leaned over and whispered, "Split 'em."

"You sure?"

He looked at me with a knowing smile.

I shook my head and tossed both sevens up for the dealer to see.

"Split 'em," I said.

Everyone watched as I slid the other two grand in front of the cards.

I smiled as he tossed an ace to the first seven, and I waved my hand over them.

For the second hand, I had to work a little harder. The first card was a two, then a three. I could hear Mike and Taz still laughing behind me. I knew Jerry was calculating odds and counting cards in his head. I was just worrying about the $4,000 bet on these two hands.

I tapped my fingers twice on the table and the dealer flipped over another seven. That made nineteen.

Now it was the dealer's turn.

He flipped over his card to show a jack. With twelve showing, he needed an eight or nine to beat my second hand.

He slid a card from the shoe and tossed it over. Another jack!

Jerry, Mike and Taz patted me on the back as everyone at the table cheered. The girl joined in with a "Jolly-bloody-good!"

"Okay," I said as I won four grand. "Time to go!"

"No," Jerry said.

"Get outta here, kid," Mike said, in between bursts of laughter, "We're staying until it's either gone, or you turn it into ten grand."

"Shit!" I said to myself.

Jerry looked at his watch, then slid two grand into the bettor's circle and said, "Time for one more hand. I gotta make some calls from the airport."

Seeing this, everybody else at the table upped their bets.

The husband and wife each had two hundred on the line, and the redhead bumped her bet up to a thousand dollars. She looked at me, winked and crossed her fingers.

Two pit bosses came over to the table. One stood on each side of the dealer and watched.

A crowd of onlookers gathered around us.

The cards were dealt and each of us played cautiously.

No one busted.

The dealer flipped over his down-card to show a seventeen. He couldn't pull another one.

We turned over our cards to show that each of us had between eighteen and twenty-one. A table of winners!

There were cheers all around as I quickly gathered up the ten grand in chips. The redhead thanked me for bringing her good luck, and I said the same to her.

I couldn't believe it. We started with a thousand dollar bet and within a few minutes I ran it up to $10,000.

I tossed a black chip to the Dealer and handed the remaining $9,900 to my cousin.

While counting and separating the cash as we left the cashier's cage, Jerry said, "Here's the original two grand for Casiano." He put the money in a wad that already had at least ten grand in hundreds wrapped with a rubber band. "There's a grand each for me, Mike and Taz," he said as he handed them the cash. Then he handed the rest to me. "And the balance is for *the gambler*."

Quickly doing some math, I said, "That's forty-nine hundred dollars, Jer! You're givin' me forty-nine hundred dollars?"

"It's found money, Juan. And you *won* it."

"Don't ever go against your cousin's hunches, kid," Mike chimed in as he and Taz folded their *piece* into their already bulging pockets.

As we walked away from the cashier I noticed the three people from the blackjack table were also cashing in.

The girl came up to me as I was pocketing my winnings and asked, "Would you like to stop into the lounge for a quick drink?"

I told her we had a car waiting to take us to the airport and that we were in a rush. "Maybe another time," I said with a smile.

I quickly found myself in formation next to Jerry as Taz led the way and Mike covered the rear.

I looked at her as we walked away. She was about an inch taller than me and around the same age. Her red hair came down just below her shoulders and her clothes were in style for the mid '70s. They helped outline a very attractive body.

She smiled back and watched as we made our way out of the casino.

By 3:55, I was standing at the gate with the guys, waiting for them to board their plane back to Jersey.

Jerry walked away to find a payphone.

I was standing between Mike and Taz as they towered above me. Taz looked down and asked, "So kid, whatcha think of your first trip?"

I took a few seconds to think of the logical and calculated answers that I could have given him. But instead, I just smiled. I still wasn't sure this was something I wanted to do again, so I didn't give a response that would show my hand.

Sure...it was profitable.

Besides the forty-nine hundred I just picked up at The Trop, I also had the sixteen hundred and seventy-five dollars I'd won at the roulette table when I first arrived at The MGM on my birthday. Earlier, as we ate lunch at The Frontier, Jerry had handed me a grand as my *salary*. I also picked up three grand at the crap table the night I spent with Michele, Sharon and Jeanette.

In total, I was leaving Vegas with $10,575 more than when I arrived.

As Taz repeated his question to my distant stare, Jerry walked over and said, "I just spoke to Vinnie. He said everything's good with last week's collections, and he thinks we'll be able to get that store in Hoboken on Washington Avenue in a month or so."

Vinnie Caputo was another one of Jerry's inner crew. He was trusted to run the Jersey operation while Jerry, Mike and Taz worked in Vegas. Vinnie was a couple of years younger than Jerry. He stood about 5'10, was very good looking and lived in Secaucus with his wife and kids. He didn't look like a mobster...*and* he had a clean record.

Vinnie ran the fronts...the businesses that Jerry ran for Casiano.

Al 'The Tailor' Nucci hooked Vinnie and Jerry up years ago. And since that introduction, Jerry and Vinnie became close friends and business associates.

Looking at him, it was hard to imagine he was a hitman. One of the best, they said. There was even talk that Vinnie might have been the *Twenty-two Caliber Killer* that the newspapers were writing about from time to time during the early to mid '70s.

"What's the store for?" I asked as we huddled together.

"Who knows?" Jerry answered. "Vinnie wants to turn it into a pizzeria, but Rocco wants to make it a butcher shop. I'm just afraid he'll use the freezer to store people he gets pissed at and whacks. Heat like that, we don't need."

Mike and Taz nodded their heads.

I decided not to ask any more questions.

A couple of minutes later, the door out to the plane opened.

I stood on my toes to reach them as they each kissed me goodbye.

Jerry squeezed me especially tight, kissed me on both cheeks, looked me in the eyes and asked, "Have a good birthday?"

He could tell from the smile on my face that I didn't need to respond.

"Call me when you get back to Jersey. We'll talk," he said as he pulled me close and hugged me again.

Then he whispered in my ear, "I'm very proud of you, Jon. I learned things I never knew about you before. You're not the little kid I used to bring toys to anymore." He choked up for a few seconds before he continued, "I'm sorry...I'm sorry I didn't notice you had grown up." He kissed me on the cheek again and repeated, "I'm very proud of you."

I knew he was being sincere...because he didn't call me *Juan* or *kid*.

I kissed him back and watched as he took his place between Mike and Taz and walked onto the tarmac, then up the steps to the United jet.

I stood there and smiled as I thought about the great twenty-second birthday he gave me.

I strolled over to the Hughes Airwest gate to wait for my flight to Burbank and began thinking about *the money*.

I started calculating.

I was averaging about fifteen hundred dollars a week from my session work. My manager took 15%, and whichever agent booked the gig got

10%. I had a lawyer who took 5% to negotiate my contracts with my manager and the agents. An accountant took 2.5% to keep my life in order, collect and deposit my checks, pay my manager, agents and lawyer, pay my bills *and* take care of my taxes. Of course, I had to keep another 30% of my gross-after-commissions in a separate account to *pay* those taxes.

I was also paying for my health and car insurance, which came to nearly $4,000 a year.

Fortunately, living and traveling expenses, such as food, hotels and airlines were always picked up by whomever was contracting me. When I was working in the New York area, I'd stay at my parents' home. And living *there* was free.

Though I was grossing at least $78,000 a year, I'd clear about $29,000, or $560 a week, after every*one* and every*thing* was paid. That wasn't bad in 1975 for a 22-year-old *kid*.

But during just one week with Jerry, I'd made nearly 40% of my annual take-home...*and* had one of the best times of my life.

Would I be able to do this trip with the boys from Hudson County once every six months and walk away with an extra ten grand, tax and commission free, every time?

I knew I'd make at least a thousand as my salary. But would Jerry's hunches always pay off? Would I always be able to pick up three grand at the crap table just on side bets?

It seemed doubtful. But...there were all those *other* perks. Taz wasn't bullshitting. He knew exactly what he was talking about.

If *I* was making a grand on each trip by being a make-believe gambler...I couldn't imagine how much Jerry and Dolan made every time they'd come here to run this scam.

But there are things you don't discuss with these guys. Even when one of them's family.

"Can I buy you that drink now?" I heard from behind me.

I turned around to see the British redhead from the blackjack table.

"What are *you* doing here?" I asked.

"My guardian has business to attend to at his office in Century City," she answered. "So before we return to Chicago, we've got to stop in Los Angeles for a few days. And yourself?"

"I'm going back to L.A. to pick up my gear and see some relatives before I head back to New Jersey."

"Are you on this flight, too?" she asked as she pointed to the jet parked outside the door.

"Yep."

Just then the doors opened.

"My name is Millicent," she said with a smile.

"I'm Jon," I said as I took her hand and shook it.

As we walked onto the tarmac and headed toward the steps of the plane we were met by the married couple.

Millicent, in her proper British dialect, quickly introduced Mr. and Mrs. Waite of Barrington Hills, Illinois.

Once we entered the plane they headed to their seats in first class. I said goodbye and made my way to a window seat in coach.

I was settling in as the stewardess walked over and asked the person sitting next to me if he would like to move to a seat that was available in first class. It only took him a second to think about it before he was gone.

I was happy for the solitude as I put my head back, closed my eyes and smiled as I continued thinking of my week in Vegas.

"I hope you don't mind," I heard a voice say as I felt someone slide into the vacant seat next to me.

I opened my eyes to see Millicent latching her seatbelt.

"Didn't like first class?"

"First class was fine," she answered. "It was the company and conversation that bored me."

"The couple you're with?"

"My guardians," she said in a frustrated tone.

I matter-of-factly asked, "Mind telling me about that?"

"Not right now." It was obvious she wanted to change the subject. "Maybe after we take off and they serve drinks."

"I guess you haven't flown from Vegas to L.A. before, have you?"

"No. Why?"

"We'll be there before you know it. They won't be serving any drinks. They barely have time to pour coffee."

"Damn!" she said under her breath.

Just then the plane taxied out to the runway and in less than five minutes we were airborne and heading west.

I was always a sucker for a British accent, particularly hers because she didn't speak like the U.K. rockers and roadies I was used to working with. She was educated and her diction was perfect. The way she moved when she walked, even the way she moved her body while she sat in an airplane seat seemed graceful, elegant and natural.

About halfway through the flight Mrs. Waite approached and knelt down in the aisle next to Millicent.

"Lady Millicent, I'm sorry to bother you, but--"

She stopped short, realizing that she'd done something wrong.

"*Please!*" Millicent said abruptly as a look of anger shot across her face. "I've asked you not to call me that. *Please!*"

"I'm sorry, it's just that--" the wife started to say.

"I don't care what the reason is," Millicent loudly whispered. "I insist that while we're in public, you do *not* call me that."

"I'm sorry. It won't happen again," Mrs. Waite responded, with her eyes looking to the floor.

Millicent took a deep breath, "What is it?"

"Mr. Waite would like to know your preferences for dinner," she replied, still looking down. "That way he can have the hotel make reservations as soon as we land."

Realizing Millicent didn't want to be socializing with these people, I jumped in.

"I'm sorry, but I was just asking Millicent if she'd allow me to take her to dinner." I looked at Millicent and said, "So?"

"Yes. That would be very nice. I'd like that very much," she answered, realizing that I knew I was rescuing her.

I asked, "Which hotel are you staying at?"

Mrs. Waite looked at me with eyes that appeared to be thanking me for rescuing her, too, and answered, "In Beverly Hills. At The Beverly-Wilshire. It's on--"

I cut her off, looked at my watch and said, "I know where it is. How about if I get there by eight?"

"That would be lovely, Jon," Millicent said as she put her head back against the seat and waved Mrs. Waite away.

The guardian smiled at me and walked down the aisle.

As we approached Burbank, I told Millicent that at some point during the evening I'd be asking her about *Lady* Millicent...and why she needed guardians.

"That depends on if you get me to a third gin and tonic, love, doesn't it?" she calmly responded.

After we landed and the jet taxied to the gate, I repeated the question the Waites tried to get answered shortly after takeoff.

"So, what kind of food *would* you like to have tonight?"

She smiled and answered, "I feel like a little Italian."

I remarked that 5'6 wasn't *that* little and smiled back.

She got the joke, laughed and asked, "Do you know of a good Italian restaurant in Los Angeles, or shall I have the hotel make a recommendation?"

"Don't worry about it," I laughed...sounding almost like my cousin Jerry to one of my many concerns. "I know of one of the best."

"Is it in Hollywood? I'd *love* to go to Hollywood! Someplace where movie stars go?"

"Yeah," I said as I leaned back into my seat and smiled. "It's in Hollywood."

After we deplaned, Millicent and I met the Waites at the luggage carousel, collected our bags and the four of us walked into the hot San Fernando Valley air.

As her husband went to find their limo to The Beverly-Wilshire, Mrs. Waite quietly took me aside and thanked me for taking Millicent to dinner.

It wasn't long before my cousin Joey drove up in one of his Jaguars. The red one.

"Here comes my ride," I said.

A visibly excited Millicent said, "A '72 XK-E Roadster Coupe. *Very* nice."

"Like it?" I asked.

"I have the same one," she answered nonchalantly. "I'd like a convertible, but they're not very practical in England."

She watched me barely fit one suitcase in the trunk and jam the other onto something resembling a back seat.

I waved goodbye to the Waites, then took Millicent's hand and said, "I'll see you in a few hours."

"I'm looking forward to it! Ta!" she replied with a smile as I slid into the Jag.

After Joey and I did the Italian kiss on the cheek, I fell back and melted into the soft leather seat. He put the car in gear and the terminal disappeared behind us.

I spent the twenty minute ride to Studio City telling him about my suite at The MGM Grand, winning at the roulette table, my birthday dinner... complete with a four showgirl accompaniment for dessert, relaxing at the spa, the *big win* at the blackjack table, meeting Lady Millicent and my dinner plans for the evening.

I said nothing about any of the guys from Jersey, the $25,000 credit line, my experiences at the crap tables in six different casinos, or the three married women from the pool.

It's not that I thought any of those events would have seemed out of place to Joey. I'm sure he had a few *wiseguy* stories himself, but since I was still uncertain of any future Vegas adventures, the less said...the better.

As we turned off of Laurel Canyon Boulevard onto Canton Drive, I asked him for a favor.

"Would you mind if I borrowed your other Jaguar tonight?"

"For the British girl? Want this one? It's newer. The other one's a sixty-eight," he answered.

"The other one's a convertible," I responded. "She'll like that."

And *did* she.

After giving Millicent the tour of Bel Air, Beverly Hills, Hollywood and the view from Mulholland Drive, we arrived at the restaurant around nine o'clock. I didn't mention the family connection, but I think the large neon '*Patsy D'Amore's Villa Capri*' sign atop the building may have given it away.

The parking lot was full, but the valet saw me and took the car with a smile, a personal greeting and a handshake. I slid five dollars into his palm.

When we walked in I saw that the bar was crowded with people who were waiting for tables.

Patsy's old friend Antonio, now working as the maître d', was at the podium.

Once he saw me he extended his arms and kissed me on each cheek.

"Hey, paisan! Good to see you! I hear you were in Vegas." He looked at Millicent, then back to me and continued, "Ah, signora! Molta bella! Dinner for two, Giovanni, si?"

I leaned toward him and quietly answered, "Si, Antonio. But we don't mind waiting. You're a little backed up. We can have a drink at the bar until something opens up."

He took a step back and said, "Don't be silly. You *always* have a seat at Patsy's table."

Upon hearing that, Millicent looked at me, squeezed my hand and smiled.

There were only a few people allowed to sit at what was called 'Patsy's Table.' This was where you found him, along with his wife and children, and those who would be granted the opportunity to sit there. It was like being allowed to sit with the king. After he died, it was reserved only for the family...or Sinatra. That was it.

It was the best table in the house.

And that night, it was just going to be me and Millicent. Sinatra was nowhere to be found.

Each waiter and busboy stopped to say "Hello" as they passed the table.

Throughout the night she got her fill of Hollywood celebrities, either eating at a table or schmoozing at the bar.

Jonathan Winters sat at a large corner table with a handful of studio heads.

Joey Bishop was at another table doing shtick with a bunch of friends.

Dean Martin sat directly across from us enjoying a bowl of fusilli and a glass of Chianti. He even started to sing as the pianist played *That's Amore!*

As we ate dinner, the chef came out from the kitchen to greet us and asked if our meals were prepared to our satisfaction, while the pianist played a couple of my favorite tunes and even dedicated *Imagine* to me.

Millicent was very impressed.

And as she predicted, it took three gin and tonics before she told me her story.

Apparently, she was related to the Royal Family back in jolly Olde England. About two months before our encounter she was involved in an automobile accident in which she was driving and her boyfriend was killed. The police found hashish in the car and it was determined that Millicent had a bit too much to drink. So the Royals decided that she should go to the States for a while...until the matter could be quietly resolved.

The Waites, American friends of Millicent's family, were responsible for keeping her out of trouble and out of the spotlight.

And now...she was in *my* hands.

After we finished eating, Millicent noticed another familiar face.

Standing at the podium and talking to Antonio was a tall, handsome man. I knew I had seen him in a couple of movies, but I couldn't remember his name.

"That's John Phillip Law!" she said in hushed excitement.

"You've seen him before?"

"Yes. Actually, I was supposed to meet him last year when he was in England shooting a film. One of my father's associates invited him to dinner and we were invited to attend. But at the last moment, someone decided they needed to shoot a scene at night, so he had to cancel."

I told one of the waiters to send Antonio over.

Within seconds, the maître d' was standing next to me and asking, "What's the problem, Giovanni? Anything wrong?"

"No, Antonio, nothing's wrong. But you see that guy you were just talking to?"

He looked back to the podium.

"Johnny Law?"

"Know him?"

"Sure I know him. He's been coming here for years," he answered. "He just dropped in to see who's around. Sometimes he stays for dinner, sometimes he has a drink and goes. He lives nearby. Up in the hills."

"See if he'd like to join us for a drink. Millicent would like to meet him," I said as she grabbed my arm and squeezed.

"Consider it done, paisan. Be right back," he said with a wink.

I winked at Millicent.

She melted into her seat.

As Antonio and John Phillip Law approached, I stood up and extended my hand. I was immediately intimidated by the height of this 6'4 actor.

As we shook hands, Antonio said, "John Law, this is Patsy D'Amore's cousin from New Jersey, Giovanni D'Amore. Giovanni and his guest would like to know if you have time to join them for a drink."

"It would be a pleasure," he responded with a smile and a deep, rich voice.

Antonio turned and walked away.

John looked down and said, "It's nice to meet you, Signor D'Amore," with that Italian flair in the pronunciation of my name.

"Please, Mr. Law, call me Jon."

"Same here," he responded.

It was the beginning of a long-standing friendship between me and Johnny Law.

"I'd like you to meet a fan," I said as I turned to my guest. "John Philip Law, allow me to present--"

The actor cut in and said, "*Lady Millicent!*"

I stood there with a foolish look on my face and slowly said, "You've... met?"

"Not actually," he answered, "But last year while I was in England shooting...uhm, *The Spiral Staircase* with Jackie Bisset, I was supposed to have dinner at someone's home. For some reason, it never happened. The next day a messenger arrived at my hotel room with a gift-wrapped box. When I opened it, there was a silver picture frame, and in it, a picture of a beautiful young lady with a note saying, 'I'm sorry I missed you at dinner last evening. I hope we have the pleasure someday.' It was signed, 'Lady Millicent.'"

"And you remembered what I looked like and what I wrote?" she asked as she looked up from her seat...with stars in her eyes.

"The picture, the frame and the note are hanging in a very prominent place in my home," he answered. "So it was *easy* to recognize you...and a pleasure to finally meet you."

He took her hand, clasped it and bowed his head.

I smiled and motioned for him to sit down.

"Isn't this Patsy's booth?" he asked.

I nodded.

"Thank you. It's *an honor*," he said. "Only a select group gets to sit here."

Millicent turned and looked at me with the same dreamy eyes she was casting toward the actor.

As he slid into the booth he told us, "I've been coming here since the late fifties and have seen a lot of people sitting with Patsy in this booth."

Millicent gushed, "Like who? I'd love to know!"

"Well, it's well known that the original Villa Capri was one of James Dean's favorite hangouts. As a matter of fact, I heard he had dinner there with Alec Guinness the night before he left to go up north."

He didn't have to finish the rest of the story. We all knew how it ended.

I immediately thought of my father's recollection of our chance meeting with Dean in July of 1955.

"But I've seen countless people at this table. Sinatra. DiMaggio and Marilyn. Jimmy Durante was one of Patsy's favorites. Patsy loved families. You would always find him, his wife and kids here with Tony Curtis and Janet Leigh...Bob Wagner, Natalie Wood...Ann Margret, Roger Smith.

All in this very booth."

Millicent gave me another dreamy-eyed look.

It wasn't long before Millicent and I were in the Jaguar following the actor's car down Hollywood Boulevard to LaBrea Avenue to Sunset Boulevard to Miller Drive…and directly into his driveway.

We spent the rest of the night drinking champagne, smoking pot and admiring The Strip while soaking in John's outdoor hot tub as Lady Millicent simultaneously made love to me and the co-star of Barbarella… and she couldn't be happier.

This was absolutely Hollywood 1975!

I pulled up to the front of the Beverly-Wilshire around 2:30 the following afternoon.

Mrs. Waite was pacing back and forth across the lobby, holding what was probably her third scotch. The look of relief was vividly apparent when she saw Millicent and I walk in.

"We've asked you several times to please call us if you intend to stay out for the evening!" the guardian wailed as she approached from across the lobby. She could see from Millicent's appearance that it was a night of debauchery.

Let's face it, the girl had a different look on her face than when I picked her up the night before.

"I was *very worried!*" Mrs. Waite said under her breath as she came within a foot of Millicent. "I'm responsible for you!"

Millicent looked at me with that starstruck smile, then calmly turned to her guardian and said, "Pardon, ma'am. But rest assured that I was in the finest sets of hands last evening. I could not have been any more safe and comfortable in my life."

With that, and in the lobby of the prestigious hotel, she put her arms around me, pressed her body tightly against mine and kissed me.

"We leave at noon tomorrow for Chicago," she said as her lips left mine. "You have my phone number. I'll be in America for a few months. Please call me. *Please.*"

Mrs. Waite watched as I promised to call, then she took Millicent's hand and led her to the elevators.

Millicent turned to me and waved. I smiled.

I drove to Benedict Canyon and took the long and scenic route to Studio City along Mulholland Drive to return the Jag…and to get some sleep.

Once there, I sat in front of a phone and made two calls.

The first was to United Airlines.

I assumed that if the Waites were flying to Chicago from Los Angeles, the primary airline for that route was United, with its major hub in Chicago. Fortunately, that was the airline I was booked to fly non-stop from L.A. to Newark. I confirmed that there was a noon flight to Chicago, so I booked myself on it with a connecting flight to Newark. If Millicent was on that flight, even in first class...I'd find her.

The second call was to Jerry to let him know I was going to be home by tomorrow night and that I'd like to see him as much as he'd like to see me...to discuss our future.

And then I went to sleep.

Round 8

On Saturday morning, September 6, Joey dropped me off at LAX a few minutes after eleven.

I wasn't wearing my normal rock 'n' roll attire, as I had when I left New Jersey to work a five-day session in San Francisco nearly a month earlier.

In that period, Patsy died and I had experienced Las Vegas in a way I imagine no other 22-year-old ever has.

Now I was wearing a combination of *Vegas-meets-Rodeo Drive*...with a touch of guinea-gangster-wannabe thrown in.

And most obvious was my hair...now several inches shorter.

I checked the luggage at the curb and made my way to the gate.

As I walked through the maze of tunnels, escalators and passageways, I thought more about Jerry's offer of returning to Vegas. Was I hit with the gambling bug? Or was it *what* they were doing and I just wanted to be a part of it?

I got to the gate and made myself comfortable.

My hunch eventually paid off.

Millicent and her guardians walked up to the counter for their seat assignments. I sat back and waited to see if she would notice me.

As Mr. Waite was pulling tickets out of his briefcase, Mrs. Waite saw me. She touched Millicent's shoulder and pointed.

A very surprised Millicent came running over and threw her arms around me.

"Did you come to see me off?" she asked excitedly.

I shook my head and held up my ticket. She took it from my hand to see the flight number.

"That's wonderful! It will be wonderful to sit with you. Where are you?"

"Coach."

"Not anymore!"

"Which means...?" I asked.

"Wait until we take off," she said as we kissed and she returned to the Waites.

Less than a half hour later I was sitting in coach and the plane was leveling off at 33,000 feet. As soon as the pilot turned the seat belt sign off, a stewardess from first class came down my aisle.

I said to the gray haired grandmother sitting next to me, "I think today's your lucky day."

"What do you mean?" she asked with a gentle-but-confused smile.

"I have a feeling that stewardess is going to tell you that there's an available seat in first class, and that she'd like you to have it."

She just smiled and looked at me in disbelief, almost as if I were crazy.

The stewardess leaned toward us and said, "Excuse me, Mr. D'Amore. There is a couple in first class that are requesting that you and the person seated next to you exchange seats with them. Would you mind?"

"Excuse me?" I said.

The stewardess repeated herself.

The woman next to me couldn't believe her ears.

Then the Waites came up behind the stewardess.

Mr. Waite looked pissed off and said, "Millicent would like your company in first class. Mrs. Waite and I would like to sit together, so instead of having Millicent come back here with you, we would like to give you and your neighbor our seats."

I turned to the woman sitting next to me and asked, "Whatdya say? Feel like sitting in first class?"

"That would be very nice," she said softly, but confused.

I looked at the stewardess and humorously commanded, "Lead the way!"

Within minutes Millicent and I were sitting in the Waites' seats, drinking champagne, kissing and wrapped in each other's arms. The little old lady sat across the aisle, in Millicent's original seat.

By the time the flight was about three-quarters to Chicago, we had a bit too much to drink and began groping one another. We decided we needed a bit more privacy than first class had to offer, so we quietly made our way to the bathroom. I went in first, but didn't latch the door. When Millicent thought no one was paying attention, she slipped in and locked it.

It was cramped, but it only took us a few minutes to strip below the waist and start to have sex in every position possible in such tight and turbulent quarters.

There were times that Millicent couldn't contain herself and would let out a short scream or erotic moan. It wasn't long before the stewardesses and some of the passengers realized what was going on.

Unfortunately, after 20 minutes or so, there were complaints that we were tying up one of the two first class toilets.

One of the stewardesses knocked on the door.

The attention drew everyone's stares as the door opened and out we strolled hand-in-hand…looking lustfully disheveled and satisfied.

As we walked down the aisle and fell into our seats, a stewardess came up to us and scolded us like school children…and loud enough so everyone would hear.

"We would appreciate that you contain yourselves for the rest of the flight! That was *rude and inconsiderate!* This is not the type of behavior--"

It only took Millicent a second to compose herself before interrupting the stewardess by raising a single index finger and reading her the riot act, British style.

"First, madam, I do not believe you know to whom you are speaking. How *dare* you use that tone with me! Secondly, to the best of my knowledge, which I'm sure exceeds yours, there is no FAA law or regulation that prohibits people from making love on a commercial jetliner…unless, of course, they're doing it on the pilot's lap."

There may *have* been a law or regulation, but the stewardess was at a loss for words.

"So be on your way," Millicent continued, "And don't you dare attempt to embarrass me or my companion again. Otherwise your days with this or any other airline will be over!"

As the stunned and embarrassed stewardess backed up, turned and walked away, Millicent said, "And bring us two more glasses of champagne!"

I sat back in the deep leather seat and looked at her. This girl had *balls*…and knew how to use them.

For the remainder of the flight, no one used the toilet Millicent and I christened. Though we left it as clean as when we went in.

As the jet touched down at O'Hare, she again made me promise that I would call her.

I decided to accompany her to the baggage area and then catch my connection to Jersey.

It only took a few moments before we were with the Waites and watching the luggage slowly pass along the carousel. As Millicent and I stood hand in hand looking for her bags, a flash went off in our faces. Then another. And another.

"Lady Millicent, is it true you were caught 'in the act' in the lavatory on your flight from Los Angeles?" I heard a male reporter ask as I was trying to get the white and blue dots out of my eyes.

"Yes," I heard her say. "But please note that it was a *first class* lavatory!"

Flash! Another one.

More questions were asked, but she refused to answer them.

She snuggled close and kissed me as another round of pictures were taken.

Suddenly the Waites rushed over and stepped in front of the photographer and reporter.

How someone from the media got there so fast, and how they found out what we did and who she was, I never understood. But it was obvious that they knew.

The Waites collected Millicent and their luggage and made their way through the crowd yelling, "No comment, goddamn it!" Millicent turned, smiled, blew me a kiss and waved.

I turned and headed toward my plane for the trip home. But I was being followed.

As I reached the correct gate, the reporter and photographer caught up with me.

"Excuse me. May I have your name?" he asked.

I smiled and said, "No, that's okay. I think I'd like to keep this private."

"Private? With a member of the Royal Family?" he responded.

The photographer snapped another picture as I smiled and made my way onto the plane.

I took my seat in coach, sat back and thought about the last few weeks. You remember stuff like that.

Round 9

It was around 7:30PM, and the early September sun was low in the sky.

I was in the air somewhere between Chicago and Newark as two Lincolns and a Caddie slowly drove along a road that bordered the southern end of the north-south runways of Newark International Airport. The cars pulled behind a nondescript office trailer in the Port of New York section of Elizabeth, New Jersey, and immediately turned off their headlights.

Out of the first Lincoln stepped the driver, George Lyman, a former Sergeant on the Hudson County Police Force who was now Tommy Dolan's enforcer. He opened the rear door for his boss as Louie Calderone and Bobby Grant stepped from the other side.

Dolan walked up to the rear of the trailer, unlocked a door and the four of them entered.

Then Mike Caruso shut the Caddie's engine, stepped out and opened the rear door for Jerry. Taz and Vinnie Caputo emerged from the passenger side.

All eight men were in the trailer when the rear door opened revealing Rocco Casiano's bodyguard, Salvatore 'Sally' Della Osa...thirty-four years old, good looking and built like the proverbial brick shit-house. He stood around 5'10 and was all muscle.

"Everything all right?" he asked as he walked in and scanned the interior.

Dolan and Jerry nodded their heads.

Della Osa tapped on the door a couple of times and it opened.

In walked the boss, Rocco Casiano.

A descending jet roared overhead as Bobby Grant and George Lyman shook Casiano's hand. The rest of the men hugged and kissed him.

"So, how'd *this* trip go?" Casiano asked.

Since Vegas was Dolan's scam, everyone knew the question was put to him.

"Gettin' better every time we go, Rocco. It's almost like they can't give our guys new lines fast enough," The Irishman answered as Louie and Vinnie lifted four sacks onto a desk and emptied their contents.

Bundles of twenties, fifties and hundreds tumbled out. There was over $450,000.

"Good," Casiano smiled. Then the smile disappeared as he asked, "What about the rest of the week?"

Dolan and Jerry each held up paper bags.

Rocco smiled again.

They were filled with Jerry's and Tommy's *take* on collections from loans, gambling bets and payoffs from the previous week.

"How much?" Casiano asked.

"Eighty-six," Dolan said proudly as he emptied his bag on the desk.

Rocco looked at Jerry and asked, "What about you?"

Dolan looked at Jerry.

"One-thirty-seven large," Jerry answered softly, as the money slid out of his bag.

"One-thirty-seven? You gotta be shittin' me?" Casiano said, loud enough for everyone in the trailer to hear.

Jerry smiled at the boss and leaned against the wall as another jet passed overhead.

Dolan turned and gave an angry stare to his crew.

Jerry smiled at his guys.

"That's five weeks in a row," Casiano said as he thumbed through the cash. "That's good, Jerry. Very good."

Rocco, Jerry and Dolan were thinking similar thoughts from different perspectives; Dolan's crew was nearly twice the size of Jerry's, and he had the lucrative territories of Bayonne, Jersey City, Newark and Elizabeth, yet his take was smaller than Jerry's for the last five weeks.

This wasn't the time or place for *anyone* to make excuses or respond to compliments. The fact that the boss knew what was handed in was all that needed to be known.

Everyone but Casiano, Dolan and Jerry walked to the far side of the trailer, leaving their bosses to divvy up the more than $670,000 sprawled before them.

Thirty-five grand was counted out and handed to Jerry.

Fifty grand was handed to Dolan.

Jerry knew that Tommy got more because he had a bigger payroll to meet. But it irked him that The Irishman was turning in less money every week.

Casiano counted out a half million, then slid the remaining eighty thousand-plus to the side and signaled Salvatore Della Osa.

As Sal filled one of the empty sacks with the eighty-plus slice, Rocco looked at his two underbosses and said, "Okay, there's a half-mil on that desk. Get it out on the street. We'll meet here in two weeks, after the next Vegas trip."

They nodded their heads.

"Now, anybody have any business to discuss?" he asked.

Another approaching jet passed overhead.

"I got a new guy, Rocco," Jerry said.

"Oh yeah? Who?" the boss asked as he flashed a quick look at Dolan.

Jerry knew Dolan had called Casiano from Vegas and reported the new face along with the $25,000 line. Casiano was acting dumb and wanted to hear what Jerry had to say.

"Jon. My cousin. You know, Rocky's kid."

"I know him?"

"You've seen him at my father's house. Me and Tommy taught him what to do at the tables and he did great."

Casiano looked at Dolan for his opinion...so he gave it.

"I got him a line at The MGM and he went through it without any problems. He was good. I didn't like that he was hanging with some broads at the tables. He's young, but he worked out well and turned in all of our money."

Casiano looked back at Jerry and asked, "He a wise guy? He gonna get us pinched?"

"I can't see it, Rocco. He grew up knowin' the rules. Between me, his father and *my* father, he knows how to handle himself. He knows how to do the right thing. Ask 'The Tailor' about him...even Frank DeNike liked the kid a lot."

"Stand up guy?" Casiano asked.

Jerry nodded.

Casiano looked across the trailer. Taz and Mike gave their approval. Louie Calderone said, "Except for the broads, he worked well at the tables." Bobby Grant ground out a cigarette and immediately lit another one as he said, "His hair's too long...and he's too young lookin' to be bettin' that kind of money."

Casiano thought for a few seconds, then said to Jerry, "Okay, he's yours. Make sure he does right, keeps a low-profile and his nose clean. I don't want no problems. And tell him to get his hair cut."

Jerry nodded.

The sun had gone down. It was time to end the meeting.

Casiano looked at Dolan and said, "I'll meet *you* tomorrow morning at the apartment in Bayonne and we'll talk."

Rocco met with each of his underbosses once a week. The Irishman didn't like the fact that *his* meeting was called so soon...on Sunday...and on Labor Day weekend. He knew there were going to be questions about the weekly take.

Jerry knew it, too.

"Jerry, I'll reach out for you in a couple of days and we'll meet at The Tailor's in Secaucus," the boss said with a smile.

The fact that Rocco didn't set a specific time to see Jerry meant the boss was happy with him. And that made Jerry and his crew happy.

Dolan knew it, too.

One at a time, the Italians hugged and kissed Casiano. Dolan, George and Bobby shook his hand.

Normally, the big Irishman hugged and kissed the boss out of respect. But tonight he felt he was being punished...and he didn't like it.

Della Osa opened the door and signaled Rocco's driver, who was waiting in the second Lincoln. Without putting the headlights on, the car approached. Della Osa opened the rear door, threw the bag of money onto the back seat, and held it open as Casiano walked directly from the trailer into the car. Della Osa got in the front. The boss made sure to sit directly behind him.

The headlights came on as the car left the parking lot and Rocco Casiano was driven away into the night...as a jet passed overhead.

Another hour went by as Jerry and Tommy split up the half-mil and sat with their men to discuss its distribution.

As Mike drove the Caddie north on the Jersey Turnpike, Jerry sat in the back with Vinnie to discuss a problem they were having with a loanshark.

"This fuckin' guy thinks he can keep a piece of the vig because he pays us *on time!*" Jerry quietly said. "He's tellin' Taz he's *saving* me money 'cause I don't have to pay someone to chase him for it."

"You're kiddin', right?" Vinnie asked.

"Taz," Jerry said, "Tell Vinnie about that shylock in Hackensack."

"The baker?" Taz asked.

"No. The other guy."

"The printer?"

"No, the real estate guy."

"Oh, him. Yeah, this guy's funny. You gotta hear this." Taz slowly turned his huge, muscular body around in the seat and continued, "We're doin' business with him for about a year now and he's always been a good payer. So I go to drop off his street-money about a month ago, sixty grand, and I tell him I'll be back in two weeks to start picking up our piece. He tells me he's gonna be movin' the sixty, plus more within the next month or so, and that as long as he pays us our-fuckin'-money back on time, he wants us to take five points off our end. I told him that the number *is* what it *is*, that's what everybody pays for the amount they move...and besides, he *has* no option but to pay us on time."

"What's his name?" Vinnie asked.

"Nicky DePasquale...but he wants to be called *Dion*."

"So what happened when you went back in two weeks?"

"The dumb fuck comes up five points short. You believe this fuckin' guy?"

"Whatcha do?"

"I tell him that I'll be back the next week to pick up his *weekly* plus the missing five, plus the vig on the missing five," Taz said with a laugh.

"And then?"

"I get there the following week and he hands me what he owes on the sixty, less another five! *Plus*, he's still short on the missing five and the vig on the missing five."

"You gotta be shittin' me?"

"No! And listen to this. He says he can get the money from another family for less, and if I come back looking for more than he wants to pay, he's gonna fuck us for the sixty large and start doin' business with some guy he says he's got across the river. Most likely Gotti," Taz said as he turned back around in his seat.

Vinnie couldn't believe his ears. He leaned close to Jerry and whispered so that only his boss could hear, "We gotta take this fuckin' real estate prick to dinner."

Jerry said, "I'll pick the restaurant."

Vinnie leaned against Jerry again and whispered in his ear, "Just pick a joint where a closet won't look too out of place."

Jerry knew what *the closet* meant.

He sat back into the deep smooth leather, looked at the Manhattan skyline and said, "Taz, make sure you get our sixty back from this DePasquale-prick the next time you see him. If he asks why? Tell him I'll talk to him about it over dinner."

Setting up a hit took some thought. The pro hitters were proud of their individual styles. Some were known and respected throughout the families for their creativity.

Vinnie Caputo was one of them. He liked restaurants.

He'd find one that would have a small private dining room out of view of the main room. And he *always* used a .22 with a silencer.

The small caliber bullet left a slight entry hole, would ricochet around the inside of the skull and rarely exited the body, so there wouldn't be a bloody mess.

A couple of hours before the hit, Vinnie would pull up to the rear of the restaurant with a van, wheel out a rolling coat closet and put it in the far corner of the room where they'd be eating.

The intended "hit" would be taken out for a friendly and informal business dinner. Usually it would be Vinnie and two other guys, either from Jerry's crew or a couple of Vinnie's hitters. At some point, Vinnie would stand up in front of the victim, draw his pistol, tell him why he was going to die...and shoot him right between the eyes...and then in the heart.

Vinnie believed in the Old Timer's rules, and he'd only whack people face-to-face. "Any cocksucker could whack *anybody* from behind. If you ain't got the balls to face the man you're gonna kill, you're not a man... you're not one of *us*," was his credo.

Then they would take the body, throw it in the closet and wheel it out to the van behind the restaurant. The most anyone would see would be a couple of guys moving a piece of furniture.

Only Vinnie knew how and where the bodies were disposed.

The owner of the restaurant usually walked away with a grand.

The foolish loanshark was no longer Jerry's concern. He was deep in thought about the $250,000 in the trunk and how he was going to tell me I'd have to cut my hair.

Round 10

Around ten o'clock on Sunday morning the phone in my parents' house rang.

I was asleep.

A couple of minutes passed before my father knocked on the bedroom door and said, "Jerry's on the phone."

I pulled myself out of bed and picked up the nearest extension.

"Yeah?" I said while trying to clear my throat and remembering not to say his name on the phone.

"What are you doing?"

"Sleeping," I answered, mid-yawn. "I got back from L.A. last night."

"Yeah, I *know*," he said, sounding somewhat perturbed.

I was wondering why he called.

"How soon can you be ready?" he asked.

"Ready for what?"

"We gotta go for a ride...to talk."

When he or anyone in his position says "We gotta go for a ride...to talk," there's no way you can say "No."

I told him, "Gimme a half hour."

"We'll be outside in twenty."

He hung up.

What was going on that he needed to speak to me in such a hurry? I didn't know what to think. Did something go wrong in Vegas? Did Casiano find out about my personal winnings and want a piece of it?

I didn't have time to think about it. I had to get ready.

"What did Jerry want?" my father asked...with an odd smile on his face.

"No idea. But he'll be here in a few minutes and I'm sure I'll find out," I answered while pulling a pair of jeans up to my waist.

I had just rinsed the toothpaste out of my mouth when my mother yelled that someone was honking a car horn. I said goodbye and flew out the door.

Mike was behind the wheel of the Cadillac. Taz was in the front seat reading the *Bergen Record's* sports section, and Jerry was sitting in the back.

As I approached, Taz got out and opened the rear door for me.

I sat next to Jerry. Once Taz returned to the front seat, the car pulled away.

"Morning, guys!" I said, then leaned over, kissed my cousin on the cheek and asked, "So, what's up?"

"Well," he said, with a long pause before continuing, "I thought you'd want to know about the conversation me and Tommy Dolan had with Rocco about you yesterday. And what *he* had to say."

I couldn't tell from his voice or facial expressions if it was good or bad, so I took a deep breath and sat back to listen.

He looked at me and said, "The report he got from Dolan was that you were approved for twenty-five grand and you went through it with no problems. You always turned in your marker money and you worked well at the tables. All that made Rocco happy." Then he leaned toward me and continued, "What Dolan didn't like was that there were times you were the center of attention at the tables, either because of women, or your--"

I interrupted him.

"It was just that once, Jer...You know what happened--"

He held up his hand, shutting me down...then continued, "Either because of women, or your age. They said you look too young and inexperienced to be gambling that kind of money."

"Hey, what can I do? I *do* look young. I'm only twenty-two! And what the fuck? I *am* inexperienced at gambling!"

Mike laughed, "Imagine if they saw you *before* you got your haircut?"

"Then we wouldn't be havin' this conversation," Jerry said. "Casiano would never let us have someone like that. He'd get pissed off if he thought you even smoked pot."

I sat there and didn't say a word. I didn't know if Jerry actually knew if I did or didn't smoke, and *I* wasn't about to say anything.

Jerry was on a roll and kept going.

"I told him you were reliable and that you know how to keep quiet about what we do. I said you were quick to learn the tables and after a couple of trips you'll be perfect. He didn't have a problem with bringing you in...considering you're family, you're my Godson, and he's known your father for around twenty-five years."

I smiled but didn't say anything.

"He just wants you to keep your mouth shut. Talk to no one about what we do and who you do it with. His boss and the goombahs on The Commission hate *any* kind of publicity. So it's important you don't do *anything* to attract attention to yourself, 'cause that'll only bring heat down on the rest of us. Capice? You understand what I mean?"

I was a little surprised that he thought he had to ask me that.

"Of course I understand! Don't you think I know that by now?"

I heard Taz and Mike trying to suppress some laughter.

Jerry tapped Taz on the shoulder.

"Hand me the front section of that paper."

As Mike continued driving and Taz was passing the newspaper to the back, I more-than-a-little-nervously asked my Godfather if there was anything else I needed to know.

He held up his hand as he took the paper and turned to the second page.

"So Juan...you say you understand and know how to keep a low profile, huh?"

Before I could answer, he said, "Lemme read the caption under the picture first."

"*What* picture?"

Now I was nervous.

Was there a picture of me in the paper with him and Tommy Dolan? Certainly he couldn't hold *that* against me.

He held up his hand again and started reading, "'Local north Jersey musician, Jon D'Amore, and England's current Royal Scandal, Lady Millicent Overton, seen here at Chicago's O'Hare International Airport, were found together in the first class lavatory during their flight from Los Angeles.'"

"Oh shit," I said, and then sunk into the seat as Mike and Taz started laughing... hysterically.

"Wait!" Jerry said. He was serious. "Let me read the article."

I put a hand over my face.

Though Mike and Taz were getting a kick out of this, I could see that Jerry wasn't.

He cleared his throat and continued, "'The pilot reported a couple locked themselves in the first class lavatory of a United Airlines flight from Los Angeles. A crewmember confirmed it was Lady Millicent Overton, England's current scandal girl, and her traveling companion, Jon D'Amore. Lady Millicent did not deny the incident and emphasized that it took place in first class, not coach.'"

Fuck. I looked at the paper to see if there was more.

He looked at me, shook his head and continued reading.

"'When questioned as to his identity and relationship with the royal relative, D'Amore refused to comment and then boarded a United flight to Newark.'"

"*See*...I know not to say *anything* when I'm being questioned," I said, hoping to get some reaction out of him.

He wasn't smiling.

"'The airline confirmed that D'Amore was traveling with Lady Millicent and seated in first class.'" He stopped reading, looked at me and said, "First class?"

By now, Mike and Taz were trying not to pee in their pants. Jerry remained straight-faced and read on. I was just grateful knowing none of these guys were gonna shoot me.

"'Lady Millicent, a member of the Queen's family, is currently facing charges of reckless vehicular homicide in the death of her twenty-eight-year-old fiancé, Charles A. Eddington III, the son of Lord Eddington. Alcohol and hashish were found at the scene of the accident and in breath and blood tests. The trial is pending upon Lady Millicent's return from America, where she is undergoing alcohol and drug treatment in the Chicago area.'"

I thought to myself, "Alcohol and drug treatment? *Yeah...right.*"

He put the paper down and looked at me.

"When the fuck did you meet this woman? Did you know who she was?"

"I met her the same time *you* did! We *all* did! She was the girl at the blackjack table at The Trop the day we left. Remember the three people sittin' there? She was the British chick with the married couple."

Jerry looked at the picture again.

"No shit?" came from Mike.

"But the four of us left the casino together. How'd you hook up with her?" Taz asked.

"After you guys boarded your plane I went to the gate for my flight to Burbank. They were on the same flight. We wound up sitting next to one another, and that night I took her to dinner. I changed my return flight to go through Chicago, where she's staying with her guardians. She had the couple move to coach and--"

Mike interrupted me and asked, "Her *guardians?* Whatdya mean *guardians?* Maybe we can do something here? They must be *loaded.* There's gotta be *some* scam we can pull."

I laughed at his suggestion, then said, "Get the fuck outta here with that." I got serious again and continued my response.

"She had the couple give up their first class seats so I could sit with her. How the fuck was I supposed to know she was some international scandal? If I was banging a *nobody* in the bathroom, it never would have made the papers. She ripped the stewardess a new asshole for yelling at us. I guess the stewardess went to the pilot."

"That's not the point," Jerry said. "Today's Sunday. It's Labor Day weekend. You *know* Casiano and Dolan are gonna read the paper. And it's right here on the second-fuckin'-page."

I sat there, unsure of what to do or say next.

He rubbed his face, took a deep breath and said, "Let me see what Rocco says. Lay low for a few days. Do your music business...and don't contact her for a while."

Unbelievable! I was just part of a team of mob guys who hit Vegas for over $450,000 in five days, but...I was being scolded for doin' a girl in the bathroom of a plane.

What an amazing world I was living in.

"Oh, by the way," Jerry held up the paper, "I told your old man about this. After he got done laughing he said, 'Yep...That's my son.'"

I smiled and eased back into the seat.

He handed me the paper and said, "I gotta admit...you make a good lookin' couple."

Then he laughed and kissed me.

I looked at the picture of me and Millicent, hand-in-hand at the baggage carousel.

He was right.

The Caddie cruised along Bergenline Avenue through North Bergen and West New York, which was void of traffic since the majority of Hudson County spent Labor Day weekend, the last official weekend of the summer, down at the Jersey shore.

The shore was another bastion of north Jersey and Philadelphia mob influence. Jerry's crew ran a dozen stands on the Boardwalk, and he and Casiano held an interest in The Bat Cave, one of the big Seaside Heights nightclubs.

"Where are we goin'?" I asked.

"See up ahead?" Jerry asked as he pointed out the front window.

"Where? What?" I answered as the car slowed down across the street from the Embassy Theater.

All three of them were looking at it.

"I need your help on something, Juan."

"I'm listening," I said, unsure of what he was going to ask.

He didn't respond...yet.

Mike made a U-turn and parked in front of the marquee.

We got out of the car and walked to the side of the building. Taz knocked on a heavy metal door and within seconds it opened. The old watchman didn't say a word, he just stepped aside while the four of us walked in. Then he turned on the houselights and led us to the stage. We stood looking at the 1,600 empty seats.

Jerry put his arm around my shoulder and said, "Juan, I gotta raise eight thousand dollars."

I raised an eyebrow and looked at him. Here's a guy who could do that on a good weekend of football or basketball games. What did he need me for?

He said, "It's gotta be *clean* money. I gotta show where I got it. Get it?"

"For?"

"My football team," he answered.

"Huh?"

He led me off the stage, up the aisle and into the mezzanine as he told me his story.

In order to maintain a good standing in Ridgefield, the affluent Bergen County town south of the George Washington Bridge where he and his father and sister owned homes and resided, Jerry coached a football team of local teenagers. And since he took over, along with Mike and Taz as his

Offensive and Defensive Coaches, they had led their league in wins for the last three years.

For kicks, Jerry, Mike and Taz even took bets on the games.

The parents wanted their kids to have the best uniforms and equipment they could find, so Jerry took the task of raising the funds.

"So...whatdya need me to do?" I asked. "Get a couple of rock groups to put on a show? I can get a friend of mine to run it. He's produced a bunch of shows in this place."

"No. I got the act," he said.

"You do?"

Oh no! Could it be who I think it was going to be? Was *I* going to run a Sinatra show?

I looked at Jerry as he said, "The kid on TV. Travolta."

"Travolta? *John* Travolta?"

"Yeah, with that new show, 'Welcome Back, Kotter.' His brother lives in Ridgefield, and he's got two kids on the team. He says he can get Travolta and one or two people from the show to do a couple of skits. Apparently the whole Travolta family's into acting and singing. He said they'd all do something and kill an hour-or-so for free to help raise the money."

"But would sixteen hundred kids pay five or six bucks-a-head to see them?" I asked.

"That's where you come in, Juan. You're gonna produce the show. And I don't want sixteen hundred seats at five or six bucks."

I looked at him and awaited his expectations.

"I want thirty-two hundred seats at ten bucks-a-head."

"*Two* shows?" I laughed. "At *ten bucks?* For *John Travolta?*"

Okay...so there were *some* things I could *never* have predicted.

Jerry smiled, nodded his head and said, "I know you can do it."

"But you only need eight grand, Jer. You're looking at more than thirty grand in tickets."

"Not really." He put his arm on my shoulder as we walked. "Here's how that works. I need a thousand comped tickets of the best seats."

"A thousand?"

"Yeah. I gotta have tickets to give to my Hudson and Bergen County police and political people for their kids. And then I need tickets for our family and the *usual* people I gotta take care of. You know?"

"That brings it down to twenty-two hundred seats. There's still twenty grand-plus comin' in," I said. "How much do you think it'll cost to rent the theater?"

"I'm sure I can get the owner to *donate* the place that night. But we'll show it on the books at five grand, fifty-five hundred, whatever."

"Can you get a receipt?"

He laughed and said, "What do *you* think?"

"Security?"

"I got people," he answered.

"Jer," I laughed, "You can't have guys like Taz and Mike walking around with this place full of kids. I'll get the security people from my friend. That'll cost about two grand."

"Okay. What else are you gonna need, and what's it gonna cost?"

"Lights and sound, tickets, stage sets, a stage crew, posters, a few radio and newspaper ads. Plus we can pick up some extra money from the food concession and posters and tee shirts."

"See! I told you I need you," he said as he handed me an envelope. "Cover your expenses with this. Let's meet on Wednesday to get the tickets and posters printed. I got a printer in Union City I want you to use. Your piece'll be twenty-five percent of the profit after all expenses."

Then he kissed me on the cheek and we headed back to the stage.

I opened the envelope. There was three grand in fifties and hundreds.

"When do you want to do the show?" I asked.

"In three weeks."

"*Three weeks!* No fuckin' way! That's too soon."

"That's what you've got. That's when the show's gotta be. On Saturday, September twenty-seventh."

"Why?" I asked.

"That's when Travolta's gonna be in Jersey visiting his family. His company's picking up the airfares and hotels, so it won't cost us anything to get him here or put him up." Then he smiled and said, "Today's Sunday the seventh. You got less than three weeks."

When we got to the car, Jerry asked where I wanted to be dropped off. I told him to take me home. I had a show to prepare.

"Where are you guys off to?" I asked.

"Down the shore," he answered. "We'll be there 'til Tuesday. It's a big weekend and there's a lot of cash to bring back. Between the stands and The Bat Cave, we're gonna be busy for the next couple of days."

"Isn't your anniversary around now?"

"She understands."

And she did.

Ten days went by. I was working on some sessions in Manhattan and took Jerry's advice about keeping a low profile. I didn't call Lady Millicent... but I certainly wanted to.

Then on Wednesday night the phone rang. It was Mike Caruso.

"Hey, kid."

"Hey! What's up?"

We knew not to say our names on the phone.

"We need you out there," he said.

"Out where?"

"Out there."

"*Where?*"

"*There.*"

Then I got it.

"For what?"

"To work."

"You call that work?"

He laughed.

"When?" I asked.

"You leave tomorrow morning. I'll meet you at the airport with your ticket and we'll fly out together."

"Isn't it too soon for me to go back?"

"You're gonna be stayin' someplace else."

I didn't say anything.

He continued, "By tomorrow afternoon you'll be layin' by the pool. We'll start workin' by six."

"For how long?"

"You can't be dropping big money too quick on your first couple of trips. So plan on staying for five, maybe six days."

"But I've got another session *here*. I gotta call my manager to see if he can reschedule it."

"You want *me* to call him?" he asked. "What's his number?"

"No!" I laughed. "I'll call and see what I can do. Gimme a number to call you back."

He said, "I'm runnin' around today. I'll call you in an hour," and then hung up.

I was able to juggle the session without pissing off my manager *too* much, and before I knew it Mike and I were on a United DC8 to Vegas.

"So," he asked as we cruised west, "How's everything going with the Travolta show?"

"Well, considering it's a week-and-a-half away, everything's contracted, paid for and running smooth. The newspaper and radio ads are running and tickets are at the outlets and they're selling, which is surprising *the shit* outta *me*. The only thing I haven't been able to do is make contact with Travolta or his people."

"Why not?"

"I've called his Los Angeles office and left a shitload of messages, and I've reached out to his brother in Ridgefield, but I haven't heard back from any of 'em. It'd be nice to know exactly what they're gonna do so we can figure out some stage, sound and lighting cues."

He said, "As soon as we land I'll call your cousin and he'll make sure someone gets to you."

"What hotel is he staying at this time?"

Mike leaned close to me and whispered, "He's not. He's in Jersey."

"He's not gonna be there?"

"No. It's just you, me, Taz and a few of our guys with lines. Dolan will be there with his whole crew."

"Why ain't Jerry comin'?"

He continued whispering, "He has to go to dinner with somebody. But if anybody asks...he was with you in Vegas as your guest in your room, which'll be under your name. Got that?"

Mike pulled out his airline ticket to show me that it was made out to Gerald D'Amore.

"See," he continued, "He's even flying with you."

"For Jerry? No problem," I whispered back. Then I asked, "So, when's Taz flyin' out?" as he nonchalantly handed me a Tropicana Casino credit application.

"Yesterday...with Dolan."

I filled in the same limited information that I used on the MGM form and handed it back to Mike.

"Good. As soon as we get there, you check in. I'll call your cousin about the Travolta thing. Then I'll find Dolan and have him set you up so we can get you gamblin' by tonight. Go lay out by the pool for a few hours and be ready for dinner by five. And this time, try not to pick up any broads until *after* Dolan and his boys leave. Okay, kid?"

I put my head back and closed my eyes. I *hated* being called "kid."

Within twelve hours after I had checked into The Trop...and another palatial suite, I had gone through six thousand of my new $25,000 line, picked up a few hundred dollars for myself from side bets, received a phone call from Travolta's brother in Ridgefield, two from Travolta's secretary and one from the future superstar himself. All the calls started with an apology for not getting back to me sooner, and how they were looking forward to coming to New Jersey to perform at the show.

Around nine o'clock on Thursday evening in Jersey, '*Big Petey*' LaVeglia, one of Vinnie Caputo's crew, pulled Jerry's Caddie up to the front of The Oyster House in Fort Lee.

"Oh good! I like this place. They make a lobster fra diavolo that I can't get enough of," the loanshark, Nicky '*Dion*' DePasquale, said from the back seat. Jerry was sitting next to him.

"Good. I'm glad you like it here. I like their linguini and clams with the red sauce," said Vinnie from the front.

As Big Petey opened the door for them, Jerry tapped DePasquale on the shoulder and said, "Come on. Let's have a nice meal and work out this problem."

The loanshark looked at Jerry and sarcastically said, "You got a problem? I ain't got no problem."

Jerry just smiled at him.

Big Petey walked into the restaurant first, followed by DePasquale, Jerry and Vinnie.

The owner saw them immediately.

"Ah, paisan!" he said with a smile as he walked toward Jerry and shook his hand. "I have a nice private table for you. Please...follow me."

Jerry made a mental note to throw him an extra five hundred for his nonchalant performance.

As they entered the backroom, Vinnie said, "Petey, make sure nobody bothers us."

Big Petey smiled, stood in the doorway outside the room and closed the door.

The seats were arranged so that the loanshark's back was to the rolling closet against the far wall.

The three of them sat down as the owner put a bottle of Chianti and a basket of warm garlic bread on the table. Then he handed each of them a menu and disappeared.

"As long as you guys are pickin' up the tab, I'm havin' the lobster," DePasquale said with a smile that irritated Vinnie.

"Good, good. Have whatever you want," Jerry responded with a grin. "We'll order first and then we'll talk business."

"Yeah, whatever," the loanshark said with a smirk, then stuck a piece of bread in his mouth and buried his head behind the menu.

DePasquale's attitude caused Vinnie to make a gesture as if he was going into his jacket for his gun. Jerry saw it and laughed. He knew his friend wanted to shoot the *stroonze*, but he motioned for him to relax...at least for a little while.

The owner returned, stood next to Jerry, looked at him and asked, "So paisan? What can I get for you tonight?"

But before Jerry could respond, DePasquale answered without raising his head from the menu.

"Start me off with a bowl of minestrone, a salad, and then I'll have the lobster fra diavolo. And get us a better bottle of wine than the shit that's on the table."

The owner looked at Jerry, who just made a face and a motion of "not to worry."

"I'll have the penne alla vodka," Jerry said.

Vinnie looked up and said, "I'll have the penne, too."

Then Jerry quietly said, "Thanks. We'll see you in about ten minutes, okay?"

"But bring that wine right away!" DePasquale yelled before the owner disappeared into the kitchen.

Jerry took a breath, then looked at his dinner guest and asked, "So Nicky, Taz tells me we haven't been getting the total from you every week. Is there a problem?"

Before DePasquale could answer, Jerry continued with his questions.

"When you wanted our money, did we give you a hard time? Didn't we always give you what you wanted when you wanted it?"

"You wanna talk business *now?*" DePasquale said with an attitude that was pissing Jerry and Vinnie off with each word. "Why you wanna ruin my appetite? I told your boy that I'll *pay* what I'll *pay*. Why the fuck should I give you more than I gotta give another family? I come up with my piece every fuckin' week. So it's five points less than you're getting from the other idiots you're doing business with. Big-fuckin'-deal! I'll move more of your money than they will and I'll come up with my piece...on time...every fuckin' week. You don't like it? Tough shit. Take it or leave it."

Vinnie looked at Jerry for a signal as the loanshark continued.

"I got the whole sixty grand back to you, plus the vig, right? Now I want--"

Jerry interrupted him.

"No you *didn't*. Who the fuck you kiddin'? You were short again by another five."

"Wait a minute. I'm not done," DePasquale said, infuriating Vinnie. "*Now* I want to talk about getting a hundred...no...make that a hundred-and-a-quarter. And I'll want it in two days. Otherwise, if you can't get me that much, or if you're still gonna bust my balls about the five points, I can get it from a guy I got over in the city." Then he paused, took a bite of bread, a drink of wine and said, "But let's talk about it after we eat, okay? And where's that guy with the wine?"

"Yeah, no problem Nicky. After we eat," Jerry calmly said. "Let me go check on that wine for you. I'll be right back."

"Yeah, good...and it's *Dion!*"

"Yeah, right. Dion," Jerry said with a satisfied smile, then he rose from the table and walked out of the room.

As DePasquale took another bite of bread, he said to Vinnie, without looking at him, "This wine sucks."

He had no idea *that* was going to be his last complete sentence.

Vinnie rose from the table, reached into his jacket and pulled out his .22 with the silencer extending from the front, and said, "You know something, you arrogant cocksucker?"

The loanshark looked up at him and immediately knew he had a problem. He stopped chewing...and his face drained of color.

Vinnie coldly stared at him and continued, "Not only are you a disrespectful bastard, but you just don't understand that this is New Jersey, and this is our territory. So if you wanna do business in our territory, you do it with the people who *run* this territory. To think you're gonna bring money here from the city and try to fuck us by puttin' it on our streets, and then you're gonna bitch about the vig...you *gotta* be outta your fuckin' mind."

"But--" DePasquale uttered.

"Shut the fuck up! I don't wanna hear another thing outta you," Vinnie said as he squeezed the trigger and put a bullet directly into DePasquale's forehead.

His body kicked backwards.

A second shot went right into his windpipe, and a third went into his heart.

The loanshark was dead in seconds.

Vinnie looked at him and said, "You dumb motherfucker. Was it really worth five points?"

Then he raised his glass of wine, sipped it and said, "And this wine *don't* suck," as he put away his pistol and tapped on the door. Big Petey came in, locked the door and helped carry the body to the closet.

They wheeled it out the back door, tipped it over and slid it into the waiting van, then returned to clean up any blood that may have made its way onto the floor or table. Vinnie picked up the three wine glasses, wrapped them in napkins, smashed them and threw them in the kitchen's trash container. Their fingerprints were on them and Vinnie was efficient.

Once they were finished, the two of them drove the van to a place only they would know.

Before DePasquale was shot, Jerry was already in his Caddie and headed less than a mile away for dinner at The Arches on Palisade Avenue, where he was met with embraces and kisses by Rocco Casiano and Salvatore Della Osa.

Jerry and his boss sat ear-to-ear.

"You think Dolan is holding back on me, Jerry?" Rocco asked in a low raspy whisper.

Before Jerry could answer, Casiano continued, "He's been short too many fuckin' weeks in a row. He's got a great piece of territory. If he's short with his weekly, how do I know he's not takin' a piece of the Vegas action, too? What do you think's goin' on?"

Jerry didn't know how to answer.

They both knew there was pilfering going on.

Everyone was at it.

When you're dealing with massive sums of cash and little or no paperwork...skimming off the top was easy.

Of the eighty-plus grand that Della Osa put in the sack that night in the trailer, Casiano's piece *should* have been around thirty grand. The remaining fifty should have been turned over to Vincente Gigante. But Gigante only saw forty. That meant Casiano skimmed the difference. Though, when you turn in over a hundred-and-fifty grand every month like *he* did, you can get away with pocketing ten or twenty large every now and then.

It's just not the kind of thing you should do too often.

Now...Rocco was thinking that Tommy Dolan had been taking advantage of that unwritten rule too many weeks in a row.

The fact that the boss wanted info on one of his closest people made Jerry nervous.

He worried that Casiano may be playing him against The Irishman.

Doing it this way, if Tommy got wind of someone keeping an eye on him, Jerry would appear to be the bad guy instead of Rocco.

Casiano was also interested in knowing about the relationship between his two most powerful and profitable underlings, and what Jerry thought about Dolan.

Rocco Casiano was paranoid. Constantly.

But then, someone in his position and occupation *had* to be.

Jerry was concerned that Rocco would tell Dolan he heard the info from Jerry.

This would cause Dolan to cover *his* ass by dropping something on Jerry.

And Jerry didn't want the headache.

"I can tell you one thing...all of the Vegas money comes back directly to you, Rocco. Tommy's count is on every time I'm there," Jerry answered.

The boss looked at him, hoping to see some sign of betrayal.

Jerry continued, "Of course, I can't vouch for the count when I'm *not* there."

Casiano backed away and loudly said, "He's out there now!"

Jerry pulled the boss close and whispered, "That's why I sent Mike and Taz."

"I was *wondering* why you're alone tonight."

"Taz and a few of my guys flew out with Dolan and his crew. The next day Mike flew out with my cousin."

"The kid?" Casiano asked. "Ain't it too soon to use him again?"

"Different hotel."

Jerry paused to see if the boss had read the article about me and Millicent.

Nothing.

Apparently nothing was ever said about it.

A wave of relief came over my Godfather as he continued, "He'll get some more experience. Mike and Taz'll take care of him, and they'll keep an eye on the business. I sent the other guys just to work the tables with Dolan's people." Jerry smiled, "I gotta make sure I have a few sets of eyes out there."

Casiano grinned, sat back and said, "You did good, Jerry." Then he leaned forward and kissed him on the cheek.

"I never understood why you got so close to him, Rocco," Jerry whispered in his boss's ear. "That Irish prick has no allegiance to *us*. You and I know at least a half-a-dozen qualified paisan who could be taking in the same, if not *more*, in Dolan's territory...and you wouldn't have to worry about them fuckin' you on the take. You know, Louie Calderone's a good guy--"

"I know Tommy Dolan since we were kids in Bayonne," Casiano quickly and sternly responded. "Besides, if you...or *any* goombah...came up with the Vegas scam and could make it work like he does, then things *would* be different. But last year he brought in six million in 'casino money' and we made more than three million puttin' it to work. He's *always* made money. He's got the contacts in Vegas and the politicians in Bayonne, Jersey City and Newark that ain't Italian." The boss began shaking his head as he continued, "I can't believe he's fuckin' me."

"I didn't say he *was* fuckin' you, Rocco." Jerry wanted to cover his ass. "I just said I don't know what he's doin' when I'm not around. As far as his weekly take...I can't answer for that."

Casiano put his hand on the back of Jerry's neck, kissed him on the cheek again and said, "Right. Good. Now let's mangia."

Suddenly, the boss thought of something and turned to Jerry again.

"You need any help with that guy…that problem guy? I can have Sally go talk to him for you."

Sal smiled.

Jerry knew Casiano was asking about Nicky DePasquale. He laughed as he answered, "No thanks. It's already taken care of. He won't be short no more."

All four men laughed and ate their meals.

Meanwhile, during my Vegas trip, I played the pass line at The Trop and don't-pass at The Frontier and Riviera. I remembered to call Bobby Grant 'Bobby.' I didn't have any women show up at the crap tables. And I had gone through all twenty-five grand by Sunday morning.

One night, Sandy, the blonde Trop dealer, smiled at me and said "Hello" as I worked one of the tables. I smiled back and gave her a wink.

Mike and Taz, along with Dolan and his boys, flew out early Sunday afternoon with the $360,000 we took from the casinos.

Earlier that day, as Mike handed me my $1,000 salary, I told him I was flying to L.A. until Wednesday morning and then back to Jersey. But as soon as his plane departed, I boarded a United flight to Chicago…and was met by Lady Millicent in her Jaguar XK-E.

We checked into The Drake Hotel, got a room overlooking Lake Michigan, ordered all of our meals and several bottles of champagne from Room Service, smoked hash and didn't step outside until she drove me back to O'Hare for my Wednesday afternoon flight back to Jersey.

I made sure that Jerry wouldn't need to have the same conversation with me twice.

Round 11

The newspapers said the Travolta show was nothing short of a success... and Jerry couldn't have been happier.

To make sure there were no last minute surprises, I had the Travolta family get to the theater the day before the show to rehearse their skits and practice with the recorded soundtracks while I worked with the lighting technicians on their cues.

Based on earlier discussions as to what they'd be doing, I had three stage-sets constructed and ready prior to the rehearsal.

The show was great and went off without a hitch.

We sold every seat in the house for both shows...well, except for those thousand tickets Jerry used. Still, that was twenty-two hundred seats at ten bucks a pop.

Just how Jerry wanted it.

He got his eight grand for the football team's equipment. I think *that* made him the happiest.

No more than four grand was paid for all of the production costs, yet we had receipts for over sixteen thousand.

Jerry let a friend of Rocco's run the food concession and the 'Welcome Back, Kotter' poster stand. As a show of respect to the boss, Jerry didn't accept the pieces that were offered for the space.

By the end of the night the ten thousand dollars we cleared, all cash... in ones, fives, tens, twenties, fifties and hundreds...sat right in front of us on a backstage desk.

Jerry counted out thirty-five hundred dollars, put it in an envelope and handed it to me.

"I know I said you'd get twenty-five percent of the net, but you went above and beyond for me, Juan. So I want you to have a bit more."

I smiled, kissed him and humbly said, "*Anything* for you, Jerry."

Mike and Taz stood beside him adding even more praise to the success of the show.

Jerry smiled, counted another fifteen hundred off the pile and said, "Here...take Travolta and his family out to eat. Whatever's left over...go take out one of your girlfriends. Have a good time."

I kissed him again as he handed me the cash.

He had just given me 50% of the profit...and told me to have a good time.

I knew he was rewarding me.

It wasn't hard for anyone affiliated with this way of life to realize that by my simple acts of love and respect...I had, once again, proven myself to him.

In Vegas several weeks earlier, he put me in the middle of a situation where I could have fallen...but didn't. A couple of weeks later, I came through again by going back to Vegas with Mike and Taz. Then he needed me to produce the Travolta show simply to help his standing in the community... and I came through with flying colors.

But to me...I was just doin' the right thing.

I was showing my relative, my Godfather...this man of *respect*...respect.

Sure, I was earning the admiration of his associates. That was good for me, too. But more important was that I was earning *his* respect.

The next night I drove to Englewood and picked up Travolta's secretary and family. The star didn't join us...choosing instead to hook up with his friends in the city. I did everything possible to spend as much as I could... but the bill only came to $900.

I took the remaining six hundred, along with my thirty-five hundred dollar piece from the Travolta show...and made some travel plans.

I arranged for Lady Millicent to fly from Chicago to San Francisco, where I'd pick her up in a rented convertible and take five days to drive 400 miles south along the California coast to Los Angeles. She'd fly back to Chicago and I'd stay in L.A. for some sessions the following week.

For obvious reasons there was an emphasis on making it a *very* low profile trip.

It was a cold and damp Monday afternoon in late October, 1975.

I pulled the rented convertible up to the Arrivals curb just as Millicent was walking out of the terminal with a redcap and her luggage in tow.

I just started laughing.

The small sports car would barely accommodate *half* of what she brought for our five day getaway.

She patiently waited as I exchanged the convertible for a car with enough room for her luggage...though it wasn't exactly what *I* wanted for a drive down the coast. I was given the choice of a Cadillac Sedan deVille, a Buick LeSabre or a Chevy Impala.

As far as I was concerned...there *was* no option.

The redcap loaded her luggage into the trunk of the Caddie and we headed into Frisco to enjoy dinner with my old friend Bill, and spend the night at the Hyatt.

While filling out the form at the Hyatt's registration desk, I figured that since I was paying for everything with cash, and we wanted to remain anonymous...I'd take Jerry's lead and use an alias.

The Lady and I checked in as Mr. and Mrs. David Toma.

By Tuesday afternoon we arrived in Carmel-by-the-Sea and checked into the La Playa. And again registered as Mr. and Mrs. David Toma.

We enjoyed the oceanside community so much that we didn't leave until Friday afternoon...making our original schedule of getting to LAX in time for her early Saturday morning return flight null and void.

After checking out of the La Playa, we continued south through Big Sur and stopped for dinner in Cambria, where we checked into a little oceanfront bed & breakfast for another three days...again, as the Tomas. We were now way behind schedule...but it didn't seem to concern either of us.

Throughout the trip, she never mentioned her guardians, her pending legal situation back in England, or the fact that she was supposed to be spending time in a rehab somewhere.

On the other hand, I saw to it that we kept our vodka martinis and gin and tonics to a minimum.

That too, was part of our low profile agreement. Of course, we did have a close call with some potential publicity.

While staying in Cambria, we took a drive to San Simeon to tour the Hearst Castle.

Somehow, we conveniently managed to fall behind the tour group and found ourselves alone in a hallway of La Casa Grande that was lined with carved wooden doors.

Without hesitation, Millicent opened one of them and pulled me in as she covered my mouth with kisses before I had the opportunity to protest... not like was I going to.

It happened to be a bathroom painted in gold-leaf, adorned with gold fixtures and portraits of conquistadors.

My hands quickly pressed her body against mine as we passionately kissed...deeper and deeper...longer and longer.

She began moaning and rubbing up against me as she felt the swelling in my jeans...all the while our lips never leaving one another.

In one quick motion she turned away from me and held up her long red hair so that I could simultaneously kiss the back of her neck and fondle her breasts as she continued to rub herself against my now full erection.

It only took a moment before she was holding onto a towel rack and our jeans and underwear were at our ankles as I was thrusting in and out of her...probably in the same bathroom that Charlie Chaplin or Errol Flynn performed a similar act with any of a dozen stars and starlets nearly half a century earlier.

Louder and louder Millicent's moans of lust became screams of pleasure, so it was no surprise that once again, about fifteen minutes later...we were caught...this time by the next tour group that came by.

The Castle's security people *politely* asked us to leave...and we laughed about it all the way back to the hotel where we completed what we started.

I was happy to see that...*this time*...there were no photographers or reporters on hand.

Meanwhile back in New Jersey, Rocco Casiano was having concerns about what was happening within his crew.

Over the past four months, Dolan rarely matched or beat Jerry's weekly take. Casiano was sure The Irishman was tapping into the street money, but...Dolan *was* bringing in a large and constant flow of cash from the Vegas scam.

Casiano certainly couldn't complain about *that*.

Besides, the boss knew that as long as Jerry was watching The Irishman in Vegas...that count would be secure.

One of the reasons Jerry's take was growing every week was because he was expanding his operations and territory. A piece of Hudson County wasn't enough for him and his crew anymore.

He was moving into Bergen County in a big way...increasing *his* revenue...and the revenue of his superiors.

Throughout the '60s and '70s, Bergen County was steadily growing.

Warehouses and freight terminals found new homes in the flat open acreage of the meadows and farmlands. Office buildings and high-rise condos were being erected everywhere. The New York Giants were building a stadium in the new East Rutherford sports complex that would also include a racetrack and a huge arena for basketball and hockey games. As rumor had it, a few pieces of the missing Teamster boss Jimmy Hoffa were probably somewhere in the cement foundation, too.

Often, word would trickle down from the capos that someone big on The Commission appreciated what Jerry was doing...and the old fashioned way he was doing it. Among other things, that meant: No drugs, no hits in public, always pay the right tribute, always do the right thing...and don't take business or territory away from an underboss in the same family... unless you had a damn good reason.

Casiano was paranoid and afraid of Jerry's increase in productivity and popularity. He didn't like his underbosses gaining too much power or recognition by The Commission.

One reason Casiano kept Tommy Dolan so close...and at such a high level in his crew...was because The Irishman would never stand a chance of being recognized by The Commission's inner circle.

That was an honor for Italians *only*.

So Rocco never had to worry about Dolan whacking him for his job.

Jerry *D'Amore*, a *paisan*, didn't have Dolan's problem...and Casiano knew it.

Jerry was street smart, good looking, a good earner, loyal, ran a good crew, always kept his eyes and ears open...his mouth shut...and never left a mess for anyone else to clean up.

Casiano worried about the weight Jerry was acquiring...and he was regretting the fact that Jerry was Frank DeNike's nephew and Godson.

The old timers *still* spoke respectfully about Frank and the traditional way he conducted the business.

Casiano knew he could easily solve his fears by killing Jerry.

But he *couldn't* kill Jerry...for a couple of reasons.

The first was because Jerry was his only underboss able to work the Vegas scam with Dolan. Jerry was a gambler. He knew what was going on... he just didn't have the casino contacts like Dolan did.

The second reason was a promise Casiano made to Frank DeNike years earlier. Frank received approval from The Commission and arranged for his territory to be turned over to Casiano...should something ever happen to him. In return, Rocco promised to look after Frank's Godson as if he were his own. He would see that no harm came to Jerry...and if it did...it had to be avenged.

Because of that...Rocco couldn't hit Jerry.

And besides, Jerry wasn't making any overtures toward Rocco's job. He was, for the moment, quite content with his current position and the benefits it brought him.

Rocco knew he was being paranoid about Jerry.

He knew that Dolan was his primary concern, and it pissed him off.

He couldn't kill Dolan because he didn't want to lose the revenue and cash flow of the Vegas scam.

Besides, if he killed Dolan, Jerry would wind up taking over most of The Irishman's territory and become even *more* powerful.

Dolan, on the other hand, wouldn't mind having Jerry out of the way.

He felt that Jerry's participation in Vegas was Casiano's way of getting to the casino contacts...and once Jerry had the contacts, they wouldn't need Dolan. The Irishman was afraid of being eliminated.

There was always that friction between Tommy Dolan and Jerry.

Millicent and I left Cambria on Monday morning and headed for Los Angeles.

The drive was uneventful...until we got to Malibu.

We ate a late lunch overlooking the ocean and watched a school of dolphin swim by. I was quite understandably taken by the sight, seeing as dolphins are rather rare off the Jersey shore.

When we walked out of the restaurant I looked at the mountain in front of me.

I felt compelled to take the first side-road off of the Pacific Coast Highway and we found our way up Las Flores Canyon Road to the mountain's top. Once there, we were awed by the majestic view of the surrounding peaks and the canyon leading out to the ocean far below.

As we made our way back to the PCH, the sun was setting on the horizon and I was deep in thought about something I rarely, if *ever* during my 22 years, thought about.

Sure, it was a momentary morbid idea, but realistically, I knew it was something that would have to be dealt with in *some* fashion, some *day*...by *somebody*. I decided that when I die...I'd want my ashes taken out to the ocean from the base of that mountain at sunset...and tossed. This is where I wanted to be.

I just hoped it wouldn't be for many years to come.

As we drove south toward Sunset Boulevard, I looked out to the ocean as long as possible...and smiled.

We made it to Hollywood that evening and Mr. and Mrs. Toma checked into the Chateau Marmont. The plan was to stay there until Thursday and then get Millicent on a plane to Chicago. I'd then move into the D'Amore home in Studio City and start my sessions that night.

On Tuesday morning, I called my lawyer's office in Jersey and told him to prepare a will with my wish to have my ashes set adrift off of Malibu.

He thought I was crazy, but since he got paid for doing what I told him to do...he did it without question.

That evening I called my father to let him know I was alive and well.

"Where are you?" he asked.

"L.A."

"Studio City?"

"No."

"Your cousin's been looking for you," he said, making it the longest sentence of our conversation.

"For?"

"Didn't ask."

"Got a number?"

"Yeah, ready?"

I wrote the number down and drew a double-ended arrow above it, knowing I needed to reverse the last four digits.

"When?" I asked.

"Tomorrow afternoon. Jersey time."

"Okay."

"You all right?" he asked.

I stared at Lady Millicent smoked a joint as she leaned against the fourth floor railing overlooking the gardens.

"Yeah...I'm fine," I said with a laugh in my voice.

"Be good!" he ordered.

"Yes, *dad*."

I heard him laughing as we hung up.

He knew who I was with.

He had been carrying that newspaper article and picture around with him for weeks, proudly showing it to his friends as if he was showing pictures of his newborn.

That night, Millicent and I stayed in and had dinner on the terrace.

Around 10:00 on Wednesday morning, I called the re-configured number my father gave me.

Taz answered.

"It's me," I said.

"Yeah, hold on. He wants to talk to you."

Within seconds my Godfather was on the phone.

"Where are you?" he asked.

"L.A."

"I left a message there last week."

"I just got to town...and I'm not staying at the house. I'm out here on vacation."

"A vacation? To Los Angeles? You practically *live* there," he laughed.

"So...what's up?"

"I'm gonna have to get back to you on that."

That meant he had to get to a payphone.

"Where can I reach you in an hour?" he asked.

I gave him the hotel's number with the last four digits reversed and told him to *come around* sometime.

"Everything okay?" I asked.

"Talk to you in an hour."

"*Wait!*" I yelled before he hung up.

"What?"

"My name. You gotta ask for me when you call."

"I'll ask for Juan," he said, meaning he'd ask for my real name.

"No. Ask for Aunt Pat's husband."

I didn't want to say the actual name...just in case someone *was* listening.

"Who?"

"Aunt Pat's *husband*."

"You mean Dave To--"

He caught himself and started laughing, "That's funny! That's *very* funny!"

It was nearly two hours before the phone rang again.

"Mr. Toma," the hotel receptionist's voice quivered, "I have a call for you from Johnny Carson."

Knowing it was Jerry, I told her to send the King of Late Night's call through.

"Hello, Johnny," I jokingly said as she connected us.

"Hello, Mr. Toma," he replied.

"What can I do for you?"

"I need you in Vegas."

I knew not to ask "Why?"

So I asked, "When?"

"How soon can you get there?"

I thought for a bit before answering.

"I should be done Saturday night by eleven. I'll get a plane out of Burbank first thing Sunday morning and be there around nine or ten."

"What time can you be ready Saturday night?" he asked.

"After the session? I guess around midnight. But there's nothing outta Burbank that late."

"Be at the Studio City house by midnight and I'll have someone pick you up and get you to Vegas."

"Where am I staying?"

"The Frontier," he answered. "Now enjoy the rest of your *vacation*. I'll see you out there."

I kissed Millicent just before she boarded her Thursday afternoon flight back to Chicago.

"Call me!" she yelled.

I nodded and smiled.

As soon as Saturday night's session was over, I put my guitars in Patsy's Cadillac and headed for Studio City. When I pulled into the driveway there was a limo waiting.

The driver flashed his high-beams and came toward me.

"Jon D'Amore?" he asked.

"Yeah."

"I'm ready when you are, sir."

So this was my ride? I couldn't believe Jerry hired a limo to take me to Vegas.

"I've got to drop off my gear and get my luggage. I'll be ready in a few minutes," I answered.

Since I was spending an equal amount of time between California and Jersey, I had a closet and dresser full of clothes in Studio City. Months earlier I started leaving three guitars there so that I wouldn't have to constantly schlep them cross-country.

I was traveling to Vegas with three suitcases. One was for suits and dress shirts, a second for casual wear and a third for toiletries.

But the third was only half full.

Between the clothes I was buying at the hotels, the numerous unopened bottles of alcohol we'd keep from the set-ups, or the gifts I would pick up for my friends and family, I needed the space to bring the stuff home.

The driver put the suitcases in the trunk and I got comfortable in the back. It was going to be nice to take the four hour drive through the desert this way. I was even hoping to get a couple of hours sleep.

I didn't pay attention to where he was driving until the limo pulled into Van Nuys Airport. He showed someone a pass, went through a gate, drove along a taxiway to the end of the field and pulled up to a Lear Jet.

He popped the trunk, took out my suitcases and loaded them into the cargo hold. When he opened the door I got out and looked at the attractive, smiling stewardess waiting at the bottom of the stairway to the cabin.

She said, "Right this way, Mr. D'Amore."

I looked on the side of the plane to see the logo of The Frontier Hotel and Casino.

Jerry got them to send a jet for me.

Un-fucking-believable.

She led me onto the plane, buckled me in and poured a flute of Dom Perignon. *This* was the way to go to Vegas.

I wasn't in the plane for more than five minutes before they started the engines and we took off.

An hour and fifteen minutes later I was in Vegas, in another limo... and at one-fifty in the morning I was greeted at the hotel by a hostess who cheerfully and slowly escorted me to the elevator as a bellman quickly got my luggage up to the suite.

"Don't I need to register?" I asked as we walked through the lobby.

"That's already been taken care of by the Casino Manager, Mr. D'Amore."

I knew to keep my mouth shut.

The elevator opened on the seventh floor and she led me down the hall.

The bellman was just leaving as she opened the double doors.

Once again, there was a magnificent living room with a beautiful view, along with a bar and piano.

The bedroom had a huge four-poster bed and a master bathroom large enough for a party. It had a sauna *and* a steam room, a bathtub *and* a shower, a toilet *and* a bidet.

As the hostess was walking out, she smiled, handed me her card and the keys to the suite.

"If you need anything, just give me a call...and enjoy your stay."

I closed the doors behind her just as the phone rang.

I knew who it would be.

"Johnny Carson?"

"Like the ride?" he asked.

"How the fuck did you get a jet?"

He laughed and asked, "What's your room number?"

"Seven-eleven. Fitting, huh?"

An entire conversation ending in questions. Amazing!

We hung up. I stood there, shaking my head and smiling.

The doorbell rang while I was unpacking.

I opened it.

Taz stood in the doorway and looked around before entering. Jerry walked in behind him, followed by Mike.

Once the door was closed, I went to Jerry and kissed him on both cheeks. Then I did the same to Mike and Taz.

They sat down, talking and laughing as I opened a bottle of champagne that came with the complimentary fruit basket.

"Okay, how did I rate two limos and a jet? What kind of line did you get me here? A hundred-fuckin'-grand?" I asked as I poured a glass for each of them.

They all laughed.

So did I. But *mine* was a nervous laugh.

Jerry answered, "Twenty-five."

"That's it?" I asked, feeling relieved.

"Yeah. They heard you did twenty-five at The MGM with a double-A rating. The old casinos are tryin' to get the customers away from the big new joints...so they're going all out to bring in gamblers, hoping to get you to come *here* instead of going *there* from now on."

"And this couldn't wait until tomorrow?" I asked. "You had to get me here by two in the morning?"

"Yeah. Well, Dolan's casino contact goes off duty by three and he's leaving for vacation tomorrow," Jerry said as he pulled a credit application from his jacket. "So fill this out. That way he can approve it before he leaves."

Once again, I filled out the minimum amount of info and handed it to my Godfather. He gave it to Mike, who checked himself in the mirror and went to meet Tommy Dolan somewhere downstairs.

Jerry and Mike returned to Jersey after the third day.

I still had nine grand left on my line.

When I wasn't hitting The Frontier's casino, Taz and I were working the don't-pass line with a bunch of Dolan's guys at The Riviera and The Sahara.

After my fifth day, I had gone through my entire twenty-five grand.

Before leaving for Jersey, Dolan and Taz came up to my suite for the final count of the cash. Dolan handed me my grand salary and said, "You did good kid. You're gettin' better."

The two of them packed $473,000...in twenties, fifties and hundreds...into two briefcases, then Dolan handed me a credit application for Caesars Palace.

"Fill this out and tomorrow call Louie Calderone at The Riv. He'll take care of it. This way, you'll be all set up for your next trip."

I looked at Taz and asked, "Jerry all right with this?"

Before he could answer, The Irishman got pissed off and barked, "I cleared it with Jerry *and* Casiano. You got a problem with that?"

I kept my eyes glued to Taz as he nodded his head, giving his approval.

"We'll need you out here around the end of November. So keep it open." Dolan said.

"I'll check to see if I've got some sessions booked before I can commit to that," I responded.

Dolan wasn't happy that I didn't readily agree with his plan.

He was in charge of the Vegas scam...and technically, that meant of me too. He expected me to respond to him as I would to Jerry.

He had another thing coming.

"Yeah...you do that," he grumbled as he slammed shut one of the cash-filled briefcases, locked it and walked out the door.

I watched him and said to myself, "I'm not one of these guys. I'm a musician, not a gambler or a mobster. I don't have to take this cocksucker's bullshit."

Taz picked up the remaining briefcase, walked over to me and said, "Enjoy yourself for a couple of days. Let the concierge know when you're ready to go back to L.A., and they'll make the arrangements."

As I walked him to the door I asked, "Taz, why do I get the feeling he don't like me?"

He stopped in front of a mirror. I smiled as I watched him check his hair and clothes.

"'Cause you're Jerry's cousin. *You know that.* How'd you think he was gonna act toward you? Tommy'd rather be out here without *any* of Jerry's guys. Besides..."

He looked at my reflection.

"...if you're worried about somebody whacking you, it wouldn't be Dolan. It'd be Bobby. He'd be the one to do ya."

My look changed.

He smiled, kissed and smacked my cheek, then said, "Take care of yourself, kid."

Louie Calderone and I met for dinner that night.

I enjoyed being in Louie's company. He was around twenty years older than me, but he didn't speak to me like I was a kid, although he did refer to me that way in his discussions with Dolan. He knew music was what I did for a living and he knew it was what I loved doing.

He also knew not to discuss anything involving our bosses.

Louie was the exact opposite of Tommy Dolan. Where Tommy was overweight and gruff in his appearance and voice, Louie had class in the way he carried himself, and was soft and pleasant in the way he spoke. His appearance was first class.

I gave Louie the credit application for Caesars and by the next afternoon I was approved for another twenty-five grand...and he was on a plane back to Jersey with the rest of Dolan's crew.

Between my salary and the money I picked up on side bets, I had over seventeen hundred dollars on me. I spent the rest of my time lying around the pool, working out at the gym, playing the piano and going to the best restaurants and shows that Vegas of 1975 had to offer...and it was all comped.

I was packing to leave The Frontier on Saturday morning when the phone rang.

"Juan?"

It was Jerry.

"Yeah," I answered.

"Why was he calling me here?" I thought.

"Where are you?" I asked.

"Jersey."

"What's the matter?"

"When are you checking out?" he asked.

"I'm packing now. They said the jet will be ready in an hour. The limo's already here."

"Cancel it. You're stayin' in Vegas."

"But I've been here for a week. I used up my line. Besides, I got things to do in Jersey," I answered. "My manager booked a session."

"I need you to stay there. We covered your marker at the first place. I want you to go back."

I knew he meant The MGM Grand. He just didn't want to say it over the phone.

"Today?" I asked.

"Yeah."

"You coming out?"

"No. Now check out and go over there. Go to the VIP desk. They'll be expecting you. I'll have someone call to let you know what's goin' on."

"I gotta call my manager," I said. "He's expecting me in Jersey and I gotta--"

"You want *me* to call him? What's his number?" Jerry offered.

"No! No! I'll handle it," I laughed. "I'll see if he can reschedule the session or get someone to cover for me."

"I'll take care of you for this. I know you weren't expecting to stay for two weeks," he said, almost apologetically.

I took a deep breath and chose my words wisely.

"I'll do anything for you. You know that. But I'm concerned about my session work. I don't want to screw that up."

I wanted him to get the message. Music first...*then* Vegas.

"I understand," he said.

"Okay," I said on the exhale of another deep breath.

That was it. By saying "Okay" I was committed. But I also knew he heard the concern in my voice about missing my work.

Vegas, for me, was fun...but music was my *business*...it was my *love*...it was my *life*.

"When will I be talking to you again?" I asked.

"I'll call you in a couple of days."

By two that afternoon, I had checked into suite 2536, the same one I had on my first trip, and was lying poolside on a chaise lounge in the 88 degree heat.

Over the speaker system I heard, "Telephone call for Mr. David Toma. Mr. David Toma, please go to a house phone."

I walked to the nearest phone and told the operator I was David Toma. She connected me and the voice asked, "Mr. Toma?"

It was Mike Caruso.

"I *knew* it was you!"

"Hey kid! Whatcha doin'?"

"Waiting for someone to tell me what's happening."

"Well then, this is your lucky call."

I laughed and asked, "You comin' out?"

"In a couple of days. I got things to do back here. But in around four hours Bobby should be getting there with three guys. I don't know who they are. He's gonna need you at The Sahara and The Dunes, and then they'll work with you at your place."

Great...I had to spend the next couple of days answering to Bobby Grant.

I wasn't going to like this.

"What about The Irishman? Is he comin' out?" I asked.

"No. There's some shit goin' on back here."

"Like?" I asked, though I really didn't expect any kind of answer.

"Nothing you need to know about. Anyway...I'll be there by Monday night, the latest. Just keep your nose clean, don't do or say anything to piss Bobby off and keep track of whatever you see happening. Then let me know how much they tap their lines for. Okay?"

"I'll do the best I can."

"You're doin' great, kid. Your cousin's very proud of you."

I didn't say anything. I just nodded my head a couple of times.

It was around 6:45 that evening.

I had showered and shaved and was walking around the suite in my underwear, just killing time until I heard from Bobby, then I was going to put on one of my best suits.

Except for Louie Calderone, no one in Dolan's crew could ever be considered a slave-to-fashion. *Especially* Bobby. So I knew that by dressing to the hilt, it would piss him off. I had a feeling Bobby was the one that made the noise to Casiano about me looking too young to be gambling big money at the tables.

I was on the terrace watching The Strip's light show and taking a few hits on a joint when the phone rang.

"Hello?"

"Yeah. Kid?" the voice asked.

It was Bobby Grant.

"Yeah," I answered...hating that I had to respond to being called that. But in this case it was better to keep my mouth shut.

"You know who this is?"

"Yeah."

"How soon can you be in the lobby at The Sahara?"

"Half hour?"

"Good."

And he hung up.

Within 20 minutes I was in a suit and walking through the MGM casino. Ten minutes later I was getting out of a cab in front of The Sahara.

It only took a few minutes to find Bobby. I just had to look for the thickest cloud of cigarette smoke.

He greeted me with, "You goin' somewhere tonight?"

He couldn't even say "Hello."

I didn't know the reason why...but this guy had a bug up his ass about me.

"No. Why?" I asked, noticing he was alone.

"What's with the outfit? You puttin' on a show for somebody? You tryin' to impress some broad? I don't want no broads at the tables while *I'm* here. You got that?"

He was coming on a bit too strong. I couldn't let him get the best of me. I had to let him know I knew the rules and that I wasn't 'puttin' on a show.'

I leaned close to him so no one would hear me as I said, "Hey! It's a *suit*, not an *outfit!* I put the *suit* on because it makes me appear *older*. That way they'll think I know what the fuck I'm doin' at a crap table. *Okay?* Now if you don't think that's the right thing for me to do while we do our thing... then just let me know. I'll go back to my fuckin' hotel and change into something that will make me look *just...like...you*. Okay?"

Then I stepped back and compared my appearance to his.

He got the point, but didn't like that a 22-year-old guinea was dishing it to him.

"C'mon," he ordered, "Let's go up to the room. I want you to meet these guys."

"Did I ever see 'em out here before?" I asked as we made our way to the elevators.

"No. They're first timers. One of 'em's like you. From California. A surfer," he answered.

"Bobby, what the fuck are you talkin' about?" I said as we entered the elevator. "You got two things wrong. I'm not from California, and I don't surf. Never did."

"I thought you live in California," he said as the elevator doors closed and he hit the button for the ninth floor.

"I work there, and I got family there. But I *live* in Jersey. I was born and raised right in Hudson County with the rest of you guys...I live in Secaucus, for Christ sake."

He smiled. It was the first time I had ever seen him do that.

"Didn't know that," he responded.

The elevator doors opened and we walked down the hall. He gave a coded knock on a door and someone opened it.

It was your standard Vegas hotel room. There was nothing special about it.

I was introduced to two non-Italians in their mid-forties, who, from their attitude and the way they were dressed, *had* to be from Bayonne...and it only took seconds for Bobby to confirm it.

He ended their introduction with, "These are two friends of Tommy's from Bayonne. They're stayin' here at The Sahara."

Then he pointed to the third guy, who would *never* be taken as a Bayonne resident, and said, "This guy here...this is Ricky Rogers. He's from Newport Beach, so Tommy calls him '*Newport*.'"

"Not any worse than '*kid*,'" I thought.

He was around 37 years old, at least 6'2, muscular and tanned, with dirty blonde hair, blue eyes and wearing a bright silk Hawaiian shirt. He owned a construction company in the Newport Beach area, and somehow hooked up with Dolan. He really looked out-of-place amongst this group.

Bobby continued, "He's stayin' at The Dunes. That's where I'm at, too."

Then he looked at me and said, "None of these guys know exactly what they gotta do at the tables."

I slowly turned, looked at him and asked, "What do you mean by *exactly*?"

"They don't know *anything*. Jerry's guy, Mike, was supposed to be here to help me get 'em up to speed, but he's busy in Jersey until Monday night. So *you* gotta help me."

With my limited experience I felt a little intimidated by the task of something so important. But Mike asked me to keep an eye on how much cash they took out of the credit lines...and this would be the best way to do it. So I gave the answer I'm sure my Godfather would have wanted me to give.

"Sure. I'll do what I can."

He took me to a corner of the room and whispered in my ear, "They all have ten thousand dollar lines. And with your twenty-five at The Grand and mine from The Dunes, after a quick three or four days we'll leave with somewhere between seventy-to-eighty grand."

I asked, "Why didn't they just send out another ten guys and do what we normally do? Why just us?"

He answered as he lit another cigarette, "Because they just had a group of ten or twelve out here last week, and--"

I interrupted him, "Yeah, I know. I was one of 'em. I've been here for a week already."

He continued as if he didn't even hear me, "...and they're plannin' somethin' big for Thanksgiving. They'll probably use you for that, too. They're lookin' to bring in around thirty-five or forty guys for that one. So they need to get you and these guys up to speed."

So *now* I understood why Jerry needed me to stay here and learn what to do, and why Dolan told me I'd be coming back at the end of November. I was going to be part of The Thanksgiving Day Massacre.

Bobby and I looked at one another and did some quick calculating in our heads. It looked like the boys from Hudson County would be taking home somewhere around $750,000 over the holiday weekend.

"They'll probably throw a party for that one," he said.

"A party?"

"Oh, that's right," he laughed, "You haven't been here for any of the parties yet, huh?"

"They good?"

He just laughed again, walked back to his cohorts and chose one of them to be the first to play the pass line.

He put his arm around the newcomer's shoulder and said, "Jon and Newport are gonna be downstairs at the same table you and me are gonna be at."

I leaned against a wall and listened.

He continued, "I'll be next to you to tell you what to do. But I don't want you acknowledging the kid or Newport at all. They're gonna be playing a different way than you are. No matter what happens, you don't *talk* to them, you don't *look* at them, you don't do *anything* that's gonna make the pit bosses think you know those guys. Got that?"

The greenhorn from Bayonne nodded his head.

Newport came over to me and asked, "You going to walk me through what we have to do?"

What I wanted to say was, "I'm gonna try."

But instead it came out as, "Yep. No problem."

Bobby said to me, "Why don't you take Newport downstairs. Hang out by the tables and show him what's going on. Then go have a drink and tell him what to do. In about a half hour give me a call up here." He wrote down the room number and the name it was registered under. "Let me know you're ready and we'll come down. I'll pick the table and get my guy set up with a marker."

He reached into his pocket, counted out twenty one-hundred dollar bills and handed them to me. "Here's two grand. Split it with Newport and use it at the table. As soon as you see the pit boss come by, get yourselves set up at the opposite end and start betting."

"Right," I answered. "I'll call you in a half hour or so."

Before walking out, I went into the bathroom to check my appearance.

While Newport and I were in the elevator, I told him that I didn't like calling him by his nickname. He told me he'd prefer to be called Rick. I had no problem with that.

We strolled around the crap tables discussing his familiarity with the rules of the game and his knowledge of the don't-pass line. We sat at one of the lounges and had a drink as I explained that we would stand next to one another and bet identically.

We'd appear as friends, with one teaching the other. I'd make sure to say "Hey, just do what I do!" a lot. That way, I'd be able to control his bets while watching what was being laid on the pass line by Bobby's guy.

I called the room and alerted Bobby that we were as ready as we'd ever be.

Several minutes later, the two of them walked into the casino. Rick and I walked over to the crap tables and hovered as Bobby chose one of them. It didn't take him long. Several minutes later, three grand in chips were in front of the new guy, and we put our first don't-pass bets down.

Bobby had his guy laying two to four hundred dollars down, with five and six hundred dollar back-up bets.

Rick caught on very quickly.

I made sure we did our job with no problems or concerns from the pit bosses.

It only took Bobby twenty-five minutes to go through the three grand, and they left the table.

Rick and I went back to the lounge and gave them time to get to the room before I called.

Bobby wanted to get another three grand out tonight and was coming down with the second guy.

Around a half hour later they walked past us to let their presence be known.

Bobby picked out a different table and it wasn't long before Rick and I stood at the opposite end laying our bets.

Again, in less than a half hour another three thousand was lost on the pass line.

And the casino had no idea what just happened.

By eleven that night, the five of us were in the ninth floor room counting chips. Bobby separated the two grand that he had given us and counted out the remaining fifty-six hundred dollars.

"We got hit with a couple of twelves on the come-out roll, so we lost four hundred. We'll make that up on side bets tomorrow when Jon and I play the pass lines in our casinos."

He looked at me and winked.

I winked back.

Then he looked at all of us and said, "Okay, get some sleep. Everybody have breakfast in their own hotels tomorrow and then meet at The Dunes at ten. Got that?"

Everyone nodded.

I said goodnight, checked myself in the mirror and walked out the door.

I went to bed as soon as I got to my suite. I knew that the next couple of days were going to be tough. I didn't just have to deal with my own $25,000 line, I now had to work with Bobby and the new guys until Mike arrived Monday night.

So much for hanging by the pool.

The phone rang at 6:20, Sunday morning. It was Bobby.

"I gotta leave," he said.

"What?" I asked as I wiped the sleep from my eyes and looked at the clock.

"I gotta leave," he repeated. "I gotta go back to Jersey."

"Why?"

Normally, I'd *never* ask that...not knowing if the other person was on a safe phone...*or* what the answer might be. But I was just awakened with some bad news and wasn't thinking straight.

"One of my kids," he answered. "It snowed in Jersey last night. He slipped and broke his arm on the way to church this morning."

I looked at the clock and remembered that it was 9:20 back in Jersey...

and it was early November. There *was* the occasional snowfall to deal with in November...in Jersey.

"What do we do about the guys?" I asked.

"No problem. Mike'll be here by tomorrow night. He'll take care of ya's. Just have everybody sit tight 'til then, and make sure nobody does anything that'll get 'em in trouble." He lit a cigarette and continued, "I gotta go. Meet me in the front of your hotel in fifteen minutes."

"*Why?*" I asked...surprising even myself.

I was naked, warm and comfortable in my round bed. I didn't want to move.

"I gotta give you something," he answered.

I *definitely* knew not to ask "What?"

"Just be there in fifteen. I'll be in a cab."

And then he hung up.

Shit!

The sun was low in the eastern sky and it was already around 70 degrees as I stood under the huge marquee. His cab pulled up and I walked over.

"Here," he said as he handed me an envelope filled with cash. "It's the seventy-six hundred. The two grand we started with, and the fifty-six from last night." He lit a cigarette and smiled. "You did good last night, kid. Now give that to Mike."

"Thanks. I'll take care of it. Now get home and take care of your kid," I said, waving him away.

He said something to the driver and the cab took off.

It looked like I'd be getting to the pool after all!

It was a little after seven by the time I got to my room and called the new guys. I told them they had nothing to do until Mike arrived the next night, and to keep themselves off their hotel's radar.

Seeing as Rick was alone at The Dunes, I invited him to The Grand for breakfast and a day at the pool.

By mid-afternoon we were on our third round of Bloody Marys, and I was mentally reminiscing about the three women I met at this very pool, and the ménage-a-quatre that followed.

He asked what I was smiling about.

I looked at him and simply shook my head.

Around four o'clock I was starting to get an itch. I wanted to do some gambling.

So did Rick.

"I've got about eight hundred bucks on me," he said.

"Your money?"

"Yeah."

I laughed.

He looked at me and asked, "What's so funny?"

I quoted Tommy Dolan.

"Rule Number One...*Never* gamble with your own money."

He understood what I meant.

"Yeah, well it looks like we won't be doing *that* until tomorrow night," he answered.

"Not necessarily," I snickered.

"What do you mean?"

"How comfortable do you feel betting the don't-pass line?" I queried.

"Fine. No problem. Why?"

"I got an idea. Let's get together with the other guys. We'll have dinner and talk," I answered.

Rick went back to The Dunes to shower and dress. Then I had the three of them come to The Grand for dinner in my suite, and to explain my plan.

It was either going to work...or I was going to piss off The Irishman, my Godfather and Rocco Casiano. The stakes were *very* high.

I made sure that no one drank any alcohol during dinner, and by nine o'clock I was standing next to one of the Bayonne boys, dressed in a suit... or as close to a suit as he could muster...as he pulled another three grand from his credit line at The Sahara. We made the same bets he made the night before with Bobby.

Meanwhile, I had Rick and the other new guy working the don't-pass line.

The particular table we were at was jammed with gamblers and onlookers, but upstairs in the Security Level above the casino, something was going on.

A '*watcher*' was looking through a scope to the casino floor.

From his perch he spoke into a small microphone and said, "I got them. They're at Table Five. I want two of you behind each of them...and another two around the table in case anyone runs."

A couple of suited men approached the table where we were playing and mixed in with the crowd.

All I remember was that I felt a push from behind, then the roller threw a 7. Across the table, chips were being taken and tossed.

At that point the watcher yelled into the microphone, "Take them... *now!*"

That's when things erupted.

Some guy standing next to me, and someone at the other end of the table were quickly and violently grabbed by four men in suits and forcibly taken away.

Everyone stopped what they were doing and stepped away from the table in confusion. A security guard quickly approached and said, "Sorry about that folks! Everything's fine. Please, excuse the interruption and go back to enjoying yourselves."

I had a feeling I knew what had just happened...and it scared me.

Rather quickly, the crowd settled down and the action on the table resumed.

As my cronies and I discreetly looked at one another, we were noticeably shaken. They looked at me, wondering if we should make a hasty exit to another hotel.

I put a sizeable bet on the table, letting them know to keep playing and act as if nothing was wrong.

A pit boss was walking around the table to get everyone back into their places. I tapped him on the shoulder, leaned toward him and asked, "What was that about?"

"Nothing to worry about, sir." He came closer and whispered, "A couple of wiseguys from Cleveland. They were working a scam...oldest one in the book. We've been onto them for a couple of days. You won't be seeing them in *this* casino anymore."

Then he stepped back, let out a hearty laugh and said, "We catch 'em. We *always* catch 'em."

I gave him a forced smile as he walked away.

By three in the morning, both of The Irishman's friends had successfully gone through the remaining $7,000 of their $10,000 credit lines...with the casino having no idea that we just hit them.

We reconvened in their room and counted over $17,000 in chips, thanks to the occasional side bets I had these guys place to make up for what we lost due to the twelves that were rolled.

I sent each of them down separately to cash in the chips. Then I went to The MGM, kept the two grand start-money on the side, and put the fifteen grand together with the fifty-six hundred from the night before. Then I went to sleep...smiling.

The next day was spent lounging at the pools of our respective hotels, awaiting Mike's arrival.

As the sun slowly warmed my body, once again I heard over the PA system, "Telephone call for Mr. Toma. Mr. David Toma, please pick up a house phone."

Knowing it was Mike, as soon as I was connected I asked, "Where are you?"

"Jersey. It don't look good."

"What's *that* mean?"

"Ain't you been watching the news?"

"What the fuck are you talkin' about? Why?"

"We're in the middle of a freak-fuckin'-snowstorm!"

I laughed as I stood in the 82 degree desert.

"They closed the airports. There's no flights outta Newark, Kennedy, LaGuardia or Philly. I don't know when I'll be able to get there. I'm hopin' sometime tomorrow."

"Geez!"

"How's it goin' there? You okay?" he asked.

"Well...yeah. But...uh," I stuttered.

"You keepin' an eye on what they're doin', how much they're takin'...right?"

"Well...yeah. I know *exactly* how much they're taking. But...uh," I re-stuttered.

"What? What's the matter? Bobby giving you a hard time?"

"Not really," I hesitated before continuing, "He's not here. He had to go back to Jersey yesterday. I thought you knew."

"*What?*"

"His kid got hurt and he had to get home. He figured since you were coming out tonight, everything would be okay."

"Shit! Your cousin's gonna be pissed!"

"Well, maybe not as pissed as you might think," I chuckled.

"Whatdya mean?"

"I'll show you when you get here."

"Huh?"

"Don't worry, big guy," I said, "And don't say anything to my cousin.

Just get out here as soon as you can."

"Okay. Sit tight. Don't do anything. Keep a low-pro, and I'll get there."

"Okay."

"I'll call you as soon as I know what flight I'll be on," he said before he hung up.

I stood there thinking for a few seconds, then called The Sahara and The Dunes and made arrangements to meet the guys in Rick's room at 8PM.

When I got to my suite, the phone was ringing. I was hoping it was Mike with good news. But instead it was The MGM's Casino Manager.

He asked if everything was okay with my accommodations. I assured him everything was fine. In a very professional and cordial way he made reference to the fact that I had been there for two full days and hadn't been to the tables to play my line. I told him that friends of mine were in town and staying at another hotel and that I was spending time with them, and as soon as they left the following day, I'd start playing.

I figured that with Mike coming in sometime tomorrow, I wasn't bullshitting this guy.

I had dinner in the suite, put on a suit and made my way to The Dunes.

All three of them were waiting for me, each pumped, dressed and ready to go.

I re-explained the details of the don't-pass bets to the Bayonne boys, and sent them to the casino to await our arrival to the tables. Then I walked Rick through the marker process and getting his chips.

Once I found a table, I kept the betting simple enough for Rick to follow, and to keep the boys at the other end of the table from fucking-up.

Except for them missing a couple of back-up bets, and a few twelves getting rolled, we went through five grand over the course of the evening and cleared forty-four hundred.

By 6:15 the following evening, we finished off the rest of Rick's line, clearing another forty-eight hundred, and then went to dinner at The Sahara.

Throughout the day, I was calling The Grand to see if Mike had left a message.

Nothing.

Back in my suite, I went to the closet and took two envelopes out of one of my suit jackets and put that day's money in with the rest of the take.

I was sure the guys back east would be happy with the $29,800, *plus* the two grand start-money, I had for them. I was only $200 short of the total of their credit lines.

It was around 9:15 when the phone rang.

"Yeah?"

"Kid?"

It was Mike.

"Yeah."

He didn't sound happy as he said, "The airport was closed all day. We really got dumped on back here. They say it'll be open tomorrow morning, but who the fuck knows?"

"Well, let's hope for the best," I answered as I looked at my watch and realized that it was after midnight back east.

He said, "I'm sure the casinos are gonna start bitchin' about these guys staying there and not gambling."

"Well, not *all* the casinos."

"Whatcha mean?"

"I took care of the three visitors," I said cryptically.

"What do you mean? You mean you did their lines?"

"Yeah."

"All of 'em?"

"Yeah. Well, except mine...and the casino *has* asked me about it. Actually, the Casino Manager called my room last night. I told him I was gonna start playing today. But I was waiting for you...so I never got to hit my--"

"*Shit!* I gotta get out there," he said, angrily.

"Don't worry," I tried to calm him down, "Everything's okay. I got everything here waiting for you."

"Whatdya mean 'everything'?"

"Only two short."

"Two *grand?*" he asked.

I laughed and said, "Two *grand?* What the fuck? Are you kidding me? Two *hundred*, man."

"You're shitting? You're only down two hundred on thirty?"

"Yep."

"You're unbelievable. Your cousin's gonna flip when he hears that. That's just great, kid!"

"Yeah, well…just get your ass out here to help me with mine so I can get the fuck outta here and into a recording studio somewhere," I said. "I got a *real* job I gotta get back to!"

"Yeah…well you ain't gonna wanna come back east. It's cold and it's a mess."

I laughed and said, "I think I'm L.A. bound when I'm done here."

He laughed and we hung up.

About ten minutes later I was in the bedroom and starting to undress when the phone rang again.

"Kid?"

"Yeah," I answered, sounding a bit pissed off.

It was Mike again.

"I called your cousin and told him," he said.

"Told him what?"

"About what you did with The Irishman's guys, and the call from the Casino Manager."

"And…?"

"He said he wants you to go down and play with three grand."

"Okay. I'll call up two of the guys and have them come over."

"No. Don't worry about them. He wants you to go down right now and start gambling. And go to a table with hardly anybody on it. That way they can watch you."

"But suppose I lose?"

"It'll be *better* if you lose. He wants you to show the casino you're gambling. Just get down there as soon as you can."

It sounded crazy. But I understood the logic behind it. We had to keep up the appearance that I came, I gambled, I lost, I left.

So I took a few hits on a joint, brushed my teeth, put my shirt and tie back on, brushed my hair, sprayed on some cologne, put on a gold watch and pinky ring, slipped on my jacket, walked out of the suite, went to a $100 crap table and called for $3,000. The pit boss brought over the marker. I signed it and three grand in chips were placed in front of me.

I started with two hundred dollars on the pass line, and backed it up with two to five hundred. Plus, I was making and hitting several side bets from time-to-time. There were times when I was up a thousand or so…and then down as much a little while later.

I played the table for more than an hour and was down around eighteen hundred dollars when the pit boss came over and started to get social.

"Having a good time, Mr. D?" he asked.

"Sure am," I said, smiling.

He handed me his card and told me to call him if I wanted to go to any shows while I was in town.

"We have this new act," he said, "Siegfried and Roy. They just got into town. Two guys. They're lion tamers and magicians. It looks like a great show."

"Thanks..." I looked at the name on the card, "...Carl. I'll be here for a few days. I'll call you."

"Good. I'm sure you and Mrs. D will enjoy it."

I said, "There's no Mrs. D," as I threw a twenty-five dollar chip to the center of the table and yelled, "A Hard Eight!" to the stickman.

"Well, if you and a friend would like to go, just give me a call."

"Suppose I have a *couple* of friends?"

He eyed his clipboard for a moment, checked my credit limit and rating, smiled, looked up and said, "I'm sure we can accommodate whatever you'd like, Mr. D."

"How long will they be here?" I asked. "I don't know if I'll have time during this trip."

"Well, their contract is for six months. After that I'm not sure. They'll probably get back to town once in a while. Will you be back in less than six months?"

I laughed to myself, because I knew I'd be back in less than four weeks... just not to this casino.

"I'm sure I will, Carl. And when I do...you're the one I'm gonna call about seein' that show."

"My pleasure, Mr. D," he said as he patted me on the back and returned to his position behind the tables.

I knew I wouldn't be able to bring Mike and Dolan's guys to a show at The MGM *this* trip, because if anyone were to see all of us together and then see them playing opposite me at the tables, they'd put two-and-two together. And I had no intention on blowin' this scam for Jerry. The last three people I wanted to piss off were Jerry, Dolan and Rocco Casiano.

Within another hour I had lost all three grand. It was time to go.

I waved to Carl, and he waved back.

Mike arrived late the next morning, and with the help of the other guys, we went through the remainder of my twenty-five thousand in three days.

We sent Rick and the Bayonne boys to their respective homes on Friday night. Saturday morning I was packing when the phone rang. It was Jerry.

"Juan, I talked to The Irishman and the other guy..." I knew he meant Casiano. "...and they want me to thank you for taking care of things out there. You did a great job."

"*Something* needed to be done," I said. "It wasn't good that the four of us were just sitting here. Besides, I had fun."

"Yeah, well, we're gonna take care of you for that."

"Whatcha mean?"

"You'll see," he laughed. "Call me in a couple of days."

"At what number?"

"My guy'll give it to you." I knew he meant Mike, who was on his way to my room. "Are you coming back to Jersey or going to L.A.?"

"It's thirty-eight degrees in Jersey and seventy in Studio City. You figure it out. I booked a couple of sessions in L.A., so it'll be another week or so before I get to Jersey."

"Whatcha doin' for Thanksgiving?" he asked.

"I hear Caesars is a nice place."

He laughed, told me he loved me and hung up.

When Mike arrived I was placing the last of the unopened liquor from the set-up into my suitcase.

"Did your cousin call?" he asked.

"Yep."

"He tell you about Thanksgiving?"

"Yep."

"You're at Caesars."

"Yeah, I know."

"Did he tell you I have to give you a phone number so you can call him next week?"

"Yep."

"Did he tell you I was gonna pay you?"

"Pay me? What about the three grand I lost when I went to the table by myself?"

"That's nothin'. That's kid shit," he laughed. "You saved the mission by making it look like you were here to *gamble*."

He took an envelope out of his pocket and laid it on the coffee table.

"This is for your week at The Grand and for running the show when Bobby left. You did a good job teachin' those guys. Because of you, they'll be okay for Thanksgiving. Besides, they're Dolan's problem...not ours. Dolan should thank you himself."

I walked over to Mike, thanked him for the envelope and kissed him on the cheek.

"I gotta catch my flight to Newark. You goin' to L.A.?" he asked.

"Yep."

And he left.

I opened the envelope. There was three grand in it.

My Godfather was proud of me. I did not let *him* or *the family* down.

When my L.A. sessions were finished I called Lady Millicent for the first time since I took her to the airport. I was going to see if she'd like me to fly to Chicago for a day or two before I returned to Jersey.

Mr. Waite answered the phone and I asked for her.

"She's not here," he rudely responded.

"Can I leave a message?"

"She's not *here*," he repeated with anger.

I changed my attitude and questioned him, "Is there a problem? You got a problem with me? Is there somethin' you want to say to me?"

Apparently he did.

"For eleven days...for eleven days we had no idea where she was! She was with *you* somewhere in California! Do you have any idea of who she *is*? Do you know the position you put me and my wife in?"

Now I understood the anger.

I listened.

"We had a responsibility to her family! To the *Royal Family*. You and Millicent jeopardized a relationship that my family's had with them for eighty-three years!"

He took a deep breath and continued.

"Her barrister called while she was missing. We didn't know what to tell him. We didn't know where she was. *Nothing!* Not even a phone call. We didn't know if she was kidnapped, killed, lost..."

As he took another deep breath I managed to say, "Mr. Waite...I apologize. I--"

He continued without missing a beat, "Scotland Yard sent a team *here*, for Christ sake! They found her car at the airport and traced the airline ticket to San Francisco. But after that, we lost track of her. She didn't show up in Los Angeles for the scheduled flight back. When she finally arrived at O'Hare, agents from The State Department took her directly to the British Embassy. Her belongings were collected from our house and they shipped her back to England the following day."

I felt terrible and apologized again.

And then he hung up on me.

But what became of Lady Millicent?

I had no way of contacting her in England.

I never knew if I would see her or hear from her again.

I hopped an early morning flight from L.A. to Newark on Thursday, November 20. I certainly wasn't looking forward to returning to New Jersey. The weather had gotten progressively worse, with the daily temperatures in the 20s and 30s, and much colder at night.

There was solace in knowing I'd be leaving for Vegas again on Tuesday the 25th for the Thanksgiving trip.

The bare trees on a dirty white landscape came into view as the plane descended out of the clouds. It was cold, gray and wet. How did I spend so many years here?

Carl, the pit boss, had the hotel arrange to have a limo pick me up and drive me to my parents' house in Secaucus.

I arrived around dinner time.

As I walked toward the front door someone called my name.

"Excuse me!" It was a man in a suit and overcoat walking from across the street. "Excuse me, are you Jon D'Amore?"

It was a question I was not fond of answering to strangers.

I put my suitcase down and answered, "Who's asking?"

His hand came out of his coat and produced a badge and identification.

"I'm FBI Special Investigator Arthur McCormick."

I took a look at the ID and handed it back to him. I figured I was going to have to answer to someone about the temporary disappearance of Lady Millicent Overton.

"So what can I do for you, Artie?"

He didn't like that I used his first name, and a look of contempt came across his face as he said, "I'd like to ask you a few questions about a trip west you recently took."

I turned up the collar on my leather jacket and said, "I just got home and I'm freezing. Any chance we can do this at a later time and someplace warmer?"

"Can we talk about it inside your house?"

I didn't think my father would want me bringing an FBI Agent into the living room.

"Nah...I don't think that's gonna happen, Artie."

He looked irritated and disappointed as he said, "Well then, would you mind stepping into my car? This should only take a few moments."

"Where is it?" I asked, cautiously.

"Right across the street," he said, pointing to a large Plymouth with its engine running.

"Waiting long?" I asked.

"On and off for the last couple of weeks."

"Couple of weeks, huh? Well, I travel a lot on business."

I figured that the Queen had a few high-level friends in the State Department and they put this guy in charge of slapping my wrists.

He opened the passenger door for me. The car was warm inside, and it looked like he actually lived in there. There were files, empty food wrappers, coffee containers and lots of electronic communication equipment.

"Mr. D'Amore...what exactly do you do for a living?" he asked as he sat behind the wheel.

"I'm a musician. And you can call me Jon, Artie."

"Oh? Have you recorded anything I might know?"

I explained my function as a session musician.

"Does that bring you to Las Vegas often?" he asked.

Why would he be asking about Vegas?

"No, it doesn't. Why?"

"Mr. D'Amore, I'd like you to take a look at some pictures," he said as he took four black-and-white photos out of a folder and handed them to me.

I figured they had some shots of me and Millicent from *somewhere*.

"Do you know any of these people?" he dryly asked.

The first one wasn't what I expected. I quickly realized this had nothing to do with my kidnapping Millicent.

The picture was of Tommy Dolan.

I couldn't show a reaction.

I flipped to the second picture.

It was Bobby Grant.

Again, I showed no expression that would make him think I knew these people.

The third picture was of Louie Calderone.

He watched me closely.

The fourth picture was of Rocco Casiano.

Casiano was the only one I never actually met...but easily could have been aware of because of the numerous newspaper articles about him, and the fact that he occasionally showed up at D'Amore family functions years earlier with Frank DeNike when I was a kid.

I held up his picture.

"I've seen this guy before," I said.

"Do you know who that is?" McCormick asked.

"Who doesn't? It's Rocco Casiano."

"Do you know what he does for a living?"

I shook my head.

"Do you know the other men?"

I scanned through the pictures again and slowly said, "Nope."

He looked at me with cold eyes, took the picture of Casiano, held it up and asked, "Are you saying that you know this man...but not these three?"

"No. I'm not saying that at all. I *don't* know that man. I know *of* him. Now, what's this about, Artie?"

"Two of these men are under Federal investigation, and it's come to our attention that you may have been in contact with one or both of them in Las Vegas a couple of months ago."

I had to think quick.

"Do you mean when I was there at the end of August?" I asked.

He scanned his clipboard for dates as I continued.

"My cousin Jerry invited me to Vegas for my birthday. But Rocco Casiano wasn't there. I never met the man." I looked at the agent and said, "I met a lot of people...but I couldn't say for sure that I remember any of them."

He saw that he wasn't going to get anywhere with me, so he ended the meeting.

He handed me his card and told me, "You're hanging out with people that could get you in big trouble, Mr. D'Amore. Maybe even hurt that music career of yours. Think about it, that's all. If you remember anything about *any* of these people, you'd be better off letting me know."

I told him, "I have no idea what you're talking about, Artie. But whatever it is, it wasn't worth sitting outside in the cold for." Then I got out of the car.

As I crossed the street I looked at his card and said to myself, "Arthur McCormick...what an asshole."

If he only knew that I'd been sitting next to him with nearly five grand of Vegas money in my pocket. Even in the cold, that thought brought a smile as I walked up the steps to the front door.

Once I got in the house, I told my father what just took place and then I took a drive to Jerry's house to tell him of the pictures and questions.

My Godfather proudly smiled, kissed me, told me that I did the right thing and that I would be rewarded for it when the time came.

I would have preferred being questioned about Lady Millicent.

Round 12

It was Tuesday. Thanksgiving was two days away and I was sitting next to Mike on a jet.

"You know something, Mike?" I whispered, "I may have to start taking another airline."

He laughed and said, "I've been taking United to Vegas for a year before you started coming out, and I *never* had a stewardess remember my name or what I drank...ever! What the fuck did you do with *her?*"

I shrugged my shoulders and nonchalantly answered, "Glad Dolan ain't on this flight," as I sipped the Chivas-on-the-rocks-with-a-splash that the stewardess brought without my asking for it...and after she greeted me by name.

"No shit," he quietly responded.

About an hour after the plane lifted off above the snow covered streets of Jersey, I started feeling something I never felt before.

Anticipation.

I was *really* looking forward to this trip.

Not for the warmth, or the money, or the pool, or the restaurants and shows. Not even for the women.

It was the excitement of knowing I was going to be a part of something big. Something really big.

It wasn't the gambling. It wasn't the thrill of rolling the dice or betting big cash.

It was because I was going to be doing something with *these guys*. With Mike and Taz...and my Godfather, Jerry.

There was no feeling of apprehension.

I wasn't nervous at all.

It was like walking on stage to perform in front of a few thousand people. I had it down. My rock group experience gave me that.

To me...it was pure excitement.

And with the excitement came confidence.

Confidence...because I knew my part. Like practicing the specific music charts for a gig before going into the recording session.

I was prepared. I knew what I had to do.

And if they needed me to do more, I had already proven I could do it.

About midway through the flight, and from out of the blue, Mike asked, "You ever hear from that British girl again?"

He caught me by surprise.

I'm sure it was Jerry who really wanted to know. Mike was just asking the question for him.

So I responded with, "Huh?"

"The one you got caught doin' on the plane. Have you seen her since then?"

I looked out the window into the distance...thinking of the times Lady Millicent and I spent together. She was a small, wonderful slice of my life filled with spontaneous fun, physical attraction and youthful adventure... along with a little 'celebrity' and a lot of lust thrown in. I missed her.

"No," I answered, my stare still far away.

Before going back to whatever magazine he was reading, he laughed and said, "You should be happy United still lets you fly on their planes. I wonder if anybody's ever been blackballed from an airline 'cause they got caught fucking in the bathroom?"

I, on the other hand, went back to thinking about Lady Millicent.

As the plane lowered its landing gear I asked him about Jerry and what would be in store for the next few days.

He whispered, "He flew out on Sunday with Taz. I'm at The Aladdin. They're at Caesars...same as you. The rest of our guys'll be at The Sahara, The Riv and The Aladdin."

"The Irishman?" I asked.

"Dolan, Louie and Bobby got to town Monday. Their guys are at The Frontier, The Trop, The MGM and The Dunes."

The more I heard, the more my inner-excitement grew.

"This is gonna be *great*," I said as we neared the runway.

Mike leaned close to me and whispered, "This is the biggest fuckin' week so far. Jerry and Dolan are gonna have nearly all of their people out here. Me, Taz, Louie, Bobby and the more experienced guys are runnin' a couple of lines. A lot of money's gonna be goin' back home from this."

Just then the plane touched down and within seconds the passengers began applauding.

Normally, I found it amusing and amateurish. But this time, with my anticipation running so high...I started clapping along.

Mike looked at me and smiled. He knew he had just witnessed the bug sinking its teeth into me. I had been bitten.

We both knew it wasn't the gambling bug. It was "the family" bug.

We found our luggage, sauntered into the dry, desert heat and grabbed an air-conditioned cab.

As we rode along Caesars statue-lined driveway, Mike said, "Go to the VIP desk and register. See if you can find your cousin. Your line's already set up."

Then we kissed each other on the cheek and made arrangements to meet for dinner.

"Good afternoon, Mr. D'Amore," said the most attractive VIP hostess I had ever seen. "We've been looking forward to your arrival."

Her Romanesque uniform covered only the most necessary of parts. Her breasts were pushed up and protruding from her outfit to such an extreme that I found it hard to look at her eyes while she spoke to me... and she was completely aware of what she was doing to my twenty-two-year-old libido.

Of all the hotels that I would eventually have lines at, my fourth floor suite at Caesars was the most ostentatious. This one was the dream-pad of every young musician-cum-pseudo-mobster with twenty-five grand to blow. And I'd lay odds that I was the only one of those in town.

The gigantic living room had the standard sofas, chairs, dining area, bar, piano and vaulted ceiling. But what set this suite apart was the bronze and marble fountain with two life-size figures of women...with water spouting from their nipples at the flip of a switch.

Sliding glass doors opened to an expansive wrap-around terrace, and the bedroom rivaled the living room for space and opulent decor. Not only did the circular bed come with the prerequisite mirror-on-the-ceiling and entertainment-controls-in-the-headboard...but it was prepared nightly with a choice of black, white or red satin sheets.

The master bathroom had a television, along with a steam room, a jacuzzi-for-four and a shower-for-many-more...all with gleaming, gold-plated fixtures.

I wasn't in the suite for more than fifteen minutes before Jerry rang the doorbell, although I hadn't called him yet.

He was alone.

"How'd you know what room I was in?" I asked as he kissed me and sat down on the sofa.

His response was simply that sly smile on his face.

"Where's Taz?" I asked.

"I wanted to talk to you alone."

He motioned for me to sit next to him.

"What's wrong?" I asked, my voice growing soft.

Even though we were alone, whenever there was a reference to a "private chat" it meant it was going to be said quietly.

He was very serious as he whispered, "From now on...whenever you're out here...when you work with any of Dolan's guys...I want you to let me know who they are and how much they take at the tables."

"Is there a problem, Jer? Are they gonna be doing the same thing to us?" I asked, my voice barely audible.

"I doubt it."

I assured him, "I'll let you know everything I see."

"*Anything* out of the ordinary...I want to know about it."

I thought that would be it, but he continued.

"And if you ever get introduced to anyone...like a Credit Manager or a Casino Manager...I want you to remember everything you can about the guy and then get me on the phone right away."

"It's never happened before. What's goin' on?"

He looked deep into my eyes as if he were asking himself how much he should tell me.

Sure, he trusted me. But realistically, should anything come down, like if I were ever questioned by Dolan or the Feds...the less I knew, the better it would be for both of us.

He was just trying to protect me.

"How many trips have you made so far?" he asked.

"This is the fourth trip...fifth line."

"You understand what's going on here?"

I nodded.

"If you see anything out of the ordinary, I want you to let me know," he ordered. "Got that?"

My voice grew louder than a whisper.

"Jerry! What the fuck? You already said that! Don't you think I'd do that *anyway?*"

He knew I'd figure it out sooner or later. He knew I wasn't a fool, and once I put two-and-two together I'd know what was happening. So he quietly filled me in.

"I want to know who Tommy's casino contacts are."

"He won't tell you?" I asked, somewhat sarcastically.

He laughed, sat back and lit a cigarette.

"He knows that if I had his contacts...we'd be able to run this show without him."

I sat back and thought about what he had just said.

Something like this couldn't happen without approval from above. Jerry *never* would have considered this move on his own. Not without permission or prior approval. He couldn't move in on the business of another underboss from the same family...unless there was a reason.

I immediately figured that the reason...and the approval...must have come from Rocco Casiano.

It was the day before Thanksgiving.

While we were having a great time in Vegas...Rocco Casiano was in the back of his Lincoln Town Car as it moved through the streets of Little Italy on its way to Jersey.

He was sitting directly behind Salvatore Della Osa.

From the passenger seat Salvatore gave the driver directions to the Holland Tunnel, while he constantly turned his head to see if the Feds or some of Gambino's boys were tailing them.

Sometimes they'd take more than an hour to make the thirty minute ride just to deviate from the normal route.

"Sal, what did you think of that? That he mentioned Jerry at the meeting. What was that about?" Casiano asked his bodyguard.

Della Osa knew the '*he*' his boss was referring to was Roberto Musarra, the 69-year-old northern New Jersey Consigliere for the Genovese family. It was a name that didn't need to be said. Della Osa *also* knew that Musarra simply mentioned Jerry as a show of recognition for the increase in money he was bringing in and passing along as a result of his newly expanded Bergen County territory. But Sal knew he couldn't say that. He knew Rocco's paranoia was rearing its head.

Sal answered, "It sounded like he was sayin' he thought you were a good boss for leadin' a guy like Jerry to do bigger and better things."

Casiano quietly leaned forward and held his fingers in the shape of a gun, aimed it at the back of Sal's head, made a shooting motion and gently whispered, "*Poowf!*"...unbeknownst to Sal.

"That's a very professional answer there, Sally. You should go into fuckin' politics with answers like that." The boss was getting pissed off, and his bodyguard heard it. "Now give me a *real* fuckin' answer."

Sal knew where he had to go with this.

"It shows that Jerry's being noticed by The Commission. He's an underboss of *yours*. If anyone should bring his name up at a meeting, it's you. You think Jerry's making contact with somebody upstairs, Rocco?"

Casiano looked out the window. He knew Jerry and our family for more than twenty-five years.

"No. I don't think he'd do that. He was brought up right. He wouldn't do it...would he?"

Sal laughed, patted the gun under his jacket and answered, "Not if he knows what's good for him."

Casiano knew that Jerry learned *respect* and *the rules* from Frank DeNike. And those rules included respecting and working for your boss... unconditionally.

Though Casiano was paranoid...he was a good boss.

If Jerry *really* wanted Rocco's job, all he had to do was wait. Whether Rocco retired or met another fate, The Commission would *never* give Dolan the position. Jerry only had to bide his time.

And for the time being he was doing quite well.

By Friday afternoon I had gone through all but $6,000 of my line at Caesars.

It was a rare occasion as Jerry, Taz and I were in our bathing suits and sitting under the awning of my reserved poolside cabana, sipping another bottle of Dom Perignon.

"I think tonight's the night," Jerry said with a smile on his face.

Taz grinned. Apparently he knew what my Godfather was talking about.

"What's tonight, Jer?" I asked.

"A party. A ten thousand dollar party."

Everything had gone according to plan. The cash was coming in left and right.

Earlier that day Mike was sent back to Jersey with over six hundred thousand dollars in a suitcase. Jerry knew there was still another two-hundred grand in unfinished lines they'd wind up with by Sunday. He also knew that Casiano...and everyone above him...would be quite happy with this week's take, so blowing ten grand on a party for the boys wouldn't be an issue.

"Where?" Taz asked, as I moved to a chaise lounge in the sun.

"One of Dolan's places. If anything goes wrong, I don't want any heat at the joints our guys are stayin' at. How's midnight sound?"

The smile on Taz's big face grew bigger.

"Yeah, that's good."

I was lying on my stomach when the sun suddenly disappeared.

Without lifting my head I called to my companions, "What the fuck just happened? We havin' an eclipse?"

"Hey...Jerry," barked the gruff, raspy voice.

The large shadow was cast by Tommy Dolan as he stood over me.

Before I opened my eyes I had hoped he was wearing some clothes and not a bathing suit. At over 300 pounds, this was *not* someone I wanted to view semi-naked.

I slowly looked up to see him wearing another pair of wrinkled slacks and an Izod shirt that was stretched to its limit. It must have been 85 degrees, yet he still wore a sport jacket to cover his girth. Sweat was soaking through his shirt and dripping from his forehead.

I wondered how this man controlled a scam that brought in millions. What kind of connections did this obese, wrinkled wise-guy have that allowed him to control an operation like this?

"Is the kid ready to finish up tonight?" Dolan asked my Godfather while ignoring me.

Jerry slowly raised his head and said, "Why don't you ask him yourself, Tommy. You're standing over him."

He looked down as I put my head back to the side...ignoring him.

"What about it, kid?"

"Sorry, I wasn't listening. What about what?" I answered, with my eyes still closed.

He knew I heard him. Everyone within a 10 yard radius heard his deep Jersey growl.

He lowered his voice and looked directly at me.

"When can you be ready to clean up your line?"

"When do you need me?"

"Be in your room, dressed and ready by six," he ordered. "I'll have a couple of guys meet you there. Take out three grand, and then another three. Got that?"

Without verbally responding, I nodded and motioned for him to allow the sunlight to hit my body.

Just as he started to walk away...Jerry called him.

"Tommy!"

The big Irishman turned around.

"Yeah?"

"I think we should have the party tonight. Don't you?"

"Why?" he answered defiantly.

"You're kidding, right?" Jerry responded.

"No," he said as he approached my cousin.

Taz immediately stopped smiling and sat up. It was a habit he acquired whenever anyone came toward Jerry.

Dolan saw it, stopped and moved back to his previous position...once again blocking the sun from my body.

Jerry took a long sip of champagne, lowered his voice and said, "These guys busted their hump to get us what we already sent home. You and I have been up every night making sure everything runs smooth. A little R&R wouldn't be such a bad idea, would it? We've had parties for less. So I don't see no problem...unless *you* got a problem with that?"

"Where?" The Irishman asked.

Jerry emptied his flute and said, "The Trop."

A look of anger came over Dolan.

"Why not here?" he asked.

"'Cause we got people at The Trop to make sure everything we need will be there. We're gonna need a suite large enough for fifty or sixty people.

Our guy there can handle that."

Tommy shot back with, "*We* don't have *anybody* there! I got *my guy* there that'll do whatever *I* say. Not what *we* say. You got that?"

Jerry just looked at him.

Tension was running *very* high for a poolside chat.

Now it was Jerry's smile that disappeared as he responded, "Listen Tommy, I got no problem with that. If you don't want to throw a party for your guys tonight, fine. Just let me know, and I'll make sure *my guys* have someplace special to go and somethin' to do when they get there. All right?"

The Irishman froze in place for what seemed like a full minute... sweating and still blocking my rays...before he said, "I'll call and take care of it. What time?"

Calmer heads suddenly seemed to prevail.

"Midnight," Jerry answered.

Dolan nodded his head, turned and walked away without saying "Goodbye" to anyone.

Had I not known of Jerry's new quest, and of Dolan's fear of losing his contacts, this episode would have had me worried.

As I watched the large figure walk past the beautiful and tanned bodies along the pool, Jerry called my name.

"Hey Juan!"

I turned to face him.

"Did he ever do anything to thank you for taking care of things when Bobby had to run back to Jersey?"

I shook my head.

He leaned toward Taz and quietly said, "If Vinnie could find a closet big enough for that wrinkled Irish fuck, I'd take him for a dinner he'd never forget."

"We could have one made," Taz quickly responded.

They sat there and laughed.

Not knowing what they were talking about, I sipped my champagne, closed my eyes and continued sunbathing.

It only took two hours to go through my six grand. So by 8:15, Jerry, Taz and I were dressed in suits and sitting in my suite having drinks.

Taz looked around and said, "You know something, kid? This is what they call a Bachelor Suite. It's for guys like you. Guys that ain't married."

Looking confused, I asked, "Why's that?"

"'Cause it's only got one door in and out of the place. If you were married, you'd have *two*. The main door into the living room, and a bedroom door to the hall."

I still didn't get it.

"Yeah? Why?"

"If your wife ever shows up at the living room door...whoever you're bangin' can go out the bedroom door. The way this room is set up...you'd be fucked...and not in a *good* way."

As the two of them laughed at his explanation, I shook my head, drank my scotch and looked at my watch.

"Okay," I said, "So what do we do between now and midnight?"

"I hear that new magic show at The MGM's pretty good," Taz replied, then turned to his boss and asked, "You think we can get in for the dinner show?"

Jerry looked at his watch and said, "It probably starts at nine, and none of our guys are at The Grand this trip, only Dolan's."

Taz shook his head and said, "And who knows where the fuck he is right now. Forget it."

"For how many?" I asked.

They looked at me, wondering why I would be asking.

I repeated the question.

Jerry smiled and answered, "Us three. Why?"

"Gimme the phone," I said to my Godfather.

I had the hotel operator connect me with The MGM Grand.

Their operator connected me to the crap pit.

When someone picked up, I said, "Carl the pit boss, please."

I assumed he was still on the night shift.

Jerry and Mike listened, not sure of what they were going to hear.

"Hello, Carl? This is Jon D'Amore." I heard the noise of the casino behind him. "We met a couple of weeks ago. I was at the tables late one night and had taken a little bath. You offered to set me up with some tickets for that Siegfried and Roy show in the main room. Think you can swing three seats for the dinner show?"

You could hear in his voice that there was no way he remembered me.

"Siegfried and Roy? For what night, sir?" he asked.

"Tonight," I said confidently.

He paused.

"Your name again, sir?"

"D'Amore. Jon D'Amore," and then I spelled it.

He put me on hold.

Jerry and Taz wanted to know what was going on.

I shrugged my shoulders.

Carl came back on the line and primed me for disappointment.

"I gotta tell you, Mr...uh, D. It's Friday night, right after Thanksgiving. It may be a little too late to...Oh? Oh! Hold on a second, Mr. D. I'll be right with you."

He put me on hold again.

Jerry said, "Someone just brought him your credit and table ratings. Watch what happens."

Taz nodded his head.

"Mr. D? This is Carl again. I'm sorry about that. I just had to check my records. Yes sir, I see you were here a couple of weeks ago, but I don't see you registered with us tonight."

I had to come up with a story...quick.

"I was in L.A. for the holiday and felt like coming in for a few hours, so me and a couple of friends just got into town. Think you can get me those seats?"

He must have gotten to the section of my record showing that in less than three months I had gambled...and lost...$50,000 in his casino.

His voice and attitude changed dramatically and instantaneously.

"For you? Three? At nine tonight? *Absolutely*, Mr. D! Just come to the casino, find me in the crap pit and I'll take care of you, sir."

"Thanks Carl. See you in around fifteen minutes."

I hung up and said, "Let's go."

Jerry smiled.

Taz gave me that "*I told you so*" look again.

Before we walked out of the suite, each of us went to a mirror to check our appearance.

Taz's hair needed to be brushed, Jerry's tie needed to be tightened and straightened, and thanks to their cigarettes, I needed to reapply some cologne.

Within fifteen minutes we were walking through The MGM casino.

Carl shook my hand and pulled his business card out of his jacket pocket. On the back of it was written, "Mr. Jon D'Amore + 2."

"I've made your reservation, Mr. D. Everything's been taken care of. Just hand this to the host at the door and he'll take care of you."

Jerry and Taz looked at me...they were impressed.

Before we walked away, I shook Carl's hand and slid him a fifty dollar bill.

As we made our way toward the podium, Taz said, "Looks like the kid knows how to use his contacts...even when he *ain't* stayin' here."

Just as I handed the card to the maître d', Jerry smiled and asked, "You got connections I don't know about, Juan? You makin' moves in this casino?"

I smiled back, knowing he was joking.

"Ah! Mr. D'Amore! Carl called and told us to be expecting you. Please, follow me. We have a table reserved for you and your guests."

The show was sold out. Every table was taken. Every table except *our* table...the one dead-center in front of the stage. As we sat down, I slid the maître d' fifty dollars.

A waitress came by to take our drink and dinner order as the lights dimmed.

Just as the food arrived the maître d' whispered in my ear, "Compliments of the casino..." and placed a bottle of champagne on the table.

It was 11:40 when the show ended. We had to get to The Trop by midnight.

I signed the comp slip and we made our way through the casino toward the main door to get a cab, where we were confronted by a line of 30 or so people...all waiting for cabs.

"This is fucked up," Taz growled, "We could *walk* there by twelve!"

We had a party to get to...so I took control.

"Come on. Follow me," I said as I started to walk back into the casino.

They looked at one another as if to say, "Who the fuck is this guy talkin' to?"

When they caught up to me, I said, "There's another entrance on the side that the tourists don't know about. There's *always* cabs there. Everybody uses the front, but only the employees, the locals and the hookers know about the side."

"How you know about it?" Taz asked.

I gave him the same sly smile that Jerry used from time-to-time and said, "This place is so huge that sometimes you gotta find a shortcut to get where you wanna go. So I found a few shortcuts. Sorta like little-known ways to get around."

"Like Enrique Claudin," Jerry said as they followed me.

"Who?" Taz and I asked in unison.

"Enrique Claudin. He was the composer who became *The Phantom Of The Opera*. He knew the secret passageways in that opera house and used the sewers to get around the city," Jerry explained. "You're like *him*, Juan. You're The Phantom!"

Jerry and Taz looked at one another and both said "*The Phantom Of The Grand!*" and started laughing.

"From now on...you're The Phantom," Jerry decreed.

"No I ain't!" I barked back.

As we climbed into a cab I told them how silly it was and that I didn't want, nor need, an alias or nickname.

It didn't matter. For the next 23 months of the Vegas scam, I was lovingly referred to by Jerry, Mike and Taz as '*The Phantom*.'

Great.

Between *Juan*, *The Kid* and *The Phantom*, I had three nicknames, none of which I wanted or even *liked*.

I can see my picture in the Fed's "Genovese Family's Pyramid of Hierarchy."

There'd be '*The Chin*' up at the top. The level under him would be a row of pictures of the family capos. Then a picture of Rocco Casiano for the Northern New Jersey region. Below him would be pictures of his underbosses, that included Thomas '*The Irishman*' Dolan and Jerry '*The Beard*' D'Amore. Under Jerry would be his *inner-crew*; Vinnie Caputo, '*Big Mike*' Caruso, Tony '*Taz*' Costa and Jon '*The Phantom*' D'Amore.

This was getting crazy.

We arrived at The Trop with time to spare and separately walked through the casino so no pit bosses would see us together. As I passed a crap table my eye caught Sandy. She looked up and smiled. I smiled back.

I met up with Jerry and Taz at the elevator bay and we made our way to the party suite.

Once we got there, Taz opened the double doors and walked in. Jerry and I entered together.

Louie Calderone and Bobby Grant were sitting on a couch. Tommy

Dolan was standing in the middle of the room talking to a tall, muscular, well-dressed, tanned man. It was obvious that this guy wasn't part of The Irishman's crew.

Dolan acknowledged Jerry, and then came toward me. He shook my hand, patted me on the shoulder and whispered in my ear...though loud enough for Jerry to hear, "Louie told me how well you did tonight with the six grand. You're doin' great, kid."

It was obvious that he was trying to get on Jerry's good side without having his own men see or hear what was going on. Maybe it took him a couple of hours after the confrontation at the pool to realize that it may be wiser to be on Jerry's good side. Who knows?

I looked at Jerry.

Jerry looked at Dolan.

Dolan cheerfully said, "Come on in guys. Have a drink. Take a look around the place. Everyone should start showing up in a few minutes. So the joint's ours 'til then."

I stepped into the perfect party suite. The living room was two floors high with spiral staircases at each end that went up to the four master bedroom suites, each with their own bathrooms and views.

As we toured the upstairs, Tommy called to Jerry.

"Jerry, c'mon down! There's someone I want you to meet."

As we approached, The Irishman said, "Jerry, this is Joe Koonce. He's the Casino Manager here. He's seen to it that everything'll be taken care of. We'll have food brought in all night long. The bartenders will be here as long as we need them. The piano player will start in a few minutes and he'll stay as long as we want. And around one o'clock, the rest of the entertainment will get here."

Jerry shook Koonce's hand and said, "Joe, it's nice to meet you. Thanks for taking care of things. I don't know why you'd ever want to leave Vegas, but if you ever make it out to Jersey...make sure you look up Tommy. If there's anything we can do for you, just let him know."

Koonce looked at Taz and said to Jerry, "I'd like to get me a couple of those one day. Got any more like *him* back there?"

Taz grinned.

"And this is my cousin, Jon," Jerry continued, while putting his hand on my shoulder and taking the rest of us by surprise. "He's very special to me." My Godfather shot a glance to Dolan. "Tommy and I would appreciate it if you'd take care of him when he comes to The Trop."

Koonce and I shook hands. He handed me his card and said, "Make sure you see me whenever you check in."

The troops started arriving as Koonce walked out of the suite.

By one in the morning the living room was full of men...and cigarette smoke. The final count was 43, mostly Italians from Hudson and Bergen County. Taz and I stood on one of the staircases drinking our scotches and looking at the crowd.

They were loud. They were speaking *Jersey*. Some were even speaking Italian...at top volume, with their hands flying all over the place.

The differences were easily visible between Jerry's crew and Dolan's. Jerry's guys wore suits. Dolan's wore multicolored shirts with unmatching slacks and shoes. It was that simple.

My Godfather walked up behind us and asked, "You ready?"

Taz smiled and nodded.

I replied, "Ready for what?"

Jerry smiled.

The suite doors opened and in swayed and slithered six of the most glamorous and beautiful women that must have ever graced Las Vegas. At least *I* thought so.

In an instant, forty-three men turned their heads and the room went silent.

These were the women that make men walk into walls as they pass them on the street.

Each cruised the room in a different direction...smiling and perfectly carrying themselves.

They oozed sophistication as they went from one man to another pleasantly introducing themselves.

To see these women in *any* other situation, one would never believe... or accept...that they could be hookers. It may seem absurd, but the word *hooker* didn't do them justice.

Call girls?

No. These were women, not girls.

"This Joe Koonce knows how to supply a party, don't he?" I asked.

"He found 'em," Jerry answered. "But *we* paid 'em. At a grand apiece they'd *better* be good."

I just nodded and smiled. I was too busy ogling the women.

After twenty minutes or so, Tommy Dolan stood against the second floor railing overlooking the party and started to make a speech.

"Gentlemen...and ladies! We've all had a great time and worked hard over the past few days, and now it's time to blow off a little steam. And because I owe a favor to someone, I want him to take his pick of these beautiful ladies and be the first to...uh...well...to just *be the first!*"

Everyone started laughing.

From his perch, Dolan asked, "Where's the kid?"

He saw me on the steps.

"Ladies, this is Jon. Jon...the ladies," he pointed and yelled down. "We have four bedrooms up here. After the kid makes his choice, everyone else is on their own."

He held up his glass and all the men applauded.

I walked into the center of the living room and looked back at Jerry. He stood along the wall next to Taz, and proudly smiled.

I had a feeling that during the past hour, Jerry had a talk with Dolan about my last trip...and this was The Irishman's penance. I was given first shot...not seconds...or somewhere even further down the line.

The six women surrounded me, each introducing themselves again, and kissing me on the cheek. We spoke for a little while until I met one I felt somewhat comfortable with. Since this was another new experience, I didn't want to rush into it...or act like a kid.

Yeah...I know I had my rule about never paying for sex. But *I* wasn't paying for it. And if I wasn't first I don't think I would have even thought about it.

She was shorter than my 5'6, with a perfectly sculptured, smiling face. Long blonde hair, and from what I could tell from her evening gown, an amazing body.

Her name was Barbie.

Of *course* it was.

She took my hand and led me upstairs into one of the bedrooms, locking the door behind her. I sat on the bed and started to make pleasant conversation.

I was never with a woman of her profession before. This was virgin territory.

She started to peel off her dress.

I remember Barbie because she was the first woman I had ever been with that had silicone breasts. They looked perfect and firm. They were large. They were round. The nipples pointed straight out. And when I touched them...they were hard as a rock. I mean solid. She could have cracked walnuts between them.

She undressed me, and then slid a condom onto where it would do the most good.

About forty-five minutes later Taz was knocking on the door.

"Hey, Phantom!"

"What?" I yelled back.

"Open the door!"

Barbie walked to the door wrapped in a towel, opened it, stepped to the side and let him in.

"What the fuck ya's doin'?" he asked us.

"What do you mean?" we each responded.

He looked at me.

"You're takin' *too long*, kid. We got a bunch of guys that want to get some of this, too," he said, pointing to her.

"Yeah? So? We weren't done yet."

"What the fuck? Are you kidding? I got guys down there that can't stay hard for ten fuckin' minutes and you're in here almost an hour? They're startin' to complain," he said with that "*I told you so*" look. "Think you can wrap it up?"

"I'll see what I can do," I laughed.

As soon as he walked out, she dropped the towel and jumped back on the bed. She knew this appreciative twenty-two-year-old was the best she was going to get that night.

I was in the room at least another half hour before I dressed and walked down the staircase. A couple of minutes later, Barbie walked out of the room to circulate again.

She walked past me as I was talking to Jerry and Taz, and whispered, "Where are you staying?"

"Caesars," and I gave her the suite number.

Taz gave me *that look* again.

Jerry just shook his head.

The three of us left while the party was still in full swing.

As we walked down the corridor, I said, "So now you know that Joe Koonce is his contact here, Jer. Now you can--"

"Bullshit!" he barked.

I looked at him.

"Remember Dolan's speech at the pool? Koonce is *his* guy...and I believe him. Dolan wouldn't just turn a Casino Manager over like that. Koonce'll go runnin' back to Dolan in a heartbeat." He lit a cigarette as we walked. "Tommy wants me to think that now that I met his contact, I'll try to make a move on him. Once I try, Koonce'll rat me out. Then Dolan has a legitimate gripe, and he'll start problems with Casiano. I don't need that."

"But if Casiano has no problem with it--" I started to say before he cut me off.

"Don't you worry about it. Stay out of it. You don't need to know that much, or be that involved."

Once the elevator doors opened, Taz checked inside and we followed him in.

Jerry continued his thought, "While Tommy's waiting for me to get to Koonce, I'll be working on three other casinos over the next few months, and we'll be ready to run this without him."

Just before we reached the lobby, he said, "The next time either of you stay here...keep an eye on this Koonce guy. See how close he is with The Irishman."

Once we got to Caesars, we went to our rooms. Taz and Jerry were leaving the next day and had to pack. I was leaving on Monday...and *didn't* have to pack.

The phone in my suite rang around ten o'clock the next morning.

"Yeah?" I answered.

"Phantom? You want to meet for breakfast before we leave?" Jerry asked.

"No thanks. I'm gonna stay in bed for awhile and have Room Service bring somethin' up. I'll call you when I get back to Jersey, okay?"

"Yeah. Listen, don't make any plans for the first week in January. I want you back out here."

"I'll see. I gotta call my manager and tell him not to book anything."

"You want *me* to call him? What's his number?"

"I'll take care of it," I said with a smile.

As we hung up I looked across the living room to the beautiful nude woman draped across the sofa, smoking a joint, and asked her..."More coffee, Barbie?"

Round 13

I went to Vegas once a month over the next six months.

Yes, the bug *had* bitten me. But it was the excitement of the scam, the thrill of hangin' with these guys, the danger of getting caught...*that's* what made my blood run faster. I was living and playing in a fantasy world that most people had no idea existed.

My music career was taking off, so I let Jerry and Dolan know I couldn't do any more impromptu trips. I told them, "Once a month, that's all I can do." After all...I was a *musician*...not a mobster.

Jerry understood, but The Irishman made some noise about it.

So my Godfather went to talk to Casiano, and everything was worked out.

Well, at least they were working out on *my* end. Things, on the other hand, were a little different for Rocco.

It was a sunny Tuesday morning in late May of 1976, and the boss had an appointment to meet with one of his soldiers, '*Cheap Benny*' Petrillo, in the parking lot of the Plaza Diner, across the street from Al Nucci's tailor shop in Secaucus.

They called him Cheap Benny because he would make everyone in his family pay full price for a meal in the restaurant he owned. They say that the most he'd throw them would be a cup of coffee, but if they wanted cappuccino or espresso...he'd charge them the difference.

Benny was in his mid-thirties and the nephew of Angelo '*The Collector*' Cutillo, a made man and one of Casiano's longtime crew, who, at the time, was doing two years in Allenwood.

Benny was running his uncle's loanshark and numbers operation in the Bayonne, Newark and Jersey City area until Angelo's release in another couple of months.

But Cheap Benny wanted to do more.

Benny wanted to run *his own* operation in Bayonne.

So he found an "investor."

Several months earlier, Cheap Benny was approached by a wannabe-wiseguy named Vito Lanni, who said he had inherited "...a shitload of money after my old man died...all in cash." He wanted to earn more than the banks were paying or the stock market was making. Besides, he didn't want to "...pay no fuckin' taxes on this money."

Benny came up with a plan where Vito would give him $250,000 to put on the street, and Vito would get twenty points, that's $50,000, over the course of a year for the use of his cash.

Seeing as Cheap Benny planned on bringing in more than $150,000 a year on the vig alone, he had no problem slicing off fifty grand to Vito. Though he'd still have to throw another twenty-five grand to Casiano as tribute and for rights to the territory, he'd be clearing seventy-five for himself, on top of what he was making at his restaurant...and skimming from his uncle's business.

Casiano repeatedly told him not to use *outside money*, but Benny insisted on bankrolling his own operation. So, it was determined that Benny would have to pass his plan in front of Uncle Angelo. If his uncle approved, *then* Casiano would meet the investor, Vito Lanni.

It took nearly five hours for Salvatore Della Osa and Benny Petrillo to drive from Bayonne to the Allenwood Federal Correctional Facility in White Deer, Pennsylvania. Sal was there to be Casiano's ears during the meeting, and to bring back the uncle's decision.

Throughout the drive Benny talked about expanding his Bergen County restaurant with the money he was going to make thanks to his new partner's cash, and it wouldn't be long before he had Lanni whacked, "...and chopped up so nobody'll ever see him again."

Cheap Benny didn't plan on having a partner. He just wanted the start-up money.

Della Osa didn't like Benny.

Once they were inside the prison, Uncle Angelo said he had no problem giving Benny a slice of the pie as long as he got a piece of the action kicked back to him for the rights to his territory.

Cheap Benny lived up to his name and squawked...until Salvatore took him aside and angrily told him, "You'll pay it 'cause it's the right thing to do, you stroonze! He could've just as easily said 'No,' you dumb fuck."

A deal was cut and the message was brought back to Casiano.

Now it was time for Vito Lanni to meet with *the boss.*

What Rocco Casiano and Benny Petrillo didn't know was that Vito Lanni was really Special Agent Robert Testa of the New Jersey State Police, working undercover specifically to get Casiano. It had taken more than a year to get "Lanni" into a position of confidence with the weakest link they could find in Casiano's operation: Cheap Benny Petrillo.

Before Lanni and Petrillo drove to Secaucus for the Tuesday morning meeting, the two new partners met at The Uptown-Broadway Diner in Bayonne. As they sat over a cup of coffee, Benny started talking.

"I've looked into you, Vito. Over the last couple-a months I had some people check you out."

"Yeah? And what they say?" Lanni asked.

"They say you're good."

Vito knew he had a fool sitting in front of him.

"Who'd you talk to?" the cop asked as the small cassette deck strapped to his leg recorded every word through the microphone that ran up his body and down his arm to within a half-inch of the shirt cuff on his left wrist.

Benny leaned forward as Lanni brought the coffee cup up to his mouth, holding it with his left hand.

"I got my people," Benny bragged. "That's all you need to know. You don't need to know who they are."

"Hey, I was just askin'. You tell me you're checkin' on me, I wanna know through who, that's all. You don't wanna tell me? I don't really give a fuck, as long as it came back good," Lanni retorted.

"We got an army out there. A fuckin' *army*," Benny proudly and loudly bragged. "I could find out any-fuckin'-thing I want. I could make a phone call and get twenty guys here. Each of 'em ready to break somebody's arms or legs...even blow their fuckin' brains out. *That's* what I got behind me. Nobody'll ever think of fuckin' with us *or* our money, Vito. Nobody!"

"Whatdya mean?" Lanni queried, "If some guy's late with a payment, you'll get someone to bust him up?"

"Nah, you don't wanna do that. We'll just stick more vig on top of what he owes. Now if he gets a *month* behind, *then* we'll send somebody to put some pressure on him. 'Cause if he's busted up, how the fuck's he gonna pay us back? But if he gets disrespectful...or two months behind, then we'll straighten him out. Maybe take his car or his business until he gets caught up."

"And this guy we're meeting today at ten-thirty in Secaucus, he's the boss?" Lanni asked, choosing just the right words to get the information he wanted on tape.

"Rocco Casiano? Yeah. Nothing happens in Jersey without *his* 'okay.' Me and Rocco are tight. So don't fuck this up, 'cause I vouched for you. He even made me go see my uncle before he agreed to see you."

"Yeah?" Lanni leaned closer and asked, "Whatcha have to see your uncle about?"

"Hey, just 'cause he's away don't mean he don't call the shots. I had to get his approval to run our thing in his territory. We gotta throw *him* a piece, too."

"There's territories?" Lanni asked, knowing that Petrillo would supply the details.

"Sure," Cheap Benny boasted. "The whole state's broken into territories. Casiano runs everything down to the Jersey shore, from Seaside Heights across to Philly and up to the New York state border. My uncle's been doin' business with Dolan and Casiano for years."

"Dolan? Who the fuck is *Dolan?*" Lanni asked, as he scrolled through The Irishman's memorized dossier in his head. He certainly knew more about Thomas '*Tommy*' Dolan than Petrillo did.

"He's an underboss for the family. *Our* business is in Dolan's territory. The piece we gotta give Casiano goes through Dolan. Uncle Angelo and Dolan are a couple of Casiano's inside guys."

"You mean from his crew?"

"Yeah, whatever," Benny said as he looked at his watch. "C'mon. We gotta get to Secaucus. You don't have a guy like Casiano wait for you. That's disrespectful."

The cop couldn't believe what he was getting on tape.

As they rose from the table, Cheap Benny tossed the receipt to Vito and said, "Vee, do me a favor and take care of this. I'll get the next one."

Benny went to start his red Sedan deVille as the undercover cop paid the check.

Throughout the twenty minute ride along the New Jersey Turnpike, Petrillo exalted more stories about the muscle behind the mob, while Lanni thought about how he was going to turn the cassette over before they met with Casiano.

As they pulled into the front parking lot of the Plaza Diner, Benny asked Lanni, "What time you got?"

The investor looked at his watch and said, "Ten-thirty on the nose."

"Perfect. He should be here in a minute."

Lanni said, "I've had to piss since we left Bayonne. I'm gonna run inside and take a leak. I'll meet ya's at a table."

Once Lanni entered the bathroom stall, he dropped his pants and flipped over the cassette. Meanwhile, Petrillo got out of his Caddie and waved to Casiano as he walked out of Al Nucci's tailor shop and crossed Paterson Plank Road.

The boss saw him...but didn't wave back.

It was then that Petrillo looked across the street and noticed Salvatore Della Osa standing in front of Al's shop, keeping his eye on the situation. That made Cheap Benny nervous.

Benny had grown fearful of Sal since their trip to Allenwood. He found out that Sal was responsible for a couple of missing soldiers...after Casiano found out they were skimming.

As he reached the car, Casiano put out his hand to shake, but Benny put his arms around the boss and kissed him on both cheeks.

"Hey! What are you? Stupid?" the boss barked as he scanned the parking lot.

"What?"

"In the middle of fuckin' town you do this? You want the fuckin' world to see this? Didn't you learn anything yet? Don't you know when and where to do the right thing?" Casiano asked as he looked across the street to Della Osa, then hunched his shoulders and raised his hands as if to say, "Are you seeing this?"

The bodyguard nodded his head and shrugged in response.

Cheap Benny stood there looking and feeling like a fool. He didn't know what to say.

"Where's your guy?" Casiano asked.

"Inside takin' a leak. C'mon. Let's get a table."

"No," Casiano quietly said, "Not in there. Too many people. I wanna take a ride."

Benny immediately grew fearful, and asked, "Is *he* coming?" as he looked across the street to Sal.

The boss looked at Benny and saw the fear in his eyes, then answered, "For what? We're just gonna talk. Do I need him? You *want* him to come?"

"No," Benny quickly answered.

The boss liked seeing fear in his subordinates every once in a while.

Benny changed the subject, "Okay...as soon as Vito's done, we'll leave."

Casiano walked up to Cheap Benny and whispered in his ear, "Listen wise guy. I told you two weeks ago that the Feds got approval to start tapping us through this fuckin' RICO law. So you better be doing *all* your business from payphones. You got that? And don't always use the same phones. If I find out you're talkin' on your home phone and we get pinched, I'll have to kill ya. You got that? We don't need no heat right now. Everything's going fine, and the last thing I need is a fuck up. You hear me, *fuck up?*"

Benny was caught by surprise. He didn't know what to say. He knew he discussed business on his home phone from time to time. But he couldn't tell that to Casiano.

"Yeah, Rocco. Sure. No problem. I do *everything* on payphones. Don't worry about it."

Vito Lanni opened the diner's door and yelled, "Hey, Benny! Come on! I'm holdin' a table in here."

"Forget the table," Benny yelled back, "We're gonna take a ride. C'mon."

Casiano was amazed at the stupidity of these guys yelling to one another in front of the diner and in the center of town. He shook his head and said to himself, "Great. I got two dumb fuckin' P.A. systems here."

Vito walked over to the Caddie as Benny said, "Vito Lanni, meet Rocco Casiano."

As they shook hands, a different feeling ran through each of them. Special Agent Robert Testa was imagining putting this man in jail for the rest of his life. And Rocco Casiano had a feeling that something about this guy wasn't right.

"Nice to meet you, Rocco."

"Yeah? Why?" Casiano shot back.

Benny and Vito were taken back by the quick, sharp reply.

"Hey, I meant no disrespect!" Lanni quickly responded. "It's just something you say when you meet somebody. You know?"

"Yeah, Rocco," Benny whimpered, "He didn't mean nothin' by it. He was just being respectful."

Casiano eyed both of them with distrust.

Petrillo shot another glance across the street to Della Osa, then quickly got behind the wheel of his car and started the engine.

Vito and Casiano walked over to the passenger side without saying a word to one another. As a show of respect, and to make amends, the investor opened the front door and held it for Rocco.

Casiano stepped to the side, shook his head and opened the back door.

Vito looked confused and said, "I thought you'd want to sit up front with Benny."

Just before Casiano slid into the back of the Cadillac, he eyed the undercover cop and asked, "You the boss?"

Confused, Lanni looked at him and answered, "No."

"Then you sit in the front..." Casiano settled into the spacious seat and continued, "...The boss *always* sits in the back."

That's all he needed to say.

Vito understood.

Rocco Casiano was *the boss*.

The down-side to that statement was that the boss, Rocco Casiano, had just said it loud and clear to the undercover cop's microphone.

The boss didn't say much during the fifteen minute ride. Instead, he listened to Benny explain the business relationship he and Lanni had made and how he planned on running the operation.

Three weeks later the headlines of all the north Jersey and New York City newspapers read: *NJ State Police Make Genovese Family Sweep!*

Based on Cheap Benny's waxing eloquent on *la famiglia* and the supposed power he claimed to have through his position...along with several conversations from his home phone...all of which made their way onto Special Agent Robert Testa's tape recorder, Casiano, Dolan, Petrillo and nine other underbosses and soldiers were picked up in an early morning raid at their homes and hit with an assortment of charges, ranging from extortion to murder.

Cheap Benny's big mouth even implicated his Uncle Angelo.

A week before Angelo 'The Collector' Cutillo was to be released, his sentence was extended for another two years.

Jerry, who had no contact with Petrillo, was never mentioned on any of the recordings.

In less than six hours everyone was out on bail and meeting with lawyers.

The business went on as before...only now, there were no phone calls.

Everyone spoke in whispers, and only into the ears of trusted ones.

After the big sweep, Dolan's attorneys told him it would be best if he didn't make any more trips to Vegas until after *The Petrillo Mess*, as it came to be known, was resolved.

Overnight, Jerry was given control of the entire Vegas scam, which *really* pissed off The Irishman. But Casiano cut a deal between his two underbosses so that a war was averted. Tommy would still get a slice of the take for being the mastermind behind the operation...and because it was the *right thing to do.*

This made Jerry *very* happy.

Besides, after two years of running the scam, Dolan was getting tired of Vegas. He was starting to look into Newark International Airport and the docks and warehouses of The Port of New York and Port Newark which were located on the bays that surround Bayonne.

Each of them were right in his own backyard.

There were daily ships, trucks and planes loaded with merchandise that he wanted to get his hands on, and thousands of dockworkers and airport personnel that needed to make bets, borrow money and pay union dues.

The Bicentennial, July 4th, 1976, was only a week away.

Jerry had a plan. It was going to be the biggest hit on the casinos so far.

By this time I was one of the *experienced* guys, able to gamble two lines during the same trip *and* run a group of Jerry's guys.

"You think you, Mike and Taz can handle a weekend like the Fourth?" Jerry asked.

"What about Dolan's guys?" I responded.

"Louie Calderone and Bobby Grant'll be there with their guys, too."

"Sure, with all of us running it, I don't think we'll have any problems. Ain't you gonna be there?" I asked.

"My birthday's on the third, and my wife and kids want me to spend the holiday with them for a change. We're gonna see the fireworks on the Hudson."

I initially found that odd. He *never* let a birthday, holiday or anniversary get in the way of making money for 'the cause.'

As soon as he noticed my look of concern, he threw in, "I made reservations for you to see Neil Diamond on Sunday the Fourth. Elvis couldn't get fucking tickets if he tried. You got six."

I smiled respectfully and thanked him. There was nothing else for me to say. If my Godfather said I was going to Vegas for the Bicentennial...I was going to Vegas for the Bicentennial.

The first bunch of us arrived on Wednesday, June 30, and by Friday night, July 2, we had sixty-four guys registered and gambling in all eight casinos.

Neil Diamond put on an outstanding show. The rumor going around was that he was paid $10,000 for every minute he performed, and that the hotel made him punch a time-clock as he walked on and off stage, even in between encores.

By Tuesday morning, July 6, Louie, Bobby, Mike and Taz were in my suite breaking up the million-plus dollars that we took the casinos for in the last six days.

Because I was running a five man team *and* two lines, I was handed thirty-five hundred dollars, all in twenties, fifties and hundreds. I folded them into four separate wads and put them in my pockets. Then I was handed a briefcase by Mike and told, "Here you go, Phantom. Don't let this out of your sight."

I looked at him and asked, "What's this?"

"Two hundred grand," he answered. "We each got one to take back."

"I never brought the take back before, Mike."

"Well...the guy in charge feels you can be trusted," he laughed.

We both knew he meant Jerry.

"That's not the point. I *know* I can be trusted. I just don't know if that's something I wanna do."

"You don't have that option, kid. It's part of the job," he explained. Then he told me to bring the briefcase to Jerry's house by 10 o'clock that night.

And that was that.

Meanwhile, back in Jersey on the Fourth of July, Jerry's wife and kids were sitting in a high-rise condo on Boulevard East facing the Hudson River and watching the spectacular Macy's fireworks celebration.

Jerry was not there.

He was perched on the back seat of a parked van and looking through the front window. In the driver's seat was Salvatore Della Osa. Sitting next to Sal was Vinnie Caputo. They were in downtown Jersey City observing a crowd of people watching the fireworks.

"You gotta admit that for *our purposes* a Lincoln makes more sense than a Caddie," Sal said with all the confidence of a man who knew what he was talking about. "Fuck the power or the ride. It's the trunk!" Jerry and Vinnie were laughing as he continued, "With a Caddie, what can you do? Get one...maybe two bodies in the back of that thing? I mean not-for-nothin'....I got a Caddie of my own, I just don't work with it. When you gotta *do* a guy or two...or even three, you gotta have a couple of shovels and rugs back there...so you need the fuckin' space. And a Lincoln's *got* the space. A Caddie? What the fuck is a good stereo and a smooth ride gonna do you when you gotta put a couple of stiffs in the trunk? Fuck it...I'll take a Lincoln any fuckin' day of the week."

"What about a Chrysler, Sal? Those Imperials and Newports have big trunks, don't they?" Vinnie asked.

"Yeah," Sal answered, "But c'mon...it's a fuckin' *Chrysler!* You wanna be seen in a fuckin' *Chrysler?*"

They joked and laughed until the big finale of fireworks around 10:15, then the crowd started to disburse. That's when Della Osa spotted the person he was looking for.

"There he is," Sal said venomously. "There's that cocksucker. Get him, Jerry. Get him and bring that dumb-fuckin'-guinea to me."

The side door slid open, Sal pointed to their target and Jerry went directly toward him.

Cheap Benny Petrillo was with his wife as Jerry approached from behind and whispered in his ear, "Benny, you know me?"

As his wife continued walking with the flow of the crowd, Petrillo quickly turned around to see Jerry standing there.

People streamed past them as Petrillo answered, "Yeah. You're Jerry 'The Beard.' I've seen you at The Tailor's a couple of times."

"There's a problem," Jerry said calmly as he lit a cigarette. "We gotta take a ride down to Bayonne. One of your people got picked up and Rocco wants to see you about it."

"So he sent *you?*"

Jerry smiled, nodded and said, "Come on. I got my car down the block."

"Who's the guy that got arrested?"

"No idea. They didn't tell me. Rocco just told me it happened, and to find you."

"How'd you know where I was?"

Jerry responded just by smiling.

"I'm with my wife." Benny was trying to stall. "Tell Rocco I'll be there as soon as I take her home. Gimme a half hour or so."

"I'll tell you what. There's a payphone right over there. He's home. Why don't you call Rocco and tell him yourself." Jerry reached into his pants pocket. "Here. I got the change."

Benny knew he couldn't call Casiano's house. *All* of their home phones were tapped now, and Benny had strict orders not to call Rocco from *any* phone.

Again Jerry gave his sly smile and said, "Don't worry about your wife, Benny. She'll find her way home. You want to keep Rocco waiting?"

As Jerry led him away from the crowd, Benny wasn't watching where he was going as he constantly turned his head to see if his wife had come back to find him.

Jerry saw Vinnie standing a few feet from the van. As they walked passed it, the side door slowly opened from inside. Vinnie stepped in front of Benny and shoved him into Sal's waiting arms, then Vinnie jumped into the van and shut the door. It all happened too fast for Benny to react and make a sound.

Jerry just kept on walking.

Vinnie held his .22 silencer against Benny's head as Della Osa said "Hello scumbag!" and put silver gaffing tape over Benny's mouth.

Then Della Osa produced a large military style .45 automatic Colt and put it to Benny's forehead. The sight of it almost caused Benny to faint.

"You move or make a sound and I'll blow your fuckin' brains all over this van, you motherfuckin' rat."

Vinnie took the tape and bound Benny's wrists, knees and ankles.

Sal said to Vinnie, while staring at his victim, "Okay, you and Jerry go tell Rocco everything's taken care of. I'll take care of this rat cocksucker."

Benny started screaming, to no avail, under the tape. He began flopping around the back of the van, causing him to hit his head on the roof as he struggled to free himself.

Meanwhile, the two nonchalantly continued their conversation.

"That's not the plan, Sally," Vinnie responded as Sal holstered his .45. "I'm supposed to take care of this. Rocco didn't want you involved except for the pick-up. He's expecting you and Jerry in twenty minutes."

"No. *I* wanna take care of this bastard," Sal said with hate in his eyes as he stared at Petrillo and began screwing on the silencer extension onto his own .22.

Before Vinnie could say another word he heard *Phffft, Phffft, Phffft, Phffft,* and watched Cheap Benny Petrillo's eyes open wide just before his body fell against the inside of the van.

Salvatore grinned and happily said, "Well…that takes care of *that.*"

Vinnie shrugged his shoulders, looked at the body and simply said, "Okay. See you later," as he slid open the door and stepped onto the sidewalk as if a murder didn't just happen before his eyes, and only ten seconds earlier.

Jerry was in his Cadillac waiting for Sal to emerge from the van. He was surprised when Vinnie walked up to the car.

"What's going on?" Jerry asked. "*You're* supposed to take the van."

"He wanted to do it alone. He said for us to let Casiano know it was all taken care of."

Della Osa smiled and waved as he drove the van past them.

"Rocco ain't gonna like this. That wasn't the plan," Jerry said with concern in his voice.

As Vinnie got into the passenger seat, he said, "I had no choice, Jer. He popped him before I could say anything."

It was obvious Jerry wasn't happy with the unplanned change as he put the car in drive and pulled away.

It was nearly eleven by the time Jerry's Caddie turned onto the Bayonne side street where Rocco Casiano's mother owned her home in the middle of the block since the 1940s. Though the boss had a mansion in Colts Neck, he stayed at his mother's house most of the time…to take care of his north Jersey business.

As Jerry drove down the block, Vinnie tapped him on the shoulder and pointed to a nondescript van parked on the corner. A dim blue light emanated from inside. Jerry acknowledged seeing it. As they cruised the entire length of the block, they spotted a large Ford with two men reading a newspaper.

Jerry recognized the situation as a Federal surveillance team. He knew it would be best not to park and go in through the front door…not unless he wanted to have his picture taken.

"I bet these bastards *still* have no idea about the backyard," Jerry said to his hitman.

Vinnie smiled as they passed the Ford and turned the next corner.

Years earlier, Rocco Casiano gave one of his mother's oldest friends, Mrs. Todisco, the money to purchase the house directly behind his mother's place and put it under Todisco's name. Then Rocco arranged to have his people come in to redesign the adjoining backyards so overhead trellises could be built, covering both yards with grapevines. The property was separated by high shrubs with a tall wooden gate that allowed access to each yard. Even helicopters wouldn't be able to see what was going on under the thick vines.

When Rocco wanted to go somewhere without anyone seeing him leave, he would walk through his backyard under the trellis, open the gate, walk under Mrs. Todisco's trellis and step into her garage where Salvatore would be waiting with his Lincoln. Rocco was never fond of being driven around in Cadillacs, so he bought Sal a Town Car.

The car would pull out and drive away...and the Feds never had any idea.

A Tony Bennett record was playing in the background as Rocco sat in the brightly lit finished basement of his mother's house feeling *very* anxious. To calm his nerves, he just needed to hear Jerry and Sal tell him that Cheap Benny was in Vinnie's hands and on his way to the Staten Island landfill. Casiano couldn't wait to tell Jerry how much he appreciated this show of respect by having Vinnie take care of the troublemaker.

Even Uncle Angelo 'The Collector' sent word to "...get rid of the no good little fuck. I gotta do another two-fuckin'-years in the joint 'cause of that greedy little bastard. He's my wife's nephew...he's no blood of mine. Don't mean shit to me. Lose him."

The boss paced the linoleum for several minutes longer than he expected. He wondered why they weren't there yet. He walked upstairs into the house, went to the third floor bedroom window and looked for their car. Immediately, he spotted the van and Ford on the corners. He knew that Jerry and Salvatore would see the surveillance team and use the rear entrance.

He went to the kitchen and paced for another five minutes before he decided to walk through the yards and meet them. With all of the problems caused by Cheap Benny, the boss needed to hear some *good news* for a change…and hearing that Petrillo's body was going to be "…pulverized and mixed with the rest of the Fourth of July garbage…" would have been *good news.*

His nerves were frazzled as he filled a tall glass with ice cold water and took a long drink. He refilled the glass to bring with him while he waited in the warm summer air.

At the same time, Jerry pulled in front of Mrs. Todisco's house and the two men got out of the car. They quietly made their way into the backyard and under the trellis. Jerry knew Casiano would be waiting in the basement.

Casiano noticed the sticky July heat as he quietly closed the back door and began walking toward Mrs. Todisco's house.

Not only was he anxious, but the explosions from the scattered firecrackers, ash cans and cherry bombs set off by the local kids were causing him to nervously swing his head back and forth every time he heard the sound that he feared most…every day of his life.

Jerry and Vinnie were about three feet from the dividing gate as Rocco lifted the latch and came through…just as he was taking a mouthful of water. Through the glass he saw Jerry's hitman, Vinnie Caputo, a face he was *not* expecting to see. His heart raced. Then, as he lowered the glass, he saw Jerry.

Casiano's paranoia immediately kicked in. Vinnie was supposed to be dumping Petrillo's body! Why was he *here?* Did they whack Sal instead? Are they here to take out the boss?

Casiano turned white.

Taken by surprise, Vinnie's first reaction was to bring his hand to the inside of his jacket for his gun.

As soon as Casiano saw Vinnie make his move, the sweat from his nervous body caused the drinking glass to slip from his hand. As it crashed to the ground, a separate, more distinct noise hit Jerry's ear as his hand reacted to Vinnie's reach for the gun, and said, "No Vinnie! It's Rocco! Stop!"

Hearing this, Rocco's fears were temporarily settled, but it was too late. Something terrible had *already* happened.

Jerry looked at Rocco as soon as he heard it.

Jerry knew what he heard. He knew what had happened.

And Rocco *knew* that Jerry *knew* it happened.

Jerry and Rocco stared at one another.

Jerry broke the silence.

"Jesus, Rocco! What are you doin' here?"

"Fuck that!" the boss barked, "What's *he* doing here? Where's Sal? What happened to him?"

"He decided to deliver the package himself," Jerry answered.

"What the fuck you talkin' about? He was supposed to come here with you! You were supposed to be here fifteen minutes ago!" The boss pointed to Vinnie and said, "*This* guy was supposed to take care of the package. Not my guy!"

Jerry looked to Vinnie as the hitter responded, "Rocco, I had every intention of taking care of my end, but before I could say anything he punched the rat's ticket. Then he said he'd take care of what was left."

The boss looked at both men angrily, but he had a more pressing and upsetting matter that he needed to take care of...quickly.

Color was slowly coming back to Casiano's face, but the look of fear and anger lingered as he said, "All right, the two of you...get out of here. I don't want to hear from you until I hear from Sally and know that everything's okay." Then he looked at Jerry and said, "I'll reach out for you when I want to see you." He paused for a few seconds and then loudly ordered, "Now get the fuck outta here!"

Vinnie expected Jerry to say something, but there was silence as they turned and walked into the darkness.

Once they hit the sidewalk, Vinnie whispered, "What the fuck just happened? Why'd he yell at us like that?"

"In the car," Jerry ordered. "Get in the car first."

Jerry sat behind the steering wheel for a long time before he turned to Vinnie and asked, "Did you hear what he did?"

Still confused over the events of the last several minutes, Vinnie could only muster, "You mean what he *said?*"

"Did you hear what he *did?*" Jerry repeated.

"I didn't hear anything except that glass breaking and you telling me not to go for my gun. Why? What did *you* hear?"

"He shit."

"He what?"

"He shit in his pants when he saw us. No, actually...when he saw *you.* He was expecting me and Sal. But when he saw you he thought we were comin' to hit *him*...and he shit his pants."

"Get the fuck outta here," Vinnie said in complete disbelief.

Jerry looked at him and chuckled as he said, "I am not *shitting* you! He shit in his pants."

The two men sat there for another several seconds laughing, then Jerry's face suddenly turned pale and he slowly said, "We...got...a problem."

Vinnie stopped laughing as he mentally caught up to Jerry.

Jerry carefully thought of each word as he said, "He can't let us live knowin' what we know. Just the fact that he thought we were coming to get rid of him means we can't trust him, and that means he'll never trust *us* from this point on. But the fact that he shit in his pants...and that I heard it...and he *knows* I heard it...means he's got to get rid of us. He can't have us walkin' around telling people we *'scared the shit out of the boss.'* Even if we swear we'll never tell anyone, *ever.*"

They looked at one another and immediately started to consider their options.

They'd have to kill Casiano...before he killed *them.*

Jerry slowly pulled the car away from the curb.

It was a long ride back to Ridgefield as he weighed his options. At best, Jerry had twenty men he could depend on, and Vinnie had a small handful of experienced hitters he could bring in. But Casiano had the crews of *all* of his other underbosses. That was more than three hundred guys that would do *anything* for la famiglia. Plus, being a made member, Casiano wouldn't need approval from The Commission to take one of his own men out... even if it was Jerry.

Jerry knew that a war with Casiano didn't seem to be a viable option. And an unsanctioned hit on a made man...a *boss*...would be even worse.

There was only one logical thing to do.

Jerry needed to have a private meeting with Casiano and work something out.

That night, Jerry couldn't sleep. He stared at the ceiling and wondered how everything could have been running so well...and then instantly change.

The following morning he got in his Caddie and drove to Hackensack to find a payphone he never used before. But when he picked it up to call Casiano, he stopped and thought about the taps that were on everyone's line. He also knew he couldn't show up, unannounced, at the boss's house.

He got back in his car and drove to Secaucus. There was one person Rocco checked in with constantly, and Jerry knew he could reach out for the boss that way.

"Al," he whispered into The Tailor's ear, "I need to see our friend, right away."

"What's the matter?" Al Nucci asked.

"Nothing you want to know about, paisan. Just set it up…as soon as you can. Okay?"

"Yeah, sure Jerry. I'll see him tomorrow. What's that, Tuesday? Call in the afternoon, around four. I'll know something by then."

The Tailor slid that morning's copy of the Jersey Journal in front of Jerry. A headline on the fourth page read, "*Small Time Hood Disappears After Fireworks.*" The story said that Benny Petrillo may have gone into hiding as a result of a recent crackdown of Genovese mobsters brought on by tape recordings that were made of Petrillo.

With a chuckle in his voice, Al said, "It says his wife reported him missing, and the State Police can't determine if he's hiding from them…or the mob."

They kissed each other on the cheek before Jerry walked to his car and drove away.

For the rest of that day, every time he got in or out of his car…Jerry wished Taz and Mike were standing next to *him*, instead of being in Las Vegas with *me*.

It was one in the afternoon on Tuesday, July 6. Vinnie Caputo stood in the storage room and held a clipboard, checking a shipment of cheese and pizza boxes that had just arrived at his pizzeria on Washington Avenue in Hoboken.

Salvatore Della Osa entered through the front door, walked to the back, smiled and shook Vinnie's hand.

Vinnie didn't know how to react, so he smiled back and asked how everything went after Sal drove away with the van the other night.

"No problem at all. I went to Staten Island and dropped off the garbage. We won't have to worry about that piece of shit no more. Rocco was a little pissed, but once he calmed down, he got over it. You know how he is. See yesterday's papers?"

"Yeah. I guess he's in hiding, huh?" Vinnie answered as both men started to laugh.

"Listen, Rocco and Jerry are gonna meet for lunch down the block at that Italian place Rocco likes, you know...Miguel's. They told me to connect with you, and for all of us to meet there," Della Osa said.

Vinnie wasn't happy about being told at the last minute...and especially by Sal Della Osa. But when the boss wants to meet you someplace, you don't say "I can't make it."

He would have preferred hearing about the meeting from Jerry, but with phone communication being so heavily monitored, it was understandable to send a messenger.

He figured this was the sit-down Jerry wanted to arrange, and it was now-or-never to appease the boss.

"Sure," responded Vinnie, "I like it there. I take the wife there all the time. When?"

Sal looked at his watch and said, "They should be there in ten...fifteen minutes."

Vinnie handed the clipboard to one of the counter workers and gave orders to finish checking the shipment. Then he went into the office to check his hair before they left.

Thanks to the stifling heat, Sal was wearing a casual shirt and didn't appear to be carrying a gun. Vinnie looked at his .22 and shoulder holster hanging next to his jacket in the closet and asked, "Too hot for a jacket, Sal?"

"It's fuckin' swelterin'."

Vinnie locked the closet door and walked over to Sal.

They leisurely strolled to the corner of Washington Avenue and turned down Fourth Street toward the restaurant. As they entered, Vinnie recognized a couple of guys at the bar.

Sal leaned into Vinnie and whispered, "They're here to ask Rocco for a favor."

This wasn't out of the ordinary, seeing as the boss liked to do business while he ate.

He also saw the owner, and said, "Ahh, Miguel! You got some nice capellini con fileto di pomodori for me, paisan?"

"Ah, Vinnie! For you, I'll make anything...even if it ain't on the menu. You know that," Miguel said as he walked over to Vinnie and kissed him on the cheek.

Vinnie and Sal went to the bar and said hello to their friends for a few moments before the owner returned and said, "Gentlemen, your table is ready."

All four men followed him toward the private room in the back.

When they entered, Sal looked at the table set for six and said, "Vinnie, you know Rocco. He likes to sit with his back to the wall." He pointed to the farthest seat and continued, "I'll sit on his right, and Jerry'll sit on his left, so you sit next to Jerry. These guys'll take the other two seats."

By Sal drawing attention to the near wall, Vinnie didn't get a chance to scan the room when he first walked in. But there didn't seem to be any reason to.

"Where's Rocco and Jerry?" Vinnie asked.

Sal shrugged his shoulders and said, "I'm sure they'll be here in a couple of minutes. No problem, we'll have a drink first."

Just as the owner finished taking their drink order, Vinnie looked around the room and noticed something.

A rolling closet along the far wall, right next to the door to the alley.

He put his hands under the edge of the table and quickly stood up, flipping it over onto Sal and one of the men. Vinnie headed straight for the doorway to the main room, but the second mobster pulled out a .22 with a silencer and fired off a shot that caught Vinnie in the back of his left thigh, causing him to fall just short of the door.

Della Osa pushed the table aside with a loud, angry grunt. The other hitter pulled out another .22 with an extension and fired a shot, just missing Vinnie's head. Not yet on both legs, Vinnie threw himself against the door, busting it open and pulling his bleeding leg along as the two mobsters began to run after him.

Women started screaming and patrons scattered and ducked under their tables.

As Vinnie passed the long bar, and just a few feet from the door to the street, he heard *Phffft* just before another bullet entered his left shoulder. He felt his shoulder blade crack as the force propelled him forward and out the door. He didn't give up and continued running...to the best of his ability...toward Washington Avenue.

The two mobsters looked back at Sal for instructions as he stood in the doorway to the private room.

The look on his face alone said, "Get him! Get him...and kill him!"

That was all they needed.

They ran out the front door with their weapons in full view. It only took a few seconds to catch up with the wounded hitman. They stood in front of him and raised their guns to his head.

Suddenly, a car drove up the street. The hitters lowered their pistols and waited for the car to pass. But in that brief instant, Vinnie gathered enough energy to punch one of them in the face and push the other against the brick wall, knocking him down and clearing the way.

Just before he made it to Washington Avenue, a silent bullet hit him in the back. It passed through his right lung and exited his body. He looked down to see blood covering the front of his shirt as he gulped to breathe.

He was only thirty feet from his pizzeria. He wanted to get there...to get to his gun.

He fell less than six feet from the door to his business. His hand was clutched in the shape of a pistol.

"Got...gotta...get...my...gun. Kill these motherfu--"

The two hitters stood over him and emptied their clips...in broad daylight, and in full view of anyone who happened to be there.

Vinnie Caputo was dead.

He was dead because he scared the shit out of the boss.

Twenty minutes after it happened, Jerry was told about the death of one of his closest friends, his best hitman and a trusted soldier.

Though he couldn't readily find out who the hitters were, in his heart he knew why Vinnie was whacked, and that the decision came down from Casiano.

It made him nervous when he heard it happened in broad daylight... in front of witnesses. That meant Casiano wanted them dead...no matter where it needed to take place or how it had to happen.

As planned, Jerry called Al Nucci around four o'clock from a payphone in Cliffside Park.

"Your friend said to stop by in two hours," The Tailor told him.

"Got it," he said, then wondered if he'd be dead in two hours and ten minutes.

He looked at his watch and cursed. Our plane from Vegas wouldn't arrive for *at least* another two hours, and we weren't scheduled to see him until ten that night to turn over the Fourth of July take.

By then he could be at the bottom of the Hackensack River, or in a pile of landfill next to Benny Petrillo, or in a combination of *both* of those places.

He would have liked to have had Mike and Taz by his side for that meeting.

He took a deep breath just before saying, "Thanks, Al. I'll see you then."

Mike, Taz and I were already airborne and heading east by the time word hit the street about Vinnie, so we had no idea what had happened.

At first, Jerry figured he'd tell his two guys when they showed up at his house. But now he worried that they'd return to find out that Vinnie *and* their boss were no longer among the living.

Jerry wanted to see his wife...considering that it might be for the last time...but he couldn't go home, just in case one of Casiano's people were waiting for him.

He picked up the payphone, called her and made arrangements to meet at Roberto's II on River Road in Edgewater. He knew the owner would give him a safe room in the back, with only one entrance and a lockable door.

Throughout the call to his wife, his voice showed no trace of what he believed the future held for him.

He was mentally prepared to face the possibility of death.

This was the life he chose. After all these years he knew what his options were. Being whacked by a paranoid boss was one of them. If he was allowed the opportunity before his execution he would quietly explain his offer of silence, and if it was denied...he would close his eyes and be dealt his cards.

And if he *was* going to die, it would be the way a man of honor would die.

As soon as he got back into his Caddie, he pulled a .38 caliber Beretta from under the seat. From habit he popped out the clip, made sure it was full and rammed it back in. He knew there were eight bullets in it, plus one in the chamber. There was no reason to check it. But just going through the motions calmed him down.

He placed the pistol next to his right thigh and headed toward Edgewater.

Throughout dinner, he and his wife spoke of their two children, school, shopping, the weather...anything and everything. He showed no hint of what he feared would shortly happen to him.

And he told her he loved her a handful of times.

He didn't need to tell her anything else.

He knew that if anything ever happened to him, she knew where the suitcases with their *retirement* cash were stashed. It would be enough for her and the two kids to comfortably exist for the next two decades.

She also knew the special heavy black briefcase was hidden in the back of the secret compartment in the basement paneling. He had never told her what was in it, but she knew it was his pistols.

Afterward, as they walked along the bank of the Hudson River to their cars, he held her and kissed her.

She drove west.

He headed south, taking River Road down to North Bergen, and then along Boulevard East atop the Palisades for what he believed would be his last look at the New York City skyline.

When he got to Secaucus, he parked behind Al Nucci's Custom Tailor Shop and slid the Beretta under the seat. He knew he'd be frisked once he got inside. Besides, bringing the pistol in and having it found would just piss Casiano off more.

It was six o'clock on the nose when he walked into Nucci's basement through the rear door.

Al was coming down the steps, yelling, "I just locked the front door. I hope he knows to come in the back. He should be here any--"

Jerry interrupted him from behind, "Hey, Al."

The Tailor turned to see him.

"Hey Jerry, I'm glad you came in that way. I just locked the front door. How ya doin'?"

Jerry responded, "How *you* doin'?"

They both nodded their heads in unison as if to say, "I'm doin' okay... considerin'," and then hugged and kissed each other.

Jerry looked to see who else was around.

He expected to see at least two guys at the door and another two or three inside near Rocco.

"He's in the office," The Tailor said as he gestured to the far side of the basement, past the cutting tables and rolls of material. "I was just telling him I locked upstairs. It's six o'clock. Time to close."

The boss was sitting behind Al's desk drinking espresso out of a demitasse cup as he watched them approach. He appeared to be alone.

Jerry scanned the room thoroughly. He didn't see Salvatore Della Osa, or *any* of Rocco's people. He even looked for a rolling closet, but seeing as it was the basement of a tailor shop, the place was *lined* with closets.

Rocco stood up as they hugged and kissed each other on the cheek. Respect *had* to be shown.

By approaching Rocco so quickly, Jerry was sure he would have caused someone to jump out and stop him, but nothing happened. Still, he was sure that there were at least five guns pointed toward his head.

Casiano said, "Al...do me a favor. Go upstairs and check the door. Take your time and make sure it's locked, okay?"

A chill ran down Jerry's back. He was sure *it* was going to happen within minutes. Maybe even seconds.

"Sure, Rocco," The Tailor responded as he immediately turned around and disappeared up the stairs...with everyone knowing full-well that the front door was already locked.

"Jerry...sit down," Casiano said in his raspy Hudson County voice. "I want to talk to you."

His underboss followed the order without making a sound.

At any moment Jerry expected someone to appear out of nowhere and put the cold barrel of a silencer up against his head, and a split-second later feel the hot projectile rip and shatter into the inside of his skull.

As he sat under the fluorescent lights, Casiano downed the rest of his espresso, took a deep breath and leaned his strong body forward across the old wooden desk...all the while his eyes were transfixed into Jerry's. The desk creaked.

"Who knows about what happened the other night?" the boss asked his subordinate.

Jerry looked him right in the eyes and said, "No one."

"Your two guys in Vegas?"

"They don't even know about Vinnie yet."

Casiano looked down at the mention of the hitman's name.

"Yeah. Vinnie. A good man," the boss said quietly and respectfully.

"Why, Rocco? Why Vinnie? He didn't--"

The boss raised his hand to stop Jerry from continuing.

"Because I had to send you a message that you'll remember for the rest of your life."

"You know we'd never say anything."

"I couldn't take that chance, Jerry. *No boss* could take that chance."

Jerry didn't respond. He just looked at Rocco, knowing what the boss had just said was the truth.

Rocco knew he could have trusted Jerry more than *any* of his underbosses. But it didn't matter. It was too late.

"There's been a lot of talk lately, Jerry. Talk that you may have a friend or two *high up*. Somebody on The Commission. People up there like you. So I got my fears. Let's just say…the other night…you brought those fears *out*."

"Rocco, I'd never do anyth--"

Again, Casiano raised his hand. Jerry shut up.

"We go back a long way, paisan," Rocco said as he leaned back in the old wooden chair. It creaked.

Jerry nodded his head.

"I made a promise to your Godfather." Casiano raised his head and looked toward the ceiling. "Frank DeNike was one of the best men that ever lived." He lowered his eyes and stared at Jerry. "He was honest, and he was fair. He loved your family, and he loved *our* family, *la famiglia*. He was there when they made the rules, and then he followed them."

Again, Jerry nodded his head as his boss continued, "When he stepped down, of all the things he could have asked me to do for him…of all the things he could've asked me to promise…he made me look after *you* as if you were my own Godson. And I *have!*" Anger was rising in his voice, "I've known your family since I started. Your father, and *the kid's* father…your Uncle Rocky. They're good people. They always did what was right for *all* of us."

He realized he was drifting, so he took a deep breath to calm down. Then he leaned across the desk again and got back to the point.

"I promised Frank I'd make sure no one fucked with you, unless you *really* tried to fuck somebody over. And if anyone ever *did* do something to you, I was to avenge it. You were good, Jerry. You turned out to be one of the best lieutenants any boss could want. You're smart. A great earner. You hustle. You chose good people for your crew. You play by the rules. You did everything I ever asked you to do, and you even offered to do the things I *didn't* ask you to do."

He took another deep breath and a long pause. He knew what he had to say wasn't going to be easy…and it bothered him that he felt that way.

"That's why what I gotta do…is so friggin' hard."

Jerry could hear his heart beating. It was just a matter of seconds before the end would come.

Though he understood why Rocco had to do what he had to do...Jerry wanted to reassure the boss that his vow of silence could be trusted.

Casiano saw that Jerry was about to say something, so he held up his hand again. He wasn't finished.

"Vinnie's dead because I had to let you know I could have done the same to you. It could've happened earlier today. I could've had ya's hit at the same time if I wanted. It could happen right now, or as you're walkin' outta here. Tomorrow...whenever I want, I can have you killed."

Jerry bowed his head and waited for the axe to fall.

"But I can't. I made a promise to Frank DeNike, and I can't kill you."

Jerry raised his head as Casiano continued, "I want you out of here. Not just out of my crew, or out of my territory...I want you out of New Jersey. I want you out of this entire fucking part of the country." Casiano started getting louder again. "You hear me? I want you so far away that--"

Jerry got the point and quietly said, "I hear you, Rocco. I hear you."

He knew Casiano was speaking from the heart.

Had the decision come from the boss's paranoid mind, Jerry knew he'd be dead by now.

"It's the beginning of July," Casiano continued, "You got two months to clean things up. Let your people know you're moving. I don't give a fuck what you tell them, just make sure it has nothing to do with this conversation. You got that?"

Jerry nodded his head.

"Sell your houses and get you and your family far away from here. And find another fuckin' occupation," Casiano ordered. "Don't have anybody calling me or any of my people looking to check you out. After you leave...I don't know any Jerry D'Amore. Capice?"

Still, something in the back of Jerry's mind made him unsure if he would ever see the outside again, so he figured he had nothing to lose by asking a question.

"With all respect and if you'll allow me...can I give my territory to Mike and Taz?"

At least that way Jerry knew his guys would send him a small piece every month...out of respect.

Casiano thought about it for a few seconds and said, "No. What happens to it is my decision. I'll split it between Dolan and the Ranouro Brothers."

Disappointed, Jerry said, "If you won't let me give it to my guys, I'd rather see it *all* go to the Ranouro Brothers."

Casiano nodded his head, smiled and said, "If that's what you want, Jerry, that's what I'll do."

For a brief moment, Rocco Casiano, a man known for his vicious and ruthless acts of violence and murder, showed compassion to the man he knew was unjustifiably about to suffer the humiliation of losing his livelihood, his crew and his territory...and was being banished from his home turf simply because he was there when the boss shit in his pants.

Jerry got up, walked behind the desk and again hugged and kissed his boss.

As they held each other, Casiano whispered into Jerry's ear, "Listen to me...the two guys that did Vinnie are dead. If anyone asks you anything about it, you don't know nothin'. You got that? *We* don't know nothin'."

Jerry nodded as he listened.

"*You* made the decision to move to wherever the fuck you're gonna go. You hear me?"

Jerry nodded again as they still hugged.

"The business will go on as usual until it's time for you to move. You'll do everything you been doin', and you'll get your piece until you leave. After that...you're on your own. Capice?"

Jerry nodded, raised his head and looked at Rocco as he continued.

"If I ever find out you come back...for any reason...or if word ever gets out about what happened the other night...I'll always know where you are, and I'll come there myself and kill you. You got that? Do I have to say it more than once?"

"I got it, Rocco. I understand."

They looked eye-to-eye for a moment, thinking of the past twenty-plus years they had known one another.

Casiano said, "I'll see you tomorrow night with the Vegas money. You're a good man, Jerry. The best. I'm gonna miss having you around."

Again, Jerry nodded.

They kissed once more before Jerry turned and walked through the basement.

It wasn't until he got outside that Jerry realized why Rocco was alone. He didn't want to take the chance of anyone standing there if Jerry were to say something about the boss crapping in his pants.

Jerry started the Caddie and quickly pulled away, just in case a hitter was waiting for him to leave the tailor shop.

It wasn't until he was several blocks away that he pulled over and gripped the steering wheel in anger. His entire world had fallen apart within the last 48 hours. Everything he worked for, everything he wanted, everything he succeeded in achieving...was gone.

And he was just told to *"get outta town,"* so-to-speak.

Where would he go? What would he do? What would he tell his family, his friends...and those closest of all...his crew? And how would he tell them about Vinnie Caputo?

He looked at his watch. It was nearly 6:30. Our plane had landed.

He headed home to prepare to meet with Mike, Taz, Louie, Bobby, Dolan and me.

Earlier that day, as Mike, Taz and I boarded the plane in Vegas, we each carried a briefcase.

None of the cases were similar in appearance, but each of us knew they held a combined $600,000. Louie and Bobby left on a flight through Chicago, carrying another four hundred grand.

They laughed at me as they stowed their briefcases in the overhead compartments. I kept mine on my lap throughout the entire five hour flight. Nothing was going to get between me and that briefcase. I wasn't going to leave anything to chance. The last thing I wanted to do was go before Jerry, Tommy Dolan and Rocco Casiano and tell them I lost their $200,000.

When the plane landed, Taz was picked up by his wife, and Mike, by his girlfriend. I paid a porter $30 to take my three suitcases...filled with clothes and liquor wrapped in Caesars Palace towels...to my car in the very-distant Long Term Parking Lot as I cautiously walked next to him with the briefcase tightly in my grip.

I never said anything to Mike and Taz, but I figured that since Dolan knew what flight I was on and that I'd be carrying big money, he could permanently get me out of the way...and he'd be picking up an extra two-hundred grand. Since I was now on the FBI's 'questioning list,' it would've appeared to have been nothing more than just another mob hit...or a robbery-gone-wrong.

The cash-filled briefcase never would have been an issue or concern to the police. They wouldn't have even known it existed.

In my mind, everyone that walked or drove past me was a potential Dolan-sent hitter. The woman wheeling the stroller. The traveling businessman with a briefcase...just like mine. The shuttle bus driver. The *porter*. I thought each of them were going to pull out a pistol and end my life...either to my face or from behind. It could have happened so fast I wouldn't know what hit me.

How did these guys do it? How did they wake up in the morning and go through a whole day not knowing if the next person that walked past them was going to be the one to end their life?

But...I put on the *tough-guy* look, or at least the best one I could muster just in case I did have to confront someone, and made it safely to my car.

I remained cautious and nervous until I pulled into my father's driveway.

I left my suitcases in the trunk and brought the briefcase right into my bedroom. It would stay there until 9:45, when I'd leave to turn it over to my Godfather.

Jerry's basement was well lit and full of cigarette smoke as he and Dolan piled the stacks of cash from the five briefcases on top of the long wooden dining table.

My Godfather looked at the group of men and said, "Thanks for bringing this here. Tommy and I want all of you to know...you did a great job. Having this million will mean a great year for all of us."

Smiles and pats on the back were made throughout the room.

But Jerry wasn't smiling.

I had never seen so much cash. I couldn't believe I was sitting in a basement in Ridgefield, New Jersey, looking at one million dollars in cash stacked in organized piles.

Jerry broke the silence and my train of thought as he continued, "But while you were gone, something happened. Something...bad."

Everyone stopped what they were doing and looked at him.

"Earlier today," he had to stop and take a breath before he continued, "Vinnie Caputo was killed outside of his pizzeria."

I never really knew Vinnie, so the news wasn't the blow to me as it was to the rest of them.

This hit was too close to home...and you could see it on their faces.

Again they looked to Jerry. This time for the reason.

"I met with Rocco. We don't know who the hitters were. All we know is that there were two of them and they used .22's, the same as Vinnie."

Mike and Taz were devastated at the loss of such a close friend and partner. They wanted answers.

Jerry thought for a few seconds before he told them, "Casiano said it *could* have come from the other side of the river. I don't know. We don't have any answers yet. We're looking into it." He was angry that he had to lie to his own men. "I just wanted to tell you before you read about it in tomorrow's paper."

The rest of the evening was somber. I didn't need to stay to watch them split up the cash. I wasn't part of what happened to the money once it got to Jersey, so there was no need for me to be there.

As I made my way through the group saying "Goodnight" and hugging and kissing the Italians, Bobby Grant came up to me and said, "Ya know, kid…when I first met you I had you wrong. You turned out to be one of the good guys." Then he ground out his permanently affixed cigarette and hugged and kissed me on the cheek. I didn't know what to say and was only able to get out a simple "Thanks."

I never expected to get *any* kind of respect from the guy I thought I'd have the most trouble with.

The rest of the summer was quiet. I was still on my once-a-month Vegas schedule and spending more and more time in Los Angeles working sessions and hanging out in the jacuzzi with Phyllis's friend, Linda Rossi.

It was on the afternoon of my birthday, August 29, 1976, while I was at my parents' new home in Fairview, when Jerry called.

"Juan, what are you doing?"

"Not much--"

Before I could say anything else, he said, "Be outside in ten minutes," and then hung up.

I was standing in the driveway as his Cadillac pulled up. He was the only one in the car, so I sat in the front seat.

"Where we goin'?" I asked.

"For a ride. We gotta talk."

From the look on his face, I could tell it was serious.

I lowered my voice and asked, "About?"

"The future."

"Yours or mine?"

"Both."

He wasn't smiling.

I was very concerned.

"You know what today is?" I asked.

He shrugged and answered, "Sunday."

I tried to lighten the mood. "Tell you what...lemme give you a hint. A year ago today we met in Vegas."

This information was like a bombshell falling on him, and it made him more upset than he already was. That's when I knew he had something *very* important on his mind.

He pulled the Caddie over to the side of the road and gripped the steering wheel.

"A year ago?" he asked. "Shit! You're twenty-*three* now? Jon...you have no idea how much has happened in the last year. How much has changed."

I had never seen him like this...ever. But before I could ask him what the problem was, he leaned over, put his arms around me and hugged and kissed me.

"Ya know, of all of our cousins...it was you. You were the only one I brought in, 'cause I knew I could count on you. You were the only one that always did the right thing. I want you to know that." Then he kissed me on the cheek again and said, "Happy birthday, Jon."

As he sat up and put the car in drive, I asked him, "Okay Jer. What is it? What's bothering you? What's so important that you forgot my birthday?"

We cruised along Boulevard East with the Manhattan skyline alongside of us as he answered me.

"I'm moving. I sold my house, my father's house and my sister's house... and we're moving."

He wouldn't be acting this way if he was just *moving*. Something was happening and I didn't understand what it was.

"All of ya's?" I asked, not comprehending exactly what he was saying.

"We're gonna open a restaurant. So we're selling everything and moving."

I was speechless.

As he drove, I stared at him and eventually asked, "Does my old man know about this? Does *he* know that his brother sold his house and is moving?"

"No one in the family knows *anything* yet. You're the first one. My father's meeting with yours tonight and he's going to tell him."

"But what about the--"

"The business?" He shook his head as he answered, "I've been thinking about that every fuckin' day since this decision was ma--" he stuttered, something he never did, then continued, "Since I made this decision."

"Where you gonna go? Whatcha gonna do? What am *I* gonna do? I ain't goin' to Vegas if I'm not doin' it for *you!*"

"I'll tell you where I'm going. But you and your father are gonna be the only ones in the family to know…for a while at least. Taz and Mike will know…but you can't say anything to anybody else. You got that?"

I nodded.

He quietly said, "We're going to Palm Springs. I found a house big enough for my parents, my sister and her husband and three kids, and my family."

Quickly counting, I said, "That's eleven people. It must be a friggin' mansion."

"More like a compound," he responded. "And we're gonna open a restaurant. *That's* what I'm gonna do from now on."

"*Why*, Jer? Why are you leaving?"

He looked me in the eyes and said, "Because right now, it's the right thing for me to be doing. Someday, some time in the future…I don't know when…I'll tell you. I can't tell you now, and believe me…it's for your own good that you don't know. But someday, I'll tell you."

"And you expect me to accept that?"

"It's the best you're gonna get, Jon. You have no choice."

I couldn't imagine what made him make this decision. Everything was running fine. The Vegas trips were flawless since he took over. To just give it up…to give it *all* up was something not just I…but *anyone* who knew Jerry…couldn't believe. And to go into the restaurant business? What did he have up his sleeve? He had to have an ulterior motive…and an alternate plan. A plan that needed a restaurant as a front, perhaps?

"Can I come out to see you when I'm in L.A.?" I asked.

"No!" he quickly responded. "I don't want *anyone* coming out for a while. You gotta respect me on that. Capice?"

I couldn't believe he was saying this to me.

"Why not?" I asked angrily.

"Because that's the way I want it for now. I'll reach out for you when the time's right. Once we get set up I'll get you a phone number if you ever need to talk to me. But other than that, I can't have no one...I don't *want* no one to know what's going on or where I am for a while."

"How long is *a while?*"

He smiled, but I could see it wasn't one of his real smiles, and said, "I'll let you know."

We drove a little longer before I asked, "What about Vegas? What about the hundred grand I owe the casinos? Am I gonna get stuck?"

"No, you won't get stuck. You'll still go...if you want. Dolan's going to be runnin' the show again."

"Fuck!" I said under my breath. "He don't like me, Jer. I can't trust him."

"You'll be fine. Mike and Taz'll be there with you. In the last year The Irishman's learned you're somebody he can depend on. Even Bobbie and Louie like you. You're a good worker, Jon. You made money for him, and he knows he can count on you to run a crew when he needs you to. I'll talk to Casiano before I go. He knows you've been there for us. Before I leave I'll make sure Tommy won't fuck with you. You'll be all right."

I leaned back into the leather seat and didn't say another word until he pulled into my father's driveway.

He turned toward me and said, "I'm leaving in a couple of days. I'm driving cross-country with my wife. Everyone else is flying out over Labor Day weekend 'cause we gotta get our kids into school. If *anyone* asks you why I left, the only thing I want you to tell them is that I decided to go into the restaurant business...and *that's it*. You got that?"

I nodded and said, "Yeah Jerry! I got it! For the tenth time, I got it!" I reached across the seat and put my arms around my cousin, my Godfather... my friend. "I don't know what the fuck this is all about, Jer. But someday, *someday*, I'm gonna want an answer about why you're doin' this."

"And someday, Jon...someday, I'll tell you."

In less than ten days, Jerry's home, and the homes of his parents and his sister were emptied, and all eleven of them were living in Palm Springs, California.

As I had felt when Patsy died...another era had passed.

From that point on...I could tell that things weren't going to be the same.

Round 14

The phone rang as Linda and I sat in her jacuzzi enjoying the warm October sun. She answered and handed me the receiver.

"It's for you. A Mr. Gazzulo."

Wally Gazzulo was Tommy Dolan's alias whenever he spoke on the phone.

He opened with, "Hi kid. Your uncle talk to you?"

I corrected him and said, "You mean *cousin?*"

"Whatever."

"I haven't spoken to him since he moved."

"Did he tell you about Vegas?"

"Just that we're doin' it with you. You need me?"

"Next week. We can use you at The Dunes."

It was obvious he was treating me differently. There didn't seem to be any lingering animosity.

On one hand, that was comforting.

On the other, I constantly felt that he was setting me up...just to get back at Jerry.

An Italian wouldn't do that. They wouldn't go after a relative to get to the primary target. But...Dolan was no Italian.

Quietly, Linda watched as he told me the day and time of my flight out of Burbank. Then I hung up and immediately got Taz on the phone.

"You gonna be there?" I asked.

"Whatdya mean, am I 'gonna be there?' I *gotta* be there. The Irishman got orders from above that you can't go there without me or the other guy." When he said that, I knew he meant Mike. "Your cousin made sure he covered you before he left. He loves you, kid. You know that, right?"

As *my* voice grew low to answer, "Yeah, I know," his grew louder and angrier as he said, "I don't know what the fuck happened! Twenty-three years I've known him. I can't figure out what could have happened to make him pack up his whole-fuckin'-family and take off like that."

"You think it had something to do with what happened to Vi--" I stopped and rethought my words. "Outside the pizzeria?"

He was quick to answer, "No. Your cousin was tougher than that. I'm sure what happened bothered him like it bothered the rest of us. But he wouldn't run because of it. No. It was something else. I just don't know *what*. *Nobody* does. Even The Irishman's pissed off, 'cause now he's gotta handle the trips again. It's interfering with everything else he's got going."

"Well, as long as I know the two of you will always be with me, I--"

He cut me off and said, "Your cousin looked out for you, kid. That's all you gotta know. Somebody'll explain it to you...someday."

Then we hung up.

I turned to Linda to tell her that I'd be going to Las Vegas the next week, but just as quickly opted to keep my mouth shut. I just looked at her and smiled. Over the past fourteen months I think she realized that there was more to my Vegas trips than I let on...and I had a feeling she got off on imagining what it could be.

We had developed a wonderful relationship during that time. It was built upon *availability*. Whenever I came to Los Angeles...Linda made herself *available*.

The trip to Vegas was uneventful and, as usual, profitable.

Once again, it got my heart racing.

When I finished gambling my line, I decided to go to Jersey instead of returning to California.

Dolan arranged to have a limo pick me up and take me to my parents' house. *That* had me a little concerned, wondering if this was going to be that *last ride* these guys worry so much about.

But those fears were once again relieved as the limo pulled into my father's driveway.

I wasn't in the house for more than 15 minutes before the phone rang.

"Hello, Jon?"

I didn't recognize the voice right off the bat.

"Yeah, who's this?"

"Al Nucci."

"Jeez! Hi Al! It's been a long time. How ya been?"

"Good, *kid*. Good."

"What's the matter, Al? What can I do for you?"

He quickly responded, "I need to talk to you about somethin'."

It *had* to be 'somethin'.' Al never called just to ask how I was doing.

"You still play in the band, kid?" he asked.

"Well, not exactly in a *band*. I'm a session musi--"

He cut me off and said, "Yeah, good. Listen, I gotta talk to you about a band. Think you can be at my shop around eleven tomorrow morning?"

He didn't give two-shits about me still being in a band, nor did he have a band he wanted to talk to me about. He just needed to tell me to be at his place "around eleven tomorrow morning." Everyone was still being tapped and no one felt safe talking on the phone.

"Yeah. Sure Al."

"Good. See you then."

When I hung up, my father asked if it had anything to do with Jerry.

"Not that I could tell," I answered. "But I'm sure I'll know more tomorrow."

I hadn't been in the tailor shop since I was 17, when my father had Al make me a suit for my high school graduation.

I had always heard that Al's tailoring was popular because he had a knack of designing sport jackets and suits so that they wouldn't accentuate the bulge of a holster and pistol underneath it. Appearance was always primary to *da guys*...and *nobody* wanted to have their piece seen. Al was good at what he did.

I crossed the electric eye's beam as I walked in the front door, causing a pleasant tone to alert The Tailor to a potential customer...and suddenly all of the memories came rushing back.

It was still the same as I remembered. Sample rolls of material lined the walls, interspersed with full-length tri-angled mirrors and dressing rooms.

And then there was the music. There was always a radio tuned to some station that only played Italian music.

But it was what lined the walls *above* the rolls of material that always caught my attention.

It was the pictures.

Autographed pictures with praises and thanks to Al...from *everyone*.

Most prized to him were the pictures of boxers. He had dozens of them. I had no idea who most of them were. But...he also had the greats that I *did* recognize. There were shots of him with Rocky Marciano, Rocky Graziano, Jack Dempsey, Carmine Basilio, Jake LaMotta, Chuck Wepner, Willie Pep, Sonny Liston, George Foreman and Cassius Clay...and signed by all of them.

There were the photos of Bobby Darin, Frankie Valli and The Four Seasons, The Young Rascals and another dozen faces you'd recognize from the Johnny Carson or Ed Sullivan shows, but not know their names, all thanking Al for making their suits and stage outfits.

Understandably, there were the Italian singers; Tony Bennett, Jimmy Roselli, Jerry Vale, Dean Martin, Vic Damone, Enzo Stuarti, Julius LaRosa...and of course...a *few* of Sinatra.

Al even had a signed picture from Ringo Starr.

As I had been years earlier, I was still captivated by these photos and stared up at them as soon as I walked in.

Al came out from the back office and yelled, "Hey *kid!* Thanks for coming. Gimme a couple of minutes, I'll be right with you."

"No problem, Al. I'll be right here," I answered, and continued my viewing.

A moment later someone walked up very close behind me.

"You Jerry's nephew?" a voice asked.

Was this it? Was this the hit I expected Dolan to take now that Jerry was gone?

I didn't turn around, but answered, "No. Cousin."

"Whatever. You Jon?"

"Can I turn around?" I asked, not wanting to piss someone off by making any fast moves.

"G'head."

As I began to turn, my peripheral vision saw Al in the back of the shop. Next to him was a figure standing in the dark. For the rest of my time in the shop the *figure in the dark* would watch every move I made.

As I completed the turn, the voice said, "You know me?"

It didn't take long to recognize the man standing two feet away.

"Yes. You're Rocco Casiano."

"How you know that?"

I respectfully bowed my head and said, "I know who you are."

I took his hand and shook it as I continued, "Besides the fact that your picture's been in the papers and on the news?" He immediately noticed that I wasn't nervous as I responded. "The FBI showed me one a few months ago, *and* I remember you from a bunch of my family's functions when Frank DeNike was alive."

At the time, had I known that he was at Margaret Hague Hospital the day I was born, I would have mentioned that, too.

I let go of his hand.

"Is there a reason you wanted to see me, Mr. Casiano?" I asked. "Is anything wrong?"

He said, "Call me Rocco." Then he leaned close and whispered, "The Irishman tells me you're a good worker and that you're close with your cousin."

As he spoke, I could sense his feeling of distrust. It was easy to see he had something on his mind, and he wanted to know what I knew.

I whispered back, "Well, as far as me being a 'good worker,' I enjoy going to Vegas...and I got no problem doin' what we do. That's all. What happens with the money they bring home...I got nothin' to do with it... and I want to keep it that way." Then I raised my voice a bit and continued, "As far as Jerry? He's my cousin. He's my *closest* cousin. He's my Godfather. Yeah, we were *very* close."

He stepped back a bit and asked, "What do you mean '*were*?'"

"I haven't spoken to him since just before he left. He just packed up and split. I don't know why...and it bothers me."

Raising an eyebrow, he asked, "You don't know why?"

I lowered my voice to a whisper again, and answered, "All I know is that after what happened to Vinnie...he changed. A couple of months later he sells his house and his whole friggin' family packs up and goes into the restaurant business."

The boss leaned close to me again and quietly said, "Yeah, I know. He went to Palm Springs. If he reaches out to you, if you talk to him, you tell him I know he's there, and if there's anything I can do for him...just let *you* know, and then you'll pass it along to The Tailor. You got that?"

I nodded.

He waved Al Nucci over.

Casiano put his arm around The Tailor's shoulder and said to me, "Al tells me he's known you since you were a kid, and everybody says you're a stand-up guy." He put his other arm around my shoulder and led us toward the back of the shop as he continued talking. "I had Al ask you to come here because I want to tell you something. Something I never want you to repeat. This is only for our ears. The three of *us*. Capice?"

"What about *his* ears?" I asked while looking at the figure in the dark.

"Him? That's Sal. Don't worry about him. He's not here. He only hears what I *want* him to hear."

I looked at the darkened hulk in the corner. Though I couldn't make out his face, from his shadowy appearance I could tell this was a person I wouldn't want to run into when he was angry...especially if he was angry with *me*.

Casiano continued, "Now, you hear what I'm sayin'? This goes no farther than this room. You got that?"

Again, I nodded.

The three of us sat in the back of the shop and leaned into one another so the conversation could be said in whispers.

Casiano looked at me and started, "A couple of days before your cousin left, he met with me..." He took a short pause to choose his words, "...and he asked me to promise him something. And as someone in my position, I--" He paused again, came even closer and asked, "You *do* know who I *am*, and what that position *is*, don't you?"

I didn't respond. From the look on my face he could tell the answer. He even saw I was insulted that he would ask me that, considering how well he knew my family.

He got back to what he was saying.

"Because of my long relationship with your Godfather...before he left, one of the things he asked was that I look after you like you were my own Godson."

I pulled my head back and looked at him.

So *this* was what Taz meant when he said, "Somebody'll explain it to you...someday."

"That's a very special honor," the boss said as a surprised Al Nucci nodded his head. "The only other time anyone's ever asked me to do that was a long, long time ago." He looked into my eyes to see if I understood the magnitude of what he was saying. "Your cousin must love and respect you very much, kid, because he could've asked me for nearly *anything*. But when the time came, the only thing he had on his mind was for me to make sure that nobody fucked with *you*."

I sat there not believing I was hearing this from the man who ran the northern half of the state for the Genovese family. It was as if Jerry had a genie grant him one wish...and he gave that wish to me.

I broke the silence.

"I don't mean to be disrespectful. But if Jerry met with you before he left, didn't he give *you* a reason for leaving? I mean...after all...because of *the business*...wouldn't he tell *you?*"

Al Nucci's eyes grew large, not believing I would ask Rocco Casiano such a question.

The boss laughed and said, "I gotta admit, kid...you got balls." Then he answered me. "He didn't tell me why. He just said he was moving to California to open a restaurant. That was it. Same as he told you." He paused and then got back to where he left off. "Now, you gonna let me finish what I was sayin'?"

I respectfully nodded.

"Before I take on the responsibility of looking after you like Jerry asked me to, I need to know something."

He sat back and looked deeper into my eyes.

Without removing his stare, he told Al to take a walk downstairs. The Tailor immediately got up and left.

"I'm going to ask you one question and I want a straight answer. If I find out you're lying," Casiano pointed to Della Osa and said, "*He* will find you."

I raised an eyebrow, nodded my head and said, "Ask away."

He leaned so close that I could feel his lips against my ear as he quietly asked, "Why did your cousin leave New Jersey? What happened to make him leave? I want to know."

Within a second after he asked me those questions, my mind raced through a half dozen thoughts. Suppose Jerry told him something else? Supposed Jerry just *told* me he was opening a restaurant...and really didn't?

I didn't flinch. I put my trust in my Godfather. I could only tell Casiano what I knew. And I only knew one thing.

"To open a restaurant," I answered.

He sat back and asked, "Is that what he told you to say to me?"

"No. He never even told me I'd be *meeting* you," I answered quickly and calmly. "That's what he told me he was going to do. He was leaving the *business* and opening a restaurant." Then I leaned forward and whispered,

"Maybe there *was* another reason. Like I said, maybe it had something to do with Vinnie getting whacked. I don't know. But the point is...he left, and I don't know why. *That's* all I know. And I was taught a *long time ago* that in this *business*...from time to time...you gotta *accept* answers like that..." I returned the stare into Casiano's eyes and continued, "...*Don'tcha?*"

I believe at that moment the boss saw the anger and the truth in my eyes.

Casiano sat back and called Al.

"From now on," he said, again without breaking eye contact with me, and as The Tailor took the seat next to him, "If you need something, if you need to talk to me, if the FBI bothers you again...you come to Al. You tell him what you wanna see me about and he'll reach out for you when I'm gonna be around."

I nodded.

He continued.

"We don't talk on phones. You don't *ever* mention my name on the phone. You hear me? If you need to talk to me, you just tell Al you gotta *come by.* That's it. *He'll* tell you when. Got that?"

I nodded.

He sat back, giving me an indication that the meeting was officially over.

I stood up to shake his hand as he asked, "What do you do for a living, kid?"

Al jumped in and said, "He plays in a band."

I wasn't going to correct him.

"Oh yeah?" Casiano responded. "Well, *that* explains the hair. You wanna play with Frankie Valli's band? How about Jay and The Americans? You wanna play with *them?*"

I laughed to myself at the ease with which he said it. Did he have so much control that musicians could be replaced just from his say-so?

"Thanks, Rocco. But I work pretty regularly. I'm a session musician."

"What the fuck's *that?*"

I explained that I played the guitar in recording studios on everything from commercials and jingles to the songs on the radio, and that I didn't play with one specific band or go on tour.

When I mentioned "recording studios" his eyebrows suddenly shot up.

"You know about tape recordings?" he asked.

"Depends. What do you want to know?"

"Can you tell if a tape's been edited or spliced? You know...cut up and put together to make a different conversation?"

"Actually, I'm pretty good at hearing edits," I responded. "And if not...I got a guy with this new computerized oscilloscope that can probably do it. Why? Whatcha got?"

Casiano and Al looked at one another as if they were speaking telepathically.

Then Al said, as if answering the boss, "Yeah. You can trust him."

"Write down your address and phone number," the boss ordered, and then asked, "Will you be home tomorrow night?"

"As of right now, I will. Why?"

"Well, don't make any plans. Somebody'll call you."

"About?"

"Don't worry about it. Just be there when they call."

Then he stood up. I went to shake his hand, but instead, he put his arms around me, kissed me on both cheeks and held me close as he whispered, "I'm going to give you *a shot*. If you do this for me, I'll take care of you *better* than Jerry asked me to. That's all you gotta know. You got that?"

"And if I can't?"

"Just do the right thing, kid. That's all you gotta do."

"That's all I *ever* do, Rocco," I responded...maybe a little more arrogantly than someone in his position is used to hearing or would tolerate. But I didn't like being questioned about Jerry.

I turned and kissed Al Nucci as he patted me on the back and said, "You did good, kid."

Then I waved to the hulking figure in the shadows as I walked through the shop, again looking at the pictures as I passed them. I stopped for a few seconds at one of the full length mirrors along the wall and checked my appearance.

Just before I reached the door I heard Casiano say, "And do something about that hair."

The next afternoon the phone rang.

"Hello, kid?"

It was Casiano himself.

"Yeah," I answered.

"Know who this is?"

"Yeah."

"Gonna be there in an hour?"

"Yeah."

And he hung up.

I turned to my father and said, "I think Rocco Casiano is gonna be here in an hour."

He froze and asked, "Why?"

"I think it has something to do with tape recordings. I'll bring him downstairs to the studio."

Concern overcame my father's face as he asked, "Is he bringing anybody with him?"

I shrugged my shoulders, shook my head and said, "No idea. He didn't say."

"Did you do or say anything yesterday to piss him off?"

"Not that I know of. As a matter of fact, Al said I '*did good.*'"

Twenty minutes later the doorbell rang.

We weren't surprised that he was 40 minutes early. We figured he had his reasons for telling us an hour on the phone. At Al's, he told me *someone* would call at *night*. These guys spoke and moved in mysterious ways, but because I grew up surrounded by this life...I understood what they were *saying*, what they were *doing* and why they did it.

Casiano walked inside as soon as I opened the front door.

I noticed the black Lincoln Town Car parked in the driveway. A person resembling *the figure in the dark* looked at me as he leaned against the car. The driver's face was hidden behind a newspaper.

Entering the living room, Casiano greeted my father and me with hugs and kisses, then said, "Rocky, do me a favor. Let me and the kid have some time together, okay?"

Being a father, Rocky asked, "With all respect, Rocco, I just want to know if my son is in any trouble? If there's something I can do to--"

Casiano, holding a manila envelope under his arm, laughed and cut him off.

"He's not in any trouble. I understand he works in recording studios, and *his* ears may hear something *ours* haven't." Then he patted the envelope and said, "I just want him to listen to something and let me know what he hears. That's all."

"What if he don't hear *anything*...or if he don't hear what you *want* him to hear?" my father asked, gingerly...and respectfully.

"Then he don't hear it," Casiano said as he shrugged his shoulders. "What am I gonna do? Make him hear somethin' that's not there?" He saw that my father needed reassuring. "I just wanna borrow his ears for a little while. That's all. He'll be okay."

"I have a tape deck in the basement," I said as I led Casiano downstairs, "We can listen down there."

My father nervously walked over to the front window, pulled aside the curtain and looked at the Lincoln in the driveway...with Salvatore Della Osa patiently and obediently standing next to it. He quickly closed the curtain and hoped that the FBI wasn't trailing Casiano.

My father was a true pro at keeping a low profile in the neighborhood and community, and was nervous about the boss's visit and Sal's visibility.

A couple of months earlier I used the Vegas income to have a small recording studio built in the basement.

Yeah...that extra cash didn't hurt.

Casiano wandered around the soundproof room admiring the two 4-track TEAC 3340S reel-to-reel tape recorders, a Tascam mixing board, a Eumig cassette deck, a couple of keyboards, guitars and amplifiers, a set of drums, and an assortment of microphones on stands and booms.

Then he sat on top of my Ampeg Gemini I.

I could see he felt comfortable being there as he asked, "Why's it sound so...so...?"

He couldn't find the right word.

"Dead?" I threw in.

He looked at me.

"It's an acoustically dead room," I explained. "No sound can get in or out of here. The walls and ceiling are four inches thick with a special insulation, all covered by a half inch of acoustic tile. Between that and the carpet on the floor and doors...you could shoot a cannon in here and my folks upstairs would never know."

He looked around the room again and said, "Maybe I gotta build one of these in *my* place."

I decided to change the subject...primarily because I didn't want to know *why* he'd want a soundproof room in his house.

"Whatcha want me to hear, Rocco?" I asked as I hit the power switch, lighting up the electronic console and tape decks with their red, blue and white lights.

He reached into his jacket, took out a cassette and tossed it to me. I slid it into the Eumig tape deck.

Then he brought over the manila envelope and said, "Follow along with this."

I opened it and pulled out a transcript about two inches thick.

The cover simply read; The State of New Jersey vs. Rocco Casiano and Benito Petrillo.

The first page said; The following transcript is dated Tuesday, May 25, 1976, and filed by New Jersey State Police Special Agent Robert Testa. Recorded subjects: Benito Petrillo a/k/a Benny, and Rocco Casiano a/k/a The Boss.

As I read it, he said, "They gotta give us a copy of all the evidence they're gonna use against us."

The recording began with Testa sitting in his car, stating the time and date, and that he was using the undercover name *Vito Lanni*.

Once I heard the undercover cop say, "I'm meeting Benny Petrillo at The Uptown-Broadway Diner in Bayonne," I realized *this* was the recording that made the headlines...and the reason for Benny's disappearance.

When I turned the volume up to hear everything going on in the background, Casiano was concerned about anyone outside the walls of the studio hearing it.

"I'm telling you, Rocco. Go stand outside that door. I'll crank it up even louder and you won't hear a thing."

He smiled and trusted what I told him.

The rest of that side of the cassette consisted of Lanni and Petrillo's banter over coffee, Lanni paying the check and Petrillo's non-stop *mouth* on the ride from Bayonne to Secaucus.

I couldn't believe the stuff he was saying to Lanni about the workings of the north Jersey mob.

I asked, "Isn't Benny Petrillo the guy that disappeared last summer? He went into hiding from the cops or something, right?"

"Yeah. Something like that. I don't know. I haven't heard from him in a long time," Casiano answered, straight-faced.

The second side of the cassette began with the cop again stating the time and date, and that he was in the men's room of the Plaza Diner...about to meet with Rocco Casiano. Then there was the flush of a toilet.

I listened as Petrillo told the cop to come out to the car.

And then I heard Rocco Casiano being introduced to Lanni.

As he listened, Casiano said, "I knew he was no good when I *met* the cocksucker."

I followed along with the transcript as Casiano asked Vito Lanni, "You the boss?" as they were getting into a car. It wasn't hard to sense the confusion in the cop's response as he answered, "No."

Then Casiano clearly said, "Then you sit in the front..." There was a pause, followed by, "...The boss *always* sits in the back."

I looked at him.

Even *I* knew that having that on tape wasn't a good thing for Casiano. He looked pissed just listening to it.

Casiano didn't say much during the short ride, and after they dropped him off at the diner the transcript consisted of more dialogue between Benny and Lanni on their ride back to Bayonne...until the tape ran out.

Casiano said, "Turn it off. I want to talk to you."

As I popped out the cassette he told me what was on his mind.

"What we talk about stays in this room. Capice?"

I nodded.

"Before Benny Petrillo disappeared, he told my attorney that some of the things on this tape weren't the same as what was said."

I raised an eyebrow.

"Benny was a shit-head and a fuck-up. But he really believed that the State tampered with this thing and I got nothin' to lose by trying to find out if he was right. If you prove they *did* tamper with it...it'll save my ass." He stared at me and continued, "Think you can do it?"

What was my option?

I thought for a few seconds, then said, "If I do this...I gotta know I can ask you stuff, *and* you'll explain it to me. Okay? And no bullshit. I'll want straight answers. I gotta be able to understand what they're talking about before I can figure out if there's been any edits. You understand that?"

He nervously laughed and said, "You *do* got balls." Then he cautiously asked, "Whatdya mean? Gimme an example."

"Like when you said that you always sit in the back. Why? Why'd you say that?"

He walked back to the amplifier and sat on it, then quietly asked, "You sure nobody can hear anything outside that door?"

I just smiled.

He laughed again and said, "It's not just *me*. It's *any* boss. You see, kid, if you sit behind the guy driving and the ride's a *set-up*, then the guy in the front passenger seat has a clear diagonal shot at you...he don't even need to put his gun over the seat. Now if you sit in the *front*, that's the worst. If someone wants to get you from outside the car...you're an open target. *Or*...the guy behind you can blow you away either *through* the seat or with a shot to the back of your head. But hey, if the guy can't face you when he kills you...he shouldn't *be* one of us, right?"

I didn't answer. Though I hoped he was speaking rhetorically. I certainly couldn't relate to what he was asking.

He continued, "I don't plan on goin' that way...that's why *I* always sit in the back...right behind the passenger seat."

Then his face changed to a very serious stare.

"Before I sit in the front...I gotta trust the guy sitting behind me like a fuckin' *brother!*" Then he laughed again, "See...by sitting behind the passenger seat...if they're gonna try to whack you, the hitter's gotta turn all the way around, putting himself out of position. That gives you enough time to hit him, or deflect the gun."

This shit was *funny* to him.

I, on the other hand, sat there trying not to let my jaw fall to the floor. I didn't know *what* to say. The proper way to assassinate someone was never one of the conversations I ever thought I'd be having.

"So...whatcha think?" he asked.

I had lost track of what he was asking me, so I responded with, "Huh?"

"The tape. Think you can hear if they made any edits?"

I sat back and thought for a few seconds before I responded.

"I'll give it a serious listen, Rocco, and I'll do the best I can."

He walked over, kissed me on the cheek and said, "What more can I ask for?"

It was more than an hour-and-a-half since we had gone down to the studio. My nervous father met us at the top of the steps and asked, "Everything all right?"

"Sure. The kid did fine," Casiano answered. Then he turned to me and said, "Stop by The Tailor's in a couple of days and let him know if you heard something we can use. All right? Then we'll get together. You hear me?"

I nodded.

As soon as he walked out, the driver started the car and Sal opened the rear passenger-side door.

As we watched, my father quietly said, "You see that guy opening the door? That's Salvatore Della Osa. Stay away from him."

He didn't say another word about Salvatore. And I could tell from the way he said it...it was something he never wanted to say to me again.

Casiano got into the car and placed himself directly behind his bodyguard.

Now I knew why he sat there.

As ordered, a couple of days later I let Al Nucci know that Casiano should stop by my house for some good news.

No more than two hours went by before the doorbell rang.

When I opened the door, Casiano quickly walked in. Behind him stood a tall, slightly overweight, mostly-bald man in a suit, carrying a briefcase.

Casiano introduced the stranger as he came into the house.

"Andy, c'mon in. This is Jon D'Amore. Jon, this is my lawyer, Andrew Herschfeld."

As I shook the attorney's hand, Casiano said, "You told Al you had good news, I thought I'd bring Andy to hear what you have to say...and to see if we can use it."

I took them downstairs to the studio and made them comfortable.

"So...you listened to the tape?" the attorney asked.

I smiled and nodded.

He continued with the questions, "Did you hear anything? Did you find any edits? Did you find anything that we can use?"

Again I smiled...but this time, I didn't nod.

I asked them, "When you listened to the tape and read the transcript, did you notice something that the cop was doing for you from the beginning to the end?"

They both looked unsure of what I asked.

Before they could utter any semblance of an answer, I continued, "Before I started listening for edits, I listened to what was going *on* on the tape."

I was *still* getting the same visual response from them.

"First, I set my watch to the time Lanni said it was and I referenced it to *other* times that were said during the conversations...*especially* when Lanni was the one mentioning those times. That way, it was always coming from *his* watch."

They looked at one another and thought about what I was saying.

I could see the attorney was slowly *getting it* as he began to smile and leaned closer to hear me say, "Then...I started listening to the ambient noise."

Casiano said, "What's that?"

"Background sounds," I answered. "Things like...what's playing on a radio, or background conversations while they were in the diner...or when they stopped someplace, like at a gas station...or at a toll booth."

Now they were *very* interested as both men leaned forward and asked, "So...whatcha hear?"

I proceeded to explain that as soon as I found an eight minute discrepancy in the *time*, I started listening to the sounds in the background. It was then that I found entire sections missing.

"But we've been told by the State that what we received was *everything* they had. That tape was supposed to be in its entirety..." the attorney said while shaking his head, "...and nothing was supposed to be deleted or altered."

Then I told them, "Not only was *time* missing, but I believe that some of the verbiage from the missing conversations were edited into some of the conversations that *are* on the tape."

"How can you tell?" Herschfeld asked.

"The background noise. When Benny and Lanni were on their way to Secaucus, there's the sound of them stopping for a toll ticket to get *on* the Turnpike. But there's nothing on the tape of them paying the toll to get *off* the Turnpike. Then on their return to Bayonne from Secaucus... there's a second, although quiet, toll booth section where they *pay*. Now we all know that there's only one toll booth where you gotta pay between Secaucus and Bayonne," I sarcastically said. "And that's only *one* of three other edits I found."

I proceeded to play the tape from the top, then set my watch to the undercover cop's and showed them the *time* discrepancies. Along the way, I pointed out the verbiage sections that appeared out of sequence, which in its new version was very incriminating to Rocco...as opposed to their original order, which was only *slightly* incriminating and not enough to put him away for the forty years he was facing.

Andrew Herschfeld could not have been happier. Casiano suddenly looked as if huge weights were taken from his shoulders.

Herschfeld's mind raced in multiple directions as he asked, "How can we show this in court? We need an expert witness. Can you be considered an expert?"

"I'm just a musician," I told him. "But I have an engineer with a degree in audio physics. He has this new thing, a computerized oscilloscope that'll show a spike every time there's an edit. As you can see, most of them are simple to pick out once you know what to listen for in the background. But he could probably find a few more."

"Can we count on this guy?" Casiano asked.

"I'm sure you can," I answered.

Casiano asked again, "Can we count on this guy?"

"I work with him in the New York studios. He's a technical-fuckin'-wizard. And besides...you're not asking him to lie. This stuff's really been played with," I answered.

He asked *again*, "Can we *count* on this guy?"

I took a shot with a different kind of answer.

"His name is Carlo Falzone."

Ah, a paisan. An Italian.

That must have been what he wanted to hear, because he smiled and stopped asking.

I wrote down Carlo's phone number and handed it to the attorney as we shook hands.

As Rocco reached over to hug and kiss me, he said, "If this works out, I'll do the right thing for you. You'll see."

What he didn't realize was that I did this for him solely because I was asked...plain and simple. And in the world I grew up in, when a person of his position asks you to do something, you just *did it*...and *not* for some kind of reward.

Besides...it was for *the family*.

I grew up within the tentacles of this way of life. And within those tentacles...I knew what was right and what was wrong.

What I was doing for him was *right*.

Yeah...I knew that these guys did wrong things, too. But I wasn't a part of *that*, and I didn't want to *know* about any of it.

I found the boundaries of participation I was comfortable working and living within...and I wanted to maintain that position...nothing more.

I did it because I believed it was part of my heritage to do so. To *do the right thing*. And if I succeeded, I would have been happy knowing that Casiano knew I had shown him respect.

Within the week, Andrew Herschfeld was in possession of legitimate documentation from his expert witness showing that the tapes used as evidence against Rocco Casiano were tampered with in order to implicate him.

The boss was happy.

On Wednesday, November 3, 1976, Tommy Dolan threw a party to celebrate what he believed would be the biggest *thing* to come his way. The day before, New Jersey voters had legalized gambling.

Atlantic City was going to be Dolan's and Casiano's new fountain of cash!

Though the first of the casinos wouldn't open for a year-and-a-half down the road, the two of them knew the Vegas scam would work even *better* in their own backyard.

It didn't take long before Casiano was locking horns with Philadelphia's Angelo 'The Gentle Don' Bruno and 'Little Nicky' Scarfo over the unions, of which Rocco expected a piece, and into which he wanted to position his best people.

The boys from Hudson County were just biding their time and waiting for the first casino to open its doors.

When the State case went to trial in early December, Benny Petrillo was a no-show.

The funny part was that the judge issued a warrant for his arrest for not appearing in court.

Casiano got a bit carried away and used the media to show that the New Jersey State Police edited the tapes in a plot to get him. For the next several days he wound up on every channel's six and ten o'clock news, and on the covers of every local...and several national...newspapers.

Of course, that was not something the bosses on The Commission wanted to see. They detest publicity.

The forty years in prison Casiano was facing due to the edited tape recording was dropped to a misdemeanor. He was charged with having an unregistered shotgun in his house. The fine was $1,000, and he was free to go.

The State Police and the prosecutor were pissed.

I was working sessions in Los Angeles during the trial.

The day it was over I got a call from my father.

"When are you coming home?" he asked.

"In about a week. Why?"

"Come home sooner. He wants to see you."

"Is that good...or bad?" I cautiously asked.

"It's good. Just get home."

"It'll be a couple of days. I'll get back as soon as I finish these sessions. I'll let you know when, and you can pick me up at the airport."

I *hated* flying from warm, sunny, friendly Los Angeles to cold, gray, snowy north Jersey in the winter.

Instead of being picked up by my father, there was a limo waiting for me...with a female driver. Taz and Mike were sitting in the back drinking champagne.

In between mouthfuls of Dom Perignon, Taz said, "Rocco had us come get ya. He wants to show his gratitude."

I told them, "Well, make sure you tell him I appreciate the ride and seeing you guys. Very nice of him."

They laughed as Mike said, "*This* ain't it, Phantom! Wait 'til we get to the restaurant."

"What restaurant? Why?"

A grin came over Taz's big face as he leaned back into the leather seat and answered, "We're havin' dinner at The Edge. Ever since the trial, he's been tellin' everybody he owes his freedom to *you*. He wants to show his thanks..."

Then the smile left his face and the humor left his voice as he took it to another level.

"…And he wants to show his *respect*."

The boss was going to show *me* respect…when all I did was determine that the tapes had been altered.

The State tampered with the evidence.

I didn't have to lie.

I didn't have to edit any tapes or say I heard something that I didn't hear…or say I *didn't* hear something I *did* hear. All I had to do was listen on a level these guys and their lawyers didn't know *how* to listen.

For that, the boss was going to show me respect.

When the limo pulled behind The Edge in Fairview, Mike and Taz led me through a back entrance into the banquet room. There appeared to be a celebration going on.

It took a minute before I realized that this gathering was for *me*.

My father and Casiano were there, along with Al Nucci, Tommy Dolan, Louie Calderone, Bobby Grant and another two dozen faces I had never seen before. I also recognized Casiano's bodyguard, but *still* wasn't introduced to him.

Casiano and my father hugged and kissed me, then the boss put his arm around my shoulder, led me to the head table and told everyone to be quiet.

"Hey! Stata-chi!"

The room quickly went silent and all eyes turned to him.

"You see this kid? This is Jon D'Amore!" he proclaimed, "Most of you know his father Rocky, his uncle Geil and his cousin Jerry." Everyone applauded. "Jon's the guy responsible for saving me from doing forty in the pen. That's the best Christmas present *anybody* could have given me and my family! *This* is the guy we're here to celebrate tonight."

The room burst into more applause and cheers of "Salute!" as these Italian *men of respect* raised their glasses to me.

I smiled and respectfully nodded my head.

Fortunately, after years of performing in front of audiences, I was pretty comfortable standing before these guys…so I calmly and *correctly* handled their reaction. This certainly wasn't the ordinary crowd of adoring concert fans or patrons of a rock club that I had been used to when I was touring. This was a very *special* audience.

Casiano continued, "This kid saved *my* ass…and the asses of some of you guys in this room. And at the same time, he made that prick-of-a-cop and the *rest* of the State Police look like the dumb fucks they are."

More applause.

I didn't know how to react to that statement. It's not like I *tried* to make them look that way. I just listened to the tapes...the edits were *there*.

Then he caught me even more by surprise.

"So from now on...he's one of us. From now on...he's to be treated with the respect you would show to a member of *my family*. From now on...I want you to treat him as if he were my own Godson."

Though I kept a straight face, I couldn't believe this was happening.

There were men in this room that would have killed for Rocco just to have him say the same about them.

I listened to a tape.

Sure, I thought he'd be appreciative. I figured he'd buy me dinner and hand me an envelope with a thousand bucks in it. But to have this banquet and to say what he's saying?

I *never* expected that.

My father, Mike and Taz looked at me with pride. I knew they were thinking of how proud Jerry would have been if he were here to see this. Even Tommy Dolan was looking at me with new-found respect.

Then I heard Casiano say something I would forever regret.

"From now on...when we talk about him...when we refer to him...he's 'The Kid.'"

Then he cupped my head with his big muscular hands and kissed me on both cheeks. The fate of my mob moniker was sealed.

I was *so* glad he didn't know about *Juan* or *The Phantom*.

I mentally went deaf as they applauded my new 'name.'

I didn't hear a thing.

I had to concentrate on keeping the forced smile on my face as I looked at my father. He knew I hated being called '*the kid*,' but he shrugged his shoulders and gave me a look as if to tell me to accept it and be quiet.

What was I gonna do? Tell the boss I didn't want to be called 'The Kid' in front of all of his underbosses and their underlings? He would have had Sal Della Osa take me out back and pop me before everyone sat down to eat.

One at a time, each of the attendees approached to hug and kiss me. They introduced themselves and told me that if I was ever in a certain part of the state and needed anything, "...just mention my name, kid. That's all you gotta do."

A couple of days later, a local travel agent called and said *a friend* gave me a two-week, all expense-paid trip for two to The Playboy Hotel and Casino on Cable Beach in the Bahamas as a Christmas present.

An hour later, Mike popped by and handed me an envelope with ten grand in it.

"A friend of yours thinks you may need some pocket money for that Bahama trip," he said with a wink before he walked out the door.

I rang in the New Year partying in the Caribbean for two weeks with Heather, a 22-year-old model from Manhattan that I was seeing at the time. But I spent a lot of my two week vacation thinking about how much more fun it might have been with Lady Millicent.

It was a cold afternoon in March of 1977, when I attended Paulie Romano's wedding. Paulie and I went to high school together. I knew his father, Tony, was connected…but I had no idea to what level. It never mattered to me. And they certainly had no idea of *my* affiliation.

As my date and I took our seats, I noticed Salvatore Della Osa sitting with five other men at a rear table. Two of them were the Ranouro Brothers, Sonny and Marco, who inherited Jerry's territory. I was introduced to them at the party Casiano threw for me a couple of months earlier. It didn't take long for them to see me and I was waved over to their table.

For the first time I was introduced to Della Osa.

He stood up, shook my hand and we kissed each other on the cheek. Face to face, he was several inches taller than me, and when we hugged I could feel that his body was all-muscle.

I also felt a chunk of metal against his chest.

At some point during the evening Tony Romano pulled me aside and whispered, "Salvatore told me about you and Rocco…and the *good thing* you did for him." He leaned forward and kissed me on the cheek as a show of respect, then continued, "I'd like you to come to my place in Secaucus after the reception. I'm having a small…private party…for some of my friends," then he gave a knowing wink. "You may want to bring your date home first," he paused and smiled. "There's gonna be *other* entertainment there."

I didn't respond, but returned the smile.

He whispered, "I got a condo in Harmon Towers, just keep it to yourself. Tell the doorman you're there to see me, and he'll send you up." Then he stepped back and proudly said, "Now, go enjoy my son's wedding!"

Apparently, Tony must have been a bit more active in the business than I thought, because about fifteen minutes later I walked into the men's room to find Della Osa, the Ranouro Bothers, Tony Romano and a couple of other guys comparing pistols.

Everyone was comparing their .38's and 9mm's like they were school boys showing off their dicks in the bathroom. But when Salvatore Della Osa put his hand into his jacket and pulled out his monstrous Colt .45 automatic, the men stood back in awe. They looked upon it as if it were a holy relic.

Standing in this bathroom, watching these grown men comparing their guns was *one* thing. But when Salvatore whipped out *his* piece...I was amazed at how they marveled at its magnificence.

I was glad I didn't take out my little .25.

After the reception, I brought my date home and drove to Secaucus.

As I walked through the Harmon Towers lobby toward the elevators, I saw Salvatore and another man. They were talking and obviously knew one another.

Sal saw me. It was too late to turn and leave.

"Hey kid! You goin' to Tony's party, too?"

"Yeah," I answered with a smile and as I walked toward them.

The elevator doors opened and we stepped inside.

As they closed, he turned to me and said, "Now you know not to say anything to our friend about me being at this party, right?"

I didn't answer, but raised an eyebrow.

"Listen *kid*. There may be some things goin' on up there he won't like. You know what I mean?" he said sternly, but with a smile.

But before I could answer, his hand went into his jacket and pulled out his .45 caliber cannon. He cocked back the hammer and put the barrel gently to the side of my head.

I froze.

He started laughing and said to his friend, "You know...if Rocco didn't love this little fuckin' guy...I'd kill him just for *bein'* Jerry's Godson."

The friend calmly stood there and smiled. I guess seeing a guy with a gun to his head wasn't something new for him...but it was a whole new experience for *me*.

Then Della Osa put his lips close to my ear and whispered, "I don't know what the fuck happened that night last July. But Rocco was *very nervous* until your cousin moved to Palm Springs. *I* had a feeling Jerry was gonna hit Rocco. And that woulda been *bad!*" He backed up a bit so that I could see his face, and continued, "But whatever it was...*you* saved Rocco's ass from goin' to prison...and for that, I gotta respect you. But if I find out he knows I'm here...the next time you see this gun...it's gonna be pointed in the same place...and I'm gonna use it. You got that? You capice?"

He backed away from me and smiled.

I nodded.

He pulled the gun away, gently released the hammer and slipped it back into his shoulder holster.

I didn't move my body. It was still in shock. I was a heartbeat away from having my brains splattered all over the inside of an elevator simply because I was going to a party attended by someone who shouldn't have been there in the first place.

The elevator doors opened.

"Now c'mon, let's go have a good time," he said as he put his arm around me and led me down the hall. I tried not to let him notice my legs wobbling.

Once we walked into the condo, it didn't take long for me to understand Salvatore's reason for keeping his presence here quiet. I immediately caught the smell of marijuana...while others were snorting unending lines of coke off the top of the Yamaha baby grand.

All of this took place as a dozen naked women walked throughout the party, occasionally taking one or two men into one of the three bedrooms.

To Rocco Casiano, drugs within his crew were verboten. Jerry, Mike and Taz made that very clear *several* times. I had assumed they had smelled recently smoked pot on me on more than one occasion when they reminded me about it.

Sal kept an eye on me, and I kept one on him. Neither of us went into the bedrooms or got high, and we departed together after an hour or so.

"You been followin' the papers over the last few weeks?" he asked as we rode the elevator to the lobby.

"No. I've been in L.A. most of the time. Why?"

"Rocco's getting' picked on by the Feds *and* the State now. They're following us *everywhere*. The newspapers give him a headline every time he sneezes. That's not good."

"What's he gonna do?"

Della Osa didn't answer. He just shook his head and shrugged his shoulders.

As the elevator doors opened, I said, "Maybe he put on too much of a show during the State trial, and now they wanna get him because of the way he made them look. He shouldn't have gone to the media...'cause now the law's gonna put him in the spotlight. They may even try to make an example of him."

"Yeah. I think you're right. I think there's a lot of *other* people who think that way, too."

We hugged and kissed in the lobby before we stepped into the cold late night air.

As we walked separate ways to our cars, I laughed as I recalled that earlier that very night the man I had just kissed had a gun to my head and said he would have blown me away just for being the Godson of a guy he *thought* was out to kill his boss.

What a life! What a *crazy fuckin' life!*

Round 15

It was late August of 1977. I was about an hour outside of Palm Springs and the sun was scorching as I filled the gas tank of Patsy's Cadillac. Then...I called my Godfather from a payphone.

I needed directions to his house.

It also happened to be my birthday...again. My twenty-fourth, this time.

Jerry had been out of Jersey for nearly a year and I hadn't seen him since he left.

After months of speaking on the phone, he invited me to visit while I was working some sessions in Los Angeles. I figured my birthday was as good a time as any.

Mine would be the first familiar face from back east to visit the relocated family, and they were looking forward to having me there.

"You're alone, right, Juan?" he asked as the sun baked down on me.

"Of course."

"We can't wait to see you. I've missed you."

"I've missed you too, Jer. Everyone back in Jersey misses *all* of you."

"You didn't tell anyone you were coming, right?"

I knew he specifically meant Taz, Mike or any of the other boys from Hudson County.

"You told me not to...so I didn't." I held back some tears and said, "I *always* do what you tell me, Jer."

He too, was holding back emotions as he told me, "Yes, you do, Juan. You always do the right thing."

"For you, Jer," I said quietly into the phone.

A short time later I drove the Caddie to the front of the compound and pressed the button at the gate.

"Hello?" came from the small speaker.

Though I wanted to say, "Hey! It's me!"...it somehow came out as, "It's...The Phantom."

The gate opened.

As I followed the long driveway, I saw him walk out of the main house.

He was alone. There didn't appear to be any of my other ten relatives around.

As soon as I got out of the car he put his arms out and hugged me tighter than I ever remember him doing before.

With his head next to mine, he said, "Is he taking good care of you back there? Nobody's messin' with you, right? Are Mike and Taz keepin' an eye on you? Are they with you when you go to Vegas?"

It was as if he was asking me all the questions he couldn't during our phone calls.

"Yeah, Jer! Yeah. Everything's fine. But look at you! You look *great!* Who would have thought that this guinea from Hudson County would wind up with a restaurant out in the fuckin' desert? How are your folks? How's *everybody?* Where *is* everybody?"

"They're at the restaurant. But I wanna spend some time with you first. Together. To talk. To catch up. I hear things from back east, but I don't know if I'm hearing the truth. I know I'll get the truth from you."

I was given a tour of the massive hideaway, eventually settling under the veranda, out of the 102 degree sun, drinking iced tea and talking.

He asked me to fill him in on my music career.

He listened with interest and genuine concern before he said, "You know, a little after I settled in out here and came to the realization that I was out of *that business* and running a legitimate one...I started enjoying it."

He said that it was *then* that he realized how much my musical passion meant to me.

"Don't *ever* give up your music for what's goin' on in Jersey and Vegas," he professed. "You can't ever do that. That would be wrong."

I quickly thought about his statement. I wasn't going to question him, but...was it *really* that hard to come out to Palm Springs and set yourself up in a home like this, probably with two or three suitcases filled with a stash of retirement cash?

Besides, I *knew* Jerry.

I had a feeling he didn't choose Palm Springs by throwing a dart at a map. He must have made *some* kind of mob connection out here first.

I even had the fantasy that he would contract himself out for the occasional sanctioned hit for a sizeable fee.

So to hear him tell me of his revelation about starting his new life made me realize *again* that he wasn't actually lying to me, but he would often tell me things that were for my own good...because sometimes it was better that I didn't know the truth.

He knew that my knowing *something* was better than my not knowing *anything*...especially when Rocco Casiano would ask me what I knew.

Besides, Jerry knew I had no intention of giving up my music career.

He knew...we *both* knew...the Mafia wasn't for me.

Of course, in the last 24 months I had become a regular on the Vegas trips. I even *ran* a couple of them. I was a major factor in saving the boss from going to jail for 40 years, was then royally dubbed his honorary Godson and given an official mob name.

And I wasn't even *trying* to get involved!

How did it happen? We both knew it was because of the family we were born into, and the rules of the life within it.

I was just following the rules...and being rewarded for doing so.

I told him about Casiano's State trial and what happened with the Benny Petrillo tapes.

"I hear Benny disappeared. He went into hiding or something, right?" Jerry coyly asked.

"Yeah. The State's after him 'cause he never showed up for the trial. He's probably far away from Jersey by now," I innocently answered.

My Godfather let out a small laugh and said, "I don't think he's *that* far from Jersey." Then he didn't say another thing about it.

He continued laughing as I told him of the party Casiano threw for me, and that I was now officially known as 'The Kid.' Then he kissed me and told me how proud he was of me for "doin' the right thing for our people."

As I spoke of Casiano's escapades with the media, Jerry said, "He better get out of the public eye. The big guys ain't gonna tolerate *that* very long."

Jerry always hated publicity. It wasn't unusual to hear him say, "Frank DeNike ran Jersey for more than two decades...and the only time you ever read his name in the paper was when he died. *That's* the way it's supposed to be."

When I mentioned meeting Salvatore Della Osa, my Godfather immediately ordered me to "Stay away from Sal. Don't get involved with him. He's a dangerous man."

From the look on his face, which was similar to my father's when he told me the exact same thing…Salvatore Della Osa was not someone I would *ever* want to piss off.

I decided not to mention the gun against my head during the elevator ride.

Finally, we discussed Vegas and how much cash was going back to Jersey since he no longer ran the operation.

"*Rarely* do we ever bring back more than three hundred grand," I said. "On the holidays, Dolan *never* gets a crew out there like you used to. And more often than not, he doesn't even show. He'll have one of *us* handle everything, and then we schlep the cash back to him."

Eventually I got up the nerve to ask him the big question.

"Jer, last August…a year ago today, as a matter of fact…I said I was gonna ask you something, and that I wanted an answer. Are you gonna answer me yet?"

He didn't say a word. He just put that sly smile on his face and waited to hear what I had to ask.

"What happened that made you pack up and leave Jersey? I won't say a word to *anyone*. I just wanna know."

He sat back in his chair and looked at the mountains in the distance. He finished his iced tea and placed the glass onto a small table before he cleared his throat and put his hand on mine.

Then he looked at me.

"There are things I can't talk about for the next few years, Juan. Not as long as guys like Casiano, or Dolan, or Della Osa are still around. Not because I'm fearful of them, but because of *respect*. I *still* have to show my respect to Casiano. *And* it's because of guys like you, Mike and Taz that if word ever got back to anyone as to my reason for coming out here… the three of you…and anyone else that knew…would be gone. And I don't want that to happen. You've got to realize that by not telling you all this time…I've been protecting you."

"I know that," I said in a whisper.

He looked back toward the mountains and said, "Someday...I don't know when...but someday, I'll tell you. Until then...all you need to know is that I wanted to get out of that business and start a life of my own." Then he looked into my eyes and asked, "Capice?"

I smiled and reassured him, "Si. Capice."

"Good," he said, "Now let's go. My mother and father can't wait to see you."

As the sun began to set, we drove out to Highway 111. It wasn't long before I saw the tall neon *Casa D'Amore* sign above the building.

Though Jerry told everyone that it was out of respect and in honor of Franklyn D'Amore's Hollywood restaurant, it *really* was a smart business decision...plain and simple.

Seeing as Palm Springs is filled with Hollywood people throughout the year, using the well-known *Casa D'Amore* brought in Franklyn's and Patsy's L.A. regulars. To tie in the Hollywood connection even closer, Jerry would bring in the 85-year-old Franklyn during the peak seasons just so he could sit at the head table and talk about the "good olda days" when the Rat Pack and countless Hollywood luminaries would hang out at their restaurants.

Usually, if Sinatra was in town, he would come by to pay his respects to Franklyn.

As soon as Jerry and I walked in the door, the champagne was popped and everyone started to sing "Happy Birthday." Unlike the year before... Jerry didn't forget what day it was.

After nearly twenty minutes of hugging and kissing, we spent the evening eating, drinking and talking as only a large Italian family could do. Throughout the night, any customer that walked into the restaurant was treated like family and invited to join the party.

I stayed at the compound and hung out with Jerry for a couple of days before heading back to Los Angeles. But before I drove away I asked him... *one more time*...why he left New Jersey. And as he had said a couple of days earlier, he would tell me...someday.

It was Tuesday, October 18, 1977, and I was airborne...on the way to my twenty-second trip to Vegas in twenty-six months. It was one of those rare times when I found myself flying with Mike *and* Taz...and it was one of the best flights I ever had. The three of us drank, joked and laughed all the way.

We even applauded as the plane touched down at McCarran.

Mike and I checked into The Trop, and Taz went directly to The MGM.

Later that night, Louie Calderone checked into Caesars and Bobby Grant went to The Frontier.

Over the next 24 hours, twenty-three guys from Jersey, and Rick Rogers from Newport Beach, arrived and were ready to get to work. It was a rare, big-money week. Dolan must have been getting some heat from Casiano about the consistent low take.

Rick was also registered at The Trop, so he was given to me and Mike for the rest of his stay.

By Saturday morning, I had already gone through my twenty-five grand and was planning on flying to Burbank the following afternoon. Linda Rossi was picking me up and we were going to dinner in Malibu.

Taz, Mike and Louie had packed their briefcases with $500,000 of the six-hundred-plus that Dolan expected. Bobby and I would work the remaining unfinished lines and he'd bring the rest of the money to Jersey by Sunday night.

Privately, I assured Mike and Taz that I'd be okay working with Bobby. Besides, later that night Rick and I were going out for dinner and drinks. Come Sunday morning, I'd have breakfast, turn over whatever cash I was responsible for and kill time until my 2PM flight to Burbank.

They checked themselves in the mirror, then we hugged and kissed before they walked out the door.

That night, I was responsible for five guys working The Trop and The MGM. Bobby took care of another eight. Everything went without a hitch. When it was over I was holding onto sixty-seven grand in cash and over eleven grand in Trop and MGM chips. The chips were in one of my dresser drawers and the cash was in the closet stuffed into the pockets of my four sport jackets.

Bobby had another $81,000 in cash and nine grand in chips from the rest of the casinos that were hit that week. He'd be carrying $168,000 back to Jersey.

With my casino work finished for the night, I headed out to meet Rick at The Jockey Club. At 6'2 and with blonde hair, I knew he wouldn't be hard to spot. I found him at the bar with two attractive women in their mid-twenties.

"Jon D'Amore, this is Patty and her friend, Debbie."

We all shook hands as Patty cooed, "Oooh! *D'Amore*. That's a very *romantic* name."

I smiled, said "Yes it is," and quickly changed the subject.

"New friends, Rick?"

He had a big Southern California surfer-dude grin on his face caused by one-too-many martinis, and said, "I met Patty here last night. She told me about Debbie, and I thought you'd like to meet her. I thought maybe we can all go out to dinner? Whatdya think?"

At 37, his tanned good looks and muscular body made the most attractive women take notice of him, and these two were *very* attractive.

I was sure they were hookers, but they looked good and as long as we didn't have to pay them I didn't mind having them around.

I smiled and responded, "Sure ladies. It would be a pleasure to have you dine with us this evening."

Using my pull at The MGM, I got us comped for dinner and then into Neil Sedaka's late show. It didn't take long to impress them.

By two-thirty in the morning we were finishing a round of drinks when Patty said, "How about coming back to my place? I have some grass and a hot tub, and the girl I share my house with won't be home for a couple of hours."

I didn't want to tell her that I had grass and a hot tub back at my place, too, because I didn't want people in the room with nearly eighty grand floating around, so I said, "Sure!"

Seeing as they never mentioned money...my thoughts of them being hookers were fading.

Then I looked at Rick and said, "You know not to mention this to anybody, *right?*"

Right after I said it, and for the same reasons, I realized I was reliving the conversation that Salvatore Della Osa had with me in the Harmon Tower elevator. But then, I didn't have a .45 caliber Colt to put against Rick's temple. I quickly shook the thought out of my head as the Californian answered, "No problem on this end."

Unfortunately, after we got to her house, I quickly found out that Rick turned into a babbling-bigmouthed-asshole once he put his lips on a bong. I guess the combination of grass and alcohol caused him to lose his inhibitions...as well as his sense of good judgment.

We were sitting in the living room getting high when Debbie innocently asked us what we did for a living, and how did I get such pull to get comped at The MGM when I was staying at The Trop?

Rick quickly blurted out, "'Cause we're scamming the hotels."

I shot him a look that could have killed.

"We get these credit lines and then scam the hotels out of the comped trips while these guys in Jersey--"

"What the fuck are you talking about?" I said, while trying not to make it appear as though he was telling the truth. I turned to the women and said, "He's got a construction company in Newport Beach, and I do session work in Los Angeles...that's all. We come out here from time to time, and we both do pretty well as far as gambling. So, we get comped at a couple of hotels when we're in town."

But Patty took what he said with some interest and asked, "What do you play, honey?"

"Craps!" he said loudly, "We work the crap tables. That's how we scam the cash from our credit lines. We bet opposite each other, and--"

"Hey, Rick," I said even louder, "What are you, an idiot? You know what the fuck you're talkin' about?"

Debbie and Patty watched as I barked at him. It was obvious that I was trying to cover something up.

"Relax Jon. These girls are cool. They won't say anything," he answered as he waved me off and took another bong-hit.

My eyes burned through him. I had to shut him up.

I got up from my seat, walked over to this big muscular guy and as he lifted his head from the bong I punched him right in the jaw. He never expected it. Neither did I.

I stared at him. Rick took the shot and looked up at my angry eyes as I said, "Just shut the fuck up, okay? You don't know what the fuck you're talkin' about. So *shut up!*"

Rick caught on and we changed the subject...but it was too late.

I tried to act as if nothing was wrong as I turned to the ladies and said, "Now...where's that hot tub?"

Around three-thirty, we were drunk, stoned and ready to get into the tub of hot, bubbling water...when Patty's roommate came home.

The front door opened and in walked a tall, attractive blonde.

I immediately recognized her.

It was Sandy, the crap dealer at The Trop...and after two years of seeing me in the casino, she recognized me, too.

We now had a problem.

A big one.

"That's Sandy," Patty quickly said. "She just got off work at the casino."

Shortly after the introductions, I said, "Rick, we gotta go."

The girls and Rick, now with a swollen jaw, looked confused.

"What? Why?" he asked.

He wanted to get laid.

"C'mon, I told your wife I'd have you back before the sun came up. Let's go." My voice got stern again as I barked, "*Now*."

We called for a cab and said our goodbyes.

On the ride to the hotel he asked, "What the fuck was that all about? Why'd you say we had to leave? We were gonna get 'em in the hot tub. Maybe even get all *three* of 'em in there!"

I pointed to the driver so that Rick would know I didn't want to discuss anything in the cab, but my anger made me say, "Shut the fuck up, and wait until we get to the hotel."

Throughout the 15 minute ride we didn't say another word.

As we approached The Trop's elevator bay, he said, "They don't know shit about us. What's the difference? We'll never see them again."

"What are you, *fuckin' stupid?*" I yelled to this man who was several inches taller than me, and more than a decade older. "You *never* talk about what we do to *anyone!* If Dolan ever heard you talk like that, you'd be dead in one-fuckin'-minute. Do you have any idea who that girl was that came home before we left?"

He shook his head.

"She's a fuckin' dealer right here at The Trop! She recognized me! And you told her roommate that we're scamming this casino. I can't fuckin' believe you *did* that!"

He got the picture and was immediately ashamed and fearful of his actions.

Once inside the elevator, I said, "Meet with me and Bobby for breakfast tomorrow at eight. And you'd better hope Patty was as fucked up as you were and that she don't say anything to her friend."

The doors opened. He was visibly nervous as he got out. I stayed on and went to my floor.

When I got to my suite, I re-counted the cash and chips, then called for a 7AM wake-up-call and went to sleep.

I approached the restaurant's podium exactly at eight, and while looking for Bobby Grant and a table of our guys I walked right into Mickey Rooney.

Actually, I slammed right into the back of him.

He turned around as I was apologizing, and when I saw who it was I immediately stopped and introduced myself.

"Oh? D'Amore?" he said, "That's a very nice name. I knew a D'Amore back in Hollywood."

I brought up The Villa Capri and Patsy.

He quickly recalled a half dozen evenings that he spent at Patsy's table.

I invited him to join me for breakfast, but he was meeting with friends and passed.

We said goodbye and I continued the search for my fellow gamblers.

As I sat down at the table of six other New Jerseyites and the blonde from Newport Beach with the swollen and now bruised jaw, I heard my name announced over the P.A. system.

"Paging Jon D'Amore. Mr. Jon D'Amore, please pick up a house phone."

I excused myself and went to the podium to take the call.

"This is Jon D'Amore," I told the operator.

"Thank you, Mr. D'Amore. Please hold a moment and I'll put your call through," she said.

A few seconds later the stern and concerned voice in the receiver said, "Is this the Jon D'Amore in suite four-o-nine?"

"Who's this?"

"Joe Koonce, the Casino Manager. Meet me in the front lobby in five minutes."

"Sure Joe. What's the problem?"

He quickly said, "See you in five," then hung up.

I went back to the table and told Bobby Grant about the conversation that had just taken place.

"I don't know what it could be about," Bobby said in between drags of a cigarette. "See what he wants. Lemme know what it is and I'll tell Dolan."

As ordered, I went to the lobby and found Joe Koonce.

I put my hand out to shake, but he didn't take it.

"Take a walk outside with me," he ordered.

It wasn't until I was going through the revolving doors that I noticed we weren't alone.

There were two large well-dressed muscle-men behind me.

We walked to a secluded section of the parking lot, then he turned to me and asked, "Do you have any idea what one of your guys did last night?"

I didn't answer.

He got angrier and said, "Don't play stupid with me. I heard *you* were there, *too*. One of your morons talked too fucking much to some *bitch* who lives with one of my dealers. She called the Casino Security Investigation Board early this morning and told them you guys were scamming the casino with your credit lines. Now every one of Dolan's casinos are gonna close up on ya's 'cause some shithead tried to impress some piece of ass! And take my word for it...None of us are gonna take the heat because of one of your *idiots* from Jersey. You got that?"

I knew this would be a bad time to correct him and tell him that Rick was from California.

I *also* knew the magnitude of what had just gone down...so I didn't utter a word.

A limousine pulled up next to us and he ordered me into the car.

"Mr. Smith and a couple of his friends from the Investigation Board are gonna explain a few things to you. See you when you get back."

As I slid into the rear seat with the two large 'escorts,' I saw another guy sitting there. He looked nervous and appeared to have been punched around a bit. He didn't speak when I nodded to him. He just turned and looked out the side window.

'Mr. Smith,' though I had a strong feeling that wasn't his real name, sat in the front with the driver. His muscle-men sat facing me and the other guy. No one was smiling.

We only drove for about fifteen minutes before we were surrounded by sand and brush. The car pulled off the paved road and continued on the sand and dirt for about a half mile before stopping. The odd part was that the low skyline of The Strip wasn't that far away.

Mr. Smith got out and opened the passenger side rear door. The driver stayed in the car as Mr. Smith, his guys, the quiet passenger and I stood in the morning sun.

The supposed Investigation Board rep looked directly at me and asked, "Any idea why I brought the two of you here?"

I looked at the other guy. He started to weep. I looked at Mr. Smith and replied, "Nope. No idea."

Mr. Smith pointed to the guy and said, "See this piece of shit? *He* tried scamming one of the casinos, too."

With that, one of Smith's men pulled out a pistol and shot the guy in the head. I jumped at the sound, then froze at the sight of the guy falling to the ground…motionless, with blood spurting from the hole in his skull. It all happened within a second.

Mr. Smith, now flanked by the steroid twins, came close to me and pushed his finger deeper into my chest with each word as he told me to "…get your fucking ass out of Vegas and go back to Jersey on the next fuckin' plane! 'Cause if you're not outta your room and outta Vegas by noon, your body'll be in a fuckin' hole in this desert by tonight, and they'll *never* find you! And tell Casiano to keep Tommy Dolan, that Irish cocksucker, outta this town! How long did he think we were gonna let ya's take our money? Now walk your guinea-ass back to the hotel, pack your shit and *disappear!*"

Then he signaled his men. One grabbed me from behind. The other punched me in the stomach. I collapsed against the limo and slid to the ground as Smith turned and went into the back seat. His boys stared at me as if they were taking a mental picture…and then one at a time they followed their boss.

The limo pulled away, leaving me in a cloud of dust…and next to a dead guy.

I didn't move for at least two minutes. And each minute seemed like an hour as I wondered what to do. Then I realized that they were two very important minutes I just wasted. I had to get back to the hotel and out of Vegas…*quick*. I had no intention of winding up in a hole in the desert.

I gathered my wits, then started the long walk. I refused to turn around and look at the body lying on the hot sand.

It took a little more than an hour and a half to reach the hotel. As soon as I entered the lobby, I rushed through the casino toward the elevator… then I realized that I had to tell Bobby what just happened.

Suddenly, someone behind me called my name.

"Hey Jon!"

I turned around to see Mickey Rooney walking toward me.

"Hey Jon! I just wanted to tell you I mentioned The Villa Capri to my friends I had breakfast with, and it turns out we *all* ate there at one time or another, and damn near all of us knew Patsy."

I didn't have time to converse…not even with Mickey Rooney. Besides,

I looked like I just walked through four miles of desert and sagebrush.

I glanced at my watch. It was 10:35. I had to be out of the hotel and on a plane headed to Jersey by noon.

I apologized for appearing rude and told him I had some *very* important business to discuss with my friends, and then I had to catch a plane back east. I shook his hand and hastily excused myself, leaving a confused Mickey Rooney in my wake.

I went to a house phone and found Bobby in his room.

"Where the fuck did *you* go?"

"I'll tell you when I get up there. Find Rick and get him in your room... *now.*"

Rick was already in Bobby's room when I opened the door. They immediately saw the anguish on my face and disheveled appearance.

"Jesus! What happened to you?" Bobby asked.

I looked across the room to Rick...who was looking down at the floor in a guilty pose.

I took a deep breath and explained what happened the previous night, minus the grass. Then I told them about the resulting limo ride and conversation with 'Mr. Smith'...and the guy with the bullet hole in his head still out in the desert.

Bobby asked Rick if what I had said was true. Rick admitted that he talked too much and blamed it on the alcohol. He knew that if he mentioned the grass, *I'd* kill him. But Rick's bruised and swollen jaw was proof to Bobby that I tried to shut Rick up.

Bobby must have smoked two cigarettes during our three minute discussion.

"Get packed and get out of here, then get back to Jersey *quick*," he told me. "I'll tell everyone to get out of town. When you get back, call Dolan and tell him what happened. When I get there, I'll back you up."

"Thanks, Bobby."

As I shook his hand, he pulled me toward him, kissed my cheek and said, "You kept your mouth shut. You did good, kid. They'll know that when I get back."

I didn't respond, but angrily looked at Rick as I walked out of the room. As I headed toward the elevator I realized I wouldn't be having dinner in Malibu later that night...and I didn't have time to call Linda to let her know.

I had to bring the bad news back to The Irishman.

Once I got to my suite, I picked up the phone and called the Bell Captain with orders to send up a bellman *right away*. I ran to the closet and took out my three suitcases, opened them and flung them on the bed. Then I yanked the drawers completely out of the dresser and turned them upside down, emptying their contents of socks, shirts, underwear, bathing suits and jewelry into the suitcases.

When I opened the drawer with the eleven grand in chips, I realized I had to do something with them. Fifty-seven hundred of it was from The Trop. The remainder was from The MGM.

I looked at my watch. I had an hour to get out of the hotel and onto a plane.

I left the liquor behind as I continued filling the suitcases with clothes from the closet. Before I jammed in the sport jackets, I pulled the $67,000 in cash out of them and stuffed it into all four pockets of my slacks. Then I took the Tropicana chips and put them in the pockets of the sport jacket I was going to wear. The remaining fifty-three hundred dollars in MGM chips were tossed into a suitcase and would be dealt with back in Jersey.

As soon as I latched the last suitcase, the bellman knocked on the door. I let him in before I realized the suite was in a shambles. Every drawer from the dresser was tossed either onto the bed or lying on the floor. Sweat was streaming down my face and my eyes were full of fear. I wanted to be out of the hotel in five minutes.

He almost seemed afraid to come into the room.

I pulled a twenty off a roll of cash, handed it to him and said, "Let's go! Now!"

As the elevator took us down, I said, "Listen. I gotta stop at the cage. You grab me a cab and get these bags into the trunk. Got it?" Then I slipped another ten off the roll and handed it to him. "Then, after the cab pulls away I want you to tell the Casino Manager that the guy in four-o-nine has left the fuckin' building. You got that?" I said as I handed him another ten.

"Yes sir."

As we passed the cashier's cage the bellman headed toward the front door and I emptied the Trop chips onto the counter.

The cashier was counting out the fifty-seven $100 bills when Joe Koonce walked up and stood behind her.

He looked at the clock on the wall.

Then he looked at me.

Before she could finish saying, "Have a nice day," I was on my way to the lobby.

The bellman had just finished putting the three suitcases into the trunk and the doorman was opening the rear door of the cab.

I handed the doorman $5, and said, "McCarran Airport. Now!" as I slid into the rear seat.

"McCarran! *Now!*" he loudly ordered to the cab driver.

I saw the steroid twins watching as the cab pulled away. I looked at my watch. I now had 45 minutes to be on a plane to New Jersey.

I had nothing to do but watch the minutes tick away.

With 26 minutes left, the car pulled up to the airport and the driver asked, "What airline?"

"*Fuck!*" I said to myself. "I don't have a ticket!"

I brought my hand up to my head and said, "Shit! I don't even know who has a flight going to Newark before noon. Oh, fuck it. Just drop me off at United."

As I inched my way up to the United counter, I looked over my shoulder to see if anyone was making sure I got out of town according to Mr. Smith's schedule.

"Good morning, sir. Can I help you?" the petite blonde asked.

"Yeah," I said…a little stressed. "I have to get to Newark."

She tapped a few buttons on her keyboard and said, "Our next flight to Newark isn't until two-forty-five, and scheduled to arrive at ten-fifteen this evening. Would you like smoking or non-smoking?"

"No! I have to get there sooner than that."

"I'm sorry, sir, but there's nothing departing for Newark any sooner. All of our morning flights have left already."

"How about to Kennedy or LaGuardia…or Philadelphia?"

She hit a few more keys and said, "LaGuardia departs at three-ten, and Kennedy departs at three-forty. Our Philadelphia flight left about 10 minutes ago."

"Shit!" I cursed under my breath. "I'm sorry," I apologized. "It's just…I have an emergency back east and have to get there right away. Listen, I don't care if you get me to Newark through Anchorage. Just get me out and on the way to Jersey startin' with your next flight."

She hit a few more keys and said, "I may be able to get you there by ten-thirty this evening, but you'll have to make two stops first...and hopefully none of your flights will be late or delayed so that you can make your connections."

"That's great, hon. What do I have to do?"

"There's a noon flight..." We both checked our watches. "...and they're boarding right now. I'll call and hold it for you. It's at gate nine. You should be able to make it." She was talking and filling out the ticket at the same time. "It's going to Denver. From Denver you'll have about fifteen minutes to get to United flight forty-seven to Chicago. From there, you'll have around twenty minutes before your flight to Newark. You should arrive around ten-thirty. Will that be okay?"

"That's great. How much?" I asked as I put a hand into my pocket to reach for the cash.

"Will that be round-trip?"

"One way."

"Smoking or--"

I interrupted her. "Non."

She told me the price and I paid from a roll of hundreds. She took my suitcases, handed me the ticket and I ran to the gate.

I was the last to board the plane.

As I settled into my seat I looked at my watch. I made it with less than a minute to spare.

Once the plane took off, I slowly started to relax, though I didn't know how I was going to explain to Dolan what had happened. Fortunately, Bobby was going to back me up when he got there. I even thought about the possibility that I may be dead by that time.

The plane arrived in Denver a few minutes earlier than expected and I had no problem getting to the connecting flight and into my seat.

As the passengers continued to board, I saw three guys from Bayonne taking assorted seats.

Once we were airborne, we met in the rear of the plane.

Each of them said that Bobby told them to get out of their hotel rooms, and out of town...*immediately.*

"Where's Bobby?" I asked.

"He couldn't get on the United flight with us, so he had to take American to Dallas. I don't know where he's going from there," said one of them.

"A couple of guys had to go through San Francisco on Continental, and a couple went through St. Louis on TWA," said another.

"Jesus! It's a friggin' exodus out of Vegas," I told them.

"What the fuck happened?" they each asked in a whisper. "All we were told was that they were on to us and we hadta get out in a hurry."

I said I was told the same thing.

A couple of hours later the plane landed at O'Hare, and the memories of Lady Millicent quickly came back to me. I sure could have used her now.

The four of us waited at the gate to catch our connection to Newark as Bobby Grant approached from his Dallas flight.

We didn't speak to one another until we were in the air.

The plane was a 707 stretch with a conference table in the rear, so once we took off, the five of us met at the table and started talking...and drinking.

"Listen," Bobby said in a whisper, "Nobody says a fuckin' thing to *anybody*. Got that? Dolan's gonna have to fix things. And he don't need people asking' him about it. Just keep your noses out of it, and when everything's up and runnin' again, we'll call ya's."

That was it. Nothing else was said about it for the rest of the flight.

We asked the stewardess for a deck of cards and another round of drinks.

It didn't take long for the alcohol to hit before Bobby and I went into our pockets and distributed twenty grand to each of the guys...and we began to play poker.

Within minutes, passengers and stewardesses formed around us as we were betting thousands of dollars on each hand.

Knowing that it would all be thrown back into the Bayonne-bound kitty, we'd think nothing of raising a thousand or two on a pair of three's.

Even in the air...we were gambling with someone else's money.

By 10:55 that evening we were standing around the baggage carousel in Newark Airport. Bobby and I went over to a payphone and called The Irishman, waking him from a deep sleep.

His voice was high and raspy as he answered, "Hello?"

"I'm sorry to wake you. It's me."

It took him a few seconds to recognize my voice.

"Kid. What's up?"

"I'm at Newark Airport with, uhm..." I couldn't say his name on the phone, so I handed it to Bobby.

"Hey, it's me."

"What's the matter?" Dolan asked.

"We had a problem. That guy from California fucked up. Things got crazy. We all had to leave, and you're gonna have a problem back there."

"Don't leave the airport. I'll pick you and the kid up in a half hour."

Bobby told him what terminal we were at and that we'd be waiting.

Forty minutes or so later, Bobby and I threw our suitcases into the trunk of a green Town Car and I was introduced to Dolan's driver and enforcer, George Lyman. The Irishman was in the front passenger seat and Bobby and I were in the back.

I explained what happened at the girls' house and what Rick had said. Bobby covered me and told Dolan that Rick confirmed his actions. Then I told them what happened when Mr. Smith brought me out to the desert, and I relayed the message exactly as it was told to me, *especially* the part where he said, "And tell Casiano to keep Tommy Dolan outta this town!" I didn't think there was a need to tell him about the "Irish cocksucker" part.

"*Shit!*" Dolan yelled, in his deep growl.

"I'm sorry, Tommy. I tried to get Rick to shut up. But he just kept talking."

"It's not your fault, kid. I'll take care of that idiot. Don't worry about *him* anymore."

His statement immediately shut me up. If he was that mad at Rick... how did he feel about me? How did he feel about the bearer of bad news?

Bobby and I turned over the cash and chips and they drove me home.

Again, it wasn't until I saw my father's driveway that I felt safe.

As I was getting out of the car, I asked, "What do we do now, Tommy? I owe five casinos a hundred-and-twenty-five grand."

He said, "I gotta talk to Casiano and see what we can do. Your lines'll be taken care of. Don't worry about that. But I gotta see if we can get this problem fixed and get everybody back out there...*soon*."

I took my suitcases out of the trunk and said goodnight.

That was the last trip we ever made to Vegas.

That was it...the end of another era. One of the greatest times of my life...and one of the greatest scams to hit Las Vegas...and it ended because some low-level idiot opened his mouth and wouldn't shut up.

And because of that, the rules changed.

The management of each of the Vegas casinos, along with the Nevada Gaming Commission, got wind of what we were doing and how we were doing it. Within a year, laws were written and enacted, not just by the Gaming Commission, but by the states of Nevada and New Jersey.

After that, the guidelines to obtain a credit line became extremely strict, often needing a certified check in the casino's account before they'd comp the gambler *anything*. After the shit hit the fan, *nobody* was able to get a credit line based on the limited information that *we* used to give them.

We changed the way the old casinos ran their businesses. From that point on...corporations and accounting firms began handling the books. And with *their* paperwork? The mob *never* would have had a chance of scamming them.

It also meant that Dolan and Casiano's plan for scamming the Jersey casinos was now nothing but a dream.

Casiano was *pissed!*

In a private meeting at Andrew Herschfeld's office, I was exonerated, thanks in large part to Bobby Grant's verification about Rick's admission of fucking up.

Then Casiano and Dolan thanked me for getting Rick out of the house before he could open his big-mouth even more...and for bringing back Mr. Smith's message without saying *anything* about *anyone* to the Casino Manager or whoever 'Mr. Smith' *was*...considering that my life was being threatened at the time.

But what scared me most was when Casiano rose from his chair, walked over and kissed me on the cheek, then said, "Sally, make sure he gets to his car."

I was positive the "thank you's" were bullshit and I was being set up for the hit that was about to take place.

As Sal and I walked out of the building, he said, "I was listening to everything they said to you, Jon. I'm impressed."

I looked at him. He didn't call me *kid*.

He continued, "Every time something comes up where they need to count on you...you come through. You always seem to do what's right...as if you weren't tryin' at all."

"I was scared shit, Sal. When I was out in that desert with those guys...I didn't know *what* to expect. And if I didn't get out of Vegas in time, I wouldn't be here right now. I'd have some friggin' cactus as a headstone."

"You did what you were supposed to do. You let Bobby know what went down. You got that dumb-California-fuck out of a situation that could have gotten worse. He may have mentioned Dolan's name, and the Feds would have tied him in with Rocco...and that would have been bad for *all* of us, especially with all the heat he's been under the last few months. And best of all, you got this guy *Rick* to admit to Bobby that he fucked up...which cleared you."

Fortunately, Rick never said anything about the weed.

"So," he continued, "I give you a lot of credit. I think you're a stand up guy, and I want you to know that. I know I can count on *you*, and I want you to feel the same about *me*. Capice?"

I just nodded and smiled. What else could I do or say to respond. I *still* thought I was about to get whacked.

When we reached my car he leaned down and embraced me.

If the hit was going to happen...it would happen now. But he turned and walked back to the attorney's office.

I stood there...afraid to move...until he was out of sight.

Three weeks later the Newport Beach police found Rick Rogers' body floating in his hot tub, riddled with a dozen bullet holes.

I decided I needed a vacation from these guys.

The first Atlantic City casino, Resorts International, opened in May of 1978. The following year, Bally's Park Place and Caesars, which was originally the Boardwalk Regency, came to town. By the early '80s, casino openings proliferated along the boardwalk and the bay. One at a time they rose. Harrah's Marina, The Sands, The Golden Nugget, The Claridge and The Tropicana.

Casiano had money coming in from the construction and labor unions working in A.C., but friction between him and Philadelphia's 'Little Nicky' Scarfo would cause the occasional body to wash ashore or be found in an oil drum at a construction site.

The Commission saw it as more unnecessary heat from the State and the Feds.

I spent the next couple of years wrapped up in my music and working sessions all around the country.

Sure...nothing compared to those 26 months I had experienced...my cousin Jerry, Mike and Taz, Rocco Casiano, the scam, the women, the cash, Lady Millicent...and living like *King Shit* just like Jerry said I would.

But it wasn't *too* hard to keep my distance either...as everyone else was preoccupied.

Jerry was on the other side of the continent running a restaurant. I went to see him and his family about once a year...but he still wouldn't answer the question.

The Vegas scam was over...and I certainly didn't have plans of going back *there* for any reason. I don't look good covered in sand.

Mike Caruso was working for Dolan, and Taz was running a chain of motels for himself and the Ranouro Brothers.

Dolan had several check-cashing offices and got heavily into running the ports...often strong-arming the stevedore companies.

Stevedore companies ran the loading and unloading of ships docked in the port. And since The Irishman ran the Jersey ports...it was easy for him to collect his piece from the companies for the assurance that there would be peace with the labor unions...which his childhood friend, Rocco Casiano, was reputed to control.

Rocco had *other* problems. Staying out of the media was one of them.

On Friday, November 21, 1980, my father called me at the Studio City house.

"You watching the news?"

"Me? The news? No," I laughed. "Why?"

"Check out what's happening in Vegas," he said just before he hung up.

I flipped through a channel or two before the screen lit up with images of smoke and fire.

The MGM Grand was ablaze.

I watched as the cameras zoomed in on the same marquee that I stood under more times than I could remember. Thick black and brown smoke rushed out of the front doors and windows of rooms on the lower floors. Then...the camera panned up showing the upper balconies. It wasn't hard to see the people standing on them, beckoning to the helicopters that were shuttling others off the roof. I knew one of those 25th floor balconies was mine.

Yes...it was still mine...even though I hadn't been there in three years.

A woman who was in the casino when the fire started told a reporter, "There was a roar...like an explosion...with smoke and flames coming out of the restaurant area at the rear of the casino."

A spokesman for the fire department said most of the devastation, which included an unknown number of people who had been immediately incinerated by the blast, was in the area of a lounge that overlooked the casino. He pointed to a floorplan to show where the restaurants were and where the flames exploded into the public area...right through the lounge.

I knew exactly where he was talking about...it was *our* lounge. It was our lookout perch.

It was the lounge where Jerry and I had our first bottle of Dom Perignon on my 22nd birthday. It was where I first met Tommy Dolan. It was from where my Godfather watched as I gambled with three beautiful women wrapped around me. It was where I had spent hours talking to the guys and killing time...during one of the best times of my life.

Who knows? Had the scam still been running, I may have been sitting there when the explosion happened.

I sat in front of the television screen until they went to a commercial... then I drove to Malibu and sat on the beach where I want my ashes spread and stared at the ocean for hours.

Two weeks and three days later, I was hit with more devastating news while hanging out with my friend John '*Jad*' DeFillipis in the basement recording studio at my father's house. Only two days earlier, Jad was contracted to be John Lennon's Road Manager for the long awaited Milk & Honey Tour to promote the newly released *Double Fantasy* album.

It was the evening of Monday, December 8. My manager called to ask if I was listening to the radio or watching television.

"No. I'm just hangin' with a friend. Why?"

"Turn on the radio," he said before he hung up.

I flipped on WNEW-FM and listened as the stunned New York disc-jockey, Vince Scelsa, gave us the bad news.

John Lennon had been shot and killed by a deranged fan.

Everything suddenly came to a halt.

The following morning I went into New York City and dropped off a letter to Yoko and Sean at The Dakota. Then I drove to Newark Airport and flew to LAX. Once I got off the plane I rented a car, drove to Malibu and sat on the beach until well past sunset. I returned to New Jersey the following day...in an emotional fog.

Left-and-right, important 'eras' in my life seemed to be coming to their end. And each was more painful than the last.

Early January of 1982 brought the end of another era when the California D'Amore's closed the doors of The Villa Capri for the last time. Gone were the studio-exec meetings and the candlelit dinners of rendezvousing movie stars...all that was left were the memories of more than four decades.

It had been nearly six-and-a-half years since Patsy died, and the corner of Yucca and McCadden was no longer in a good area of Hollywood. In fact, at that time...there weren't many good areas of old Hollywood left.

Then on January 19 of that year, and after a life that included five attractive and much younger wives, Patsy's brother Franklyn passed away of natural causes at 90 years old.

Throughout the early '80s, Rocco Casiano did whatever he could to keep a low profile and was in the papers only a quarter as much as he used to be.

The Commission still wasn't happy with that and thought it was too much exposure.

But Casiano had other problems...problems that were more important than his court cases.

Apparently, one evening in the middle of December, 1985, around five o'clock, while going out for a nice steak dinner, Big Paulie Castellano, the leader of the Gambino family, along with his bodyguard, Tommy Bilotti, was shot and killed outside of Manhattan's Sparks Restaurant. Castellano's position was filled by the man who was eventually convicted of arranging his murder: John Gotti.

Once in his new position, Gotti started to make moves into northern Jersey...primarily in Bergen and Hudson County.

Casiano was heard to say, "If Jerry and Vinnie were here, they'd never let that happen, I can tell you that," and brought his complaint of 'territory infringement' to The Commission.

It would be a battle that would take time to resolve.

By November, 1987, Rocco Casiano was once again on the front page of the papers and on the evening news. This time the Feds charged him with racketeering, claiming he ran the Hudson County waterfront.

Also charged in the same case...for racketeering and extortion of a stevedore company in exchange for labor peace...was Tommy Dolan.

This time, Casiano was claiming he wasn't mentally competent to stand trial...even going as far as appearing to have a heart attack in court, then blaming it on the Feds for putting the stress of the trial on an innocent man.

And he thought *I* had balls?

There were entire days when he would stare out the courtroom window, appearing oblivious to what was taking place inside, not even responding to the prosecutor's or the judge's questions.

Each afternoon Casiano would be cited for contempt. But the following morning his lawyer would produce a doctor, or a psychiatrist, or a neurologist...all testifying to Casiano's inability to deal with the proceedings due to some possible boxing injury from decades earlier.

Also watching and reading about the trial were Vincente Gigante and the rest of the family heads that ran things from Philly to Rhode Island. They all started saying the same thing; Rocco Casiano is making too much unwanted noise...and he's got to be told to stop.

Casiano was summoned to upstate New York for a sit-down with The Chin and Consigliere Roberto Musarra. In so many words he was told to stop making headlines, and if he had to go to jail...then go to jail. Do the time. His wife and daughter would be taken care of until he got out, and then he'd get his territory back. But first and foremost...*shut up*.

There was no option. He was told what to do.

But there was a problem.

Rocco Casiano didn't *want* to give up his territory, even temporarily... and he *certainly* didn't want to go to jail.

Over the Christmas holidays he once again made the daily papers. Only this time, he really *did* have a heart attack, causing the trial to be postponed until he was physically capable of appearing in court.

Of course, it wasn't long before he was running everything from a bed in Saddle Brook's General Hospital. By the end of the first week, his room looked like the backroom of any union office in Hudson County.

His captains, all of them smoking cigarettes, would be walking in and out of his room as they conversed with their lieutenants who were standing outside of his door. The lieutenants would then wander throughout the hospital's halls using different payphones to cryptically relay orders to their people.

But the bosses on The Commission weren't happy about the way things were turning out. Rocco wasn't following their orders of keeping a low profile and staying out of the spotlight.

Rocco Casiano was no longer one of the Genovese family's favorite sons.

He wasn't doing what he was told. He wasn't doing the right thing.

By March of 1988, Casiano was released from his doctor's care and the Federal trial was scheduled to start the next month.

No sooner did it begin before he was miraculously acquitted of the racketeering charges...but The Irishman was found guilty.

Dolan was told to get his affairs in order as he would be sentenced within the next several weeks. He was facing up to ten years in prison.

I was in San Francisco during the last week of April when the phone in my hotel room rang.

"Kid?" the recognizable voice asked.

It was Rocco Casiano.

"Yeah. What's the matter? You okay?"

"I'm fine. I got the number from your father. I hope that's all right?"

He was asking *me* if it was all right?

"Yeah, sure. What's wrong?"

"When you comin' home?"

"I don't know. A week or so. This is a big session. Why?"

"I got somethin' I need you to listen to when you get back. Think you can do that for me?"

"Sure. As soon as I get back. No problem." I paused, then asked, "You okay? You don't sound good."

"There's a lot goin' on," he answered. "I'll tell you when I see you. Let The Tailor know when you get back, and I'll come over to your father's house. All right?"

"Sure."

Then he hung up.

On Thursday morning, May 5, I called Al The Tailor and told him I was back in Jersey. Less than two hours later, Casiano, alone, pulled into the driveway in a brown Buick.

When I answered the door, he was standing there holding a large cardboard box.

"Jesus, Rocco! You look like shit...with all due respect."

I ushered him in, took the heavy box from his arms and led him down to the basement studio.

As I went through the box's contents of audio cassettes and reams of paper, he began to explain.

"They're comin' at me again...and they're gonna keep comin' 'til they get me." Then he pointed to the box and said, "These are copies of all the tapes and transcripts the State and the Feds have on me. I need you to find something. I need you to see if they edited any of 'em. You gotta find something. You gotta do that for me."

I wondered if the State and Federal prosecutors were crazy or stupid enough to make the same mistake twice. I didn't think so.

Then he went into his jacket pocket and took out an envelope. It had $5,000 in it.

He handed it to me, then put his big, strong arms on my shoulders and whispered, "This is for listenin'. If you find somethin' that gets me off...I'll set you up in a business and you'll never have to work again for the rest of your life."

I stared at the box and the distraught man in front of me, then I handed the envelope back to him and said, "I'll...I'll do whatever I can. But it's not for *this*. I'll do it because it's for *la famiglia*, the *family*, not for the reward... and because it's the right thing to do. *That's* what I was always taught, Rocco."

A smile came across his worried face, then he said, "You know somethin', Jon? When your cousin asked me to look after you, he told me somethin'. He said you were a good guy, a stand-up guy...trustworthy." He paused a few seconds as he looked around the room, and then continued. "He was right."

I was happy just to hear him call me *Jon*.

"You wanna come to dinner with me tonight?" he asked. "I gotta see Dolan about somethin'. Nothin' too important, so it'd be no problem if you wanna come. You can meet us at the restaurant in Kearny."

I thought about it, but decided to decline.

"No thanks, Rocco. I'm gonna stay home and start listening to these tapes. I should get to work on them as soon as possible."

He appreciated my dedication, then leaned over and kissed me.

At seven o'clock that evening, Salvatore Della Osa tapped the remote button in his pocket and the electric door to Mrs. Todisco's garage opened. George Lyman slowly and carefully backed in his green Lincoln. Della Osa tapped the button again and the door closed. Then, like good soldiers, they waited for their boss.

A few moments earlier, Rocco Casiano was sliding on his gold pinky ring and adjusting his gray sport coat. He counted out $2,500, mostly in hundreds and fifties, folded it into two wads, wrapped each with a rubber band and put them into his pants pocket. He didn't carry a wallet. He *never* did.

He walked out the back of his mother's house and through the gate into Mrs. Todisco's backyard. He followed the path under the trellis to the rear door of the garage and walked in.

He immediately noticed that it wasn't *Sal's* Town Car. As he approached the passenger side, he looked in to see Lyman in the driver's seat, with Dolan sitting behind him. Seated next to Dolan in the back seat was Salvatore Della Osa.

Casiano looked into the open window and said, "What the fuck is this?"

"Oh Jeez, Rocco! Christ! You scared me!" the big Irishman said. "I was tellin' Sal about that horse down in Freehold. We didn't know you'd be right on time. Sorry. Come on, get in! Let me finish telling him this story. We'll be at the restaurant in fifteen minutes anyway, and it'll take me that long to tell it."

Casiano made a face that showed he was pissed off, but considering Dolan and Della Osa were his closest people, and the restaurant *was* only 15 minutes away...he opened the door and slid into the front seat.

The garage door opened as Della Osa tapped the remote in his pocket.

"I'm glad to see you remembered the remote, Sal. Now where the fuck is *your* car?" Casiano asked.

"Tune up and new tires. Remember? I told you last week," Sal answered.

Casiano looked pissed and pointed forward as Lyman pulled the car out of the garage.

As they turned into the street, Lyman looked into the rear view mirror and said, "Shit, Sal! The friggin' door didn't close."

Casiano said, "Sal. Hit the button."

"I did," the bodyguard responded, "The battery musta died."

Casiano said to Lyman, "Stop the car and go hit the button, will ya?"

Lyman got out, walked into the garage and tapped on the wall button. As the garage door closed, he walked to the side door to exit. But once he was out of view and before he returned to the car, he took a small roll of cotton out of his jacket pocket and stuffed a little into his left ear.

Lyman got back in and began driving. Casiano sat back and listened to Dolan.

"...and he's got a jockey who says he could inject this shit into the horse just before they go to the gate..."

The car cruised along a quiet street in Kearny as Dolan continued talking. But as he spoke, both he and Salvatore began to fill their ears with pieces of cotton.

Drops of rain began to streak the windows, so Lyman turned on the windshield wipers.

Casiano could see the lights of the restaurant a few of blocks away and said to Lyman, "Madone, I'm hungry."

"...so we make a deal with the cocksucker. The day of the race we *all* have a shitload of cash on this horse to win..."

As Dolan rambled on, Salvatore slowly pulled the .45 caliber Colt from inside his jacket and put it about two inches from Rocco's head.

"...They're at the gate. The bell rings and they take off...except for this fuckin' horse. He drops dead *right there at the fuckin' gate!*"

Lyman, Casiano and Dolan were laughing as Sal looked out each side window to make sure there were no cars next to them, then quietly said, "*Poowf!*"...and fired the first shot.

The blast was *LOUD.*

Lyman screamed and grabbed his right ear.

The powerful .45 slug tore the top of the boss's skull in two, blowing his scalp, along with pieces of bone and brains into the front window.

Casiano's head jerked forward and then back against the headrest. A second shot blew out his left eye. Blood splattered all over the dashboard and across the windshield.

Lyman momentarily couldn't see and had to wipe the blood, brains and bone fragments from the glass. Rain began to leak in from the two bullet holes in the windshield.

Amazingly, Casiano wasn't dead yet.

He somehow contorted his body to face his assassin and looked at him as if to say, "Et tu, Salvatore?" Then he raised his hand to protect himself.

Sal didn't want to see the face of the man he had once loved, respected and worked for...and was now killing, so he fired again. This time the bullet went through Casiano's hand and hit him in the chest, causing blood to shoot across the car, spraying the passengers in the back.

Della Osa had had enough. He leaned over the front seat, pinned the near-lifeless body against the dashboard and fired another five bullets into the head and face of Rocco Casiano.

The boss was dead.

Dead...because he didn't abide by his own rule.

Several days before he murdered Casiano, Salvatore Della Osa was awakened by the doorbell just as the sun rose above the horizon. He lived in Holmdel, no more than ten minutes from his boss's home, as all good bodyguards and right-hands do.

Outside of Sal's immediate family, Casiano was the only person with a remote control to get through the gate.

Holding his .45 and wearing a robe, Sal went to the front door and barked into the intercom, "Who's there?"

"Salvatore, it's me," the voice responded from the outside.

It was *not* his boss's voice.

"Who the fuck's *me?* And how'd you get through the gate?"

"Listen to me...open the door. It's important. Somebody...somebody important...wants to talk to you. *Now.*"

Sal thought he recognized the voice.

"Mondu? Is that you?"

"Yeah. Now open the fuckin' door."

Della Osa cocked the pistol's hammer and slowly unlocked and opened the door.

Armand 'Mondu' Guardino, the deliverer of messages from The Commission, was standing there. Behind him was a Cadillac limousine.

"Somebody wants to talk to you," Guardino said, then stood aside so Sal could see the limo.

The rear electric window went down to reveal the face of Consigliere Roberto Musarra.

Sal immediately knew that whatever was going to be said...was going to be important. The Consigliere didn't come all the way down to Holmdel shortly after sunrise just to have coffee.

"Does he want to come in?" Sal quietly and respectfully asked Mondu.

"He wants to go for a ride."

They both looked down at Sal's robe.

"Right *now?* Like *this?*"

Mondu shook his head.

Sal nervously said, "Tell him I'll be dressed and ready in ten minutes."

Just before Sal closed the door, Guardino called out, "Oh, Sally? One more thing."

Sal stopped and looked at him.

Mondu smiled and said, "Keep the cannon at home."

Sal respectfully nodded and gently closed the door.

Less than ten minutes later Della Osa was dressed and seated next to Roberto Musarra.

The driver tapped a button, the gate opened and the limo pulled into the street.

"How'd you get the code to the gate?" Sal asked Mondu, who was seated across from them.

Mondu just smiled.

Sal smiled back, realizing that these guys could get into any place they wanted.

The Consigliere looked at him, and with an Italian accent that accentuated the vowel at the end of Sal's name, said, "Salvatore." Sal turned and looked at Musarra as he continued, "As you know, there's concern from up-above about Rocco."

Sal lowered his head. He knew where this conversation was going, yet he had no option but to hear it...and obey.

"If he had only listened," Musarra said as he angrily clasped his hands and shook them up and down. "He was asked. Months ago, he was asked to do what was right. To do what would be best for *all* of us." The Consigliere's voice began to shake and get louder as he continued, "This publicity, these newspaper articles...these antics in the courtroom. This is wrong, Salvatore. This is *very* wrong."

Sal's head rose and their eyes connected.

"The Commission has...made a decision. Rocco's become too much of a risk. Too much of a burden for us to care for. Too much of a...come-se-dice? How-you-say? Renegade? A renegade. A *wise guy!* We can't have that. We need someone who's respected. Someone who can take care of things the way they *used to* be taken care of." Then he looked deep into Sal's eyes and asked, "Capice? Do you understand what I mean, Salvatore?"

Sal knew *exactly* what he meant.

The Commission had sanctioned the removal of Rocco Casiano.

There was only one answer that Della Osa could give.

"Si, Consigliere. I understand."

With those words, Salvatore Della Osa had just made an agreement with The Commission that he would relieve them of their burden, and for doing that...he would become 'the boss of northern New Jersey.'

Sal quickly ran things through his head.

If Jerry were still around, it would have been *him* sitting in the limo with Musarra.

Dolan, on the other hand, would never have been made this offer *regardless* of his power or money-making abilities. Everyone always knew that.

Salvatore knew he alone was the next logical choice. He had the muscle and the balls. He knew all of Casiano's underbosses and union contacts... and they respected him. He knew everything about Casiano's operation.

And he knew how to show respect to the people above him.

In time, he would know how to run everything as efficiently as Casiano did...but without the problems.

Sal was told to go to a bakery in Staten Island to meet Dickie Pignatello, and "...a couple of other guys." They would walk him through certain details and be his only contact to Musarra until "after the package was delivered."

The limo eventually returned to Della Osa's driveway. The driver tapped the remote button and the gate opened. Sal took Musarra's hand and kissed it. In return, Musarra kissed Sal on the cheek.

The contract was now signed.

Sal drove his Cadillac Seville to Staten Island, walked into the back of the bakery and shook hands with Dickie Pignatello. Dickie was around 43, and served as a go-between for The Commission and the underbosses. Sal knew Dickie from the meetings he attended with Casiano.

"Sal," Dickie said, while pointing to the two men standing behind him, "For obvious reasons...it's best you don't know the names of these two guys. You understand?"

Sal nodded. He knew that when a hit like this was going to happen, *advisors* would be brought in as liaisons to those above. They were there to make sure the plan went down exactly as ordered by The Commission.

Dickie continued, "From this point on, they're just *friends* of *our friend*. And what *they* say is just as good as it coming from *him*. Got that?"

Sal nodded. He knew the friend Dickie was talking about was Vincente Gigante.

"And what they see...*he* sees. Understand?"

Sal nodded again.

Sal drove the two men to the Truck Haven Rest in Carlstadt, New Jersey, where they gave him a .38 caliber revolver.

"This is clean. The serial number's been filed off. It can't be traced. Use it close...and use it all," he was told.

Sal walked into the high weeds of the swamp behind the restaurant and test fired the gun several times.

With each shot...he thought harder, and his mind began to fill with the desire and power of becoming *the boss*.

But he didn't like the .38. He wanted to use his .45. He trusted his .45.

They told him to use the .38. And they told him how to get rid of it after it was used.

Over the next several days, Salvatore began putting his plan together.

He needed another friendly face.

Someone Rocco trusted.

Sal needed to have a diversion so that he could physically be behind the boss when the time came for the hit.

For *this* hit...Sal couldn't do it face-to-face.

After more than a decade of working for Casiano...he deeply loved and respected the man. He knew he couldn't bring himself to face Rocco when it was time to kill him. Sal was angry at himself for having to do it that way.

He requested a sit-down with Dickie Pignatello, and a plan was put together.

The two liaisons agreed with Sal's plan, and they were never seen again.

One night in early May, from a payphone in Jersey City, Tommy Dolan received a call from Pignatello. The Irishman was told to get George Lyman and go to a restaurant called The Dug Out in North Bergen...and tell no one.

The Irishman didn't ask why. He knew not to. He just knew that a call from Pignatello meant it was going to be important.

When Dolan and Lyman entered the restaurant, they were brought to a back room guarded by three six-foot-plus, well-dressed monsters. One of them frisked Lyman, relieving him of a 9mm Beretta.

Lyman gave it up without an argument.

Seated at a large, comfortable booth were Roberto Musarra and Salvatore Della Osa.

Dolan and Lyman quickly scanned the room. There were no rolling coat closets visible. That made them feel better. But as they sat down, they were still very nervous.

"Tommy," Musarra quietly said, "I've asked you here for a reason. It's a reason that must never leave this table. What I'm about to tell you has come from *the top*. The *very* top. Do you understand?"

Dolan nodded as the Consigliere softly continued, "I hope we can count on your assistance."

The Irishman looked at Della Osa and asked, "What's this about, Sally?"

But instead, Musarra quietly answered, "Salvatore is about to move up in our family. In *la famiglia*. Capice?"

Tommy Dolan immediately understood.

Rocco Casiano, his friend since childhood, was about to be removed from power.

But why was *he* being told about it?

Again, the big Irishman and his enforcer scanned the room for a closet.

"Tommy," Della Osa said in a whisper, "It's been decided...from way above you and me...that Rocco's become too much of a liability. Over the past year, The Commission's been telling him to back off. Even to do his time in the can if he had to. They wanted him to just back off and cut the publicity. But he didn't. You *know* that."

Dolan silently stared at Della Osa.

Della Osa stared back at the large man sitting before him and softly said, "I've been asked to fix the problem and take control."

There was a moment of silence before Dolan whispered, "And what do you want from me?"

"When the time comes to do what I have to do...I want you with me. You and George."

Everyone sat quiet and motionless as they thought of the enormity of what was being said.

Sal broke the silence as he whispered, "And then after that...I want you to be my closest underboss...just as you were with Rocco."

Dolan was angry. He had always been a big moneymaker, not just with Vegas, the docks and airports, but with a territory that *always* brought in a profit. He was angry at being passed over by The Commission for this young tough-guy. He was also angry that within the next couple of weeks he would be sentenced for his racketeering conviction.

But Tommy knew the rules. He knew it for years. He knew he'd never be treated as an equal to the Italians. It was just that it really *was* his turn and he wanted what he felt should be his rightful position.

Sal knew he needed Dolan on his side. And in order to do that, he needed to give him something for his loyalty. He also had to take into consideration that Dolan was pissed off about being overlooked because he wasn't Italian.

"For doing this with me," Sal said...still very quietly, "You'll get Staten Island."

Dolan's eyes widened as he looked at Musarra and Della Osa. The Irishman took a long, deep breath before he softly responded, "Don't you think the Gambinos are going to have somethin' to say about that? And besides...my lawyer's tellin' me I'm goin' away for at least six or seven years."

The Consigliere got up from the table and said, "I think *that* is something Salvatore wants to speak to you privately about. I'll be back in a few minutes." Then he left the room.

The three conspirators huddled together in a very tight circle and spoke in whispers.

Sal began, "Tommy, there's people above us who know what you've done for them over the years. I have their assurance that for your loyalty... your time in the can is gonna be minimal. Two, two-and-a-half years...the most. And you won't have to go in for at least another six months. Maybe even a year."

Dolan raised his eyebrows but didn't say anything. He knew there would be a catch somewhere.

Sal continued, "If something were to happen to Rocco..." he paused and took a breath. He couldn't believe he was going to say what was about to come out of his mouth, "...It would appear that it was a hit by the Gambinos. Rocco and Gotti have been pissing each other off big-time for a year or so now. Gotti's been trying to move into north Jersey...everybody knows that. And everybody knows Rocco had a justifiable reason when he bitched to The Commission about it. So if he disappears...all fingers are gonna point to Gotti...not to us. On the other hand, The Commission will appreciate that we did our own...house cleaning."

"He's been too public," Dolan interjected. "All the families know he's been called on the carpet by the big guy for makin' too much noise. That's no secret, either. They'd *know* the hit came from within. And how you figure Gotti's gonna let me walk in and take Staten Island? How's that gonna happen?"

"We're gonna take care of him, too."

Dolan and Lyman sat back. They couldn't believe what they just heard Sal say.

Sal motioned them closer and softly said, "Getting rid of Casiano is only the beginning. Once word gets out about Gotti killing Rocco without any approval, it'll start a war...and who the fuck wants a war? So no one's gonna question it when Gotti gets whacked. Once he's gone...the war will be over, and we'll look like the good guys after the dust settles. Gotti'll be gone, and you'll have Staten Island...and you'll have it when you get out of the joint, too. You have my word."

"Upstairs know about this?" Dolan asked.

Sal paused a few seconds, looked at The Irishman's blue eyes and quietly said, "You think Roberto Musarra would be here if they didn't?"

Dolan knew that to be true.

He asked, "What do you want from me, Sally?"

In a whisper, Sal explained how he needed to have George drive his car while Dolan and Della Osa sat in the back talking, causing a trusting Casiano to sit in the front. Sal would take care of the rest.

Again, Dolan leaned back into his seat...thinking hard.

Rocco Casiano was one of his oldest friends. Rocco brought him in and gave him the ability to have a very comfortable life.

But this was *business*. And Dolan knew that as long as it was sanctioned from above...there was no option. There was nothing he could do to get them to change their minds. He was just grateful no one was discussing *his* elimination.

After another moment, Dolan looked at Sal...and gave a nod. That was all.

But that was all Sal needed.

It meant Dolan bought into the plan.

Roberto Musarra returned to the table and asked, "So...is the *first* problem taken care of?"

All the men nodded.

The Commission's representative looked at Sal and asked, "And the *other* matter?"

Sal nodded...meaning Dolan was *in* on the Gotti plot.

Musarra sat down, looked at Dolan and Lyman, extended his hand to them and said, "Good. Good," as they shook. Then he looked at Sal and quietly said, "We want the first part of this to happen within the week. Capice?"

Sal nodded.

In less than a week...*he* would be the new boss.

Musarra rose from the table and kissed Sal. Then he shook hands with the non-Italians, and left the restaurant...but not before one of the men guarding the room handed Lyman back his Beretta...without its clip of ammunition.

The three of them sat quietly for several minutes before Dolan and Lyman rose from the table.

The large Irishman opened his arms and embraced Della Osa in a new show of respect.

Nothing was said. It was a hard moment for these three men, each of whom had come to love and respect Rocco Casiano. But they also knew that Rocco had become his own worst enemy.

George Lyman bowed as he shook and clasped Della Osa's hand. Then he and Dolan left the restaurant.

Salvatore Della Osa sat at the table for a while. He had a lot on his mind.

What he didn't know was that the FBI had a microphone wired into the light fixture four feet above his head, and it transmitted to a tape recorder in an apartment across the street.

Casiano's dead body was crumpled and lying upside-down on the floor of George's Lincoln as blood still oozed out of the large bullet holes that perforated his head and chest. Rain water dripped off the dashboard and mixed with the blood.

Lyman was now driving from Kearny to the swamps of Carlstadt. Remnants of Casiano's skull were spread across the dashboard and shattered windshield.

Between the smell of gunpowder and Casiano's blood and excrement, the stench in the car was so foul they quickly opened all of the windows just to breathe. The rain blew in, but they didn't care.

Once they got to the Truck Haven Rest, Lyman drove the Lincoln through the parking lot to the edge of the swamp. Then he popped open the trunk from which Salvatore removed a large pair of fireman's gloves and a body-bag.

Dolan and Lyman watched as Della Osa stood in the rain and pulled the bloodied body from the car and laid it in the mud. He reached into the pants pockets and pulled out a set of keys and the two wads of cash. He took the keys and threw them as far as he could into the weeds...and stuffed the cash back into the pockets. Then he loosened Casiano's belt buckle, pulled down the zipper, opened Rocco's pants and turned the body over so that its bullet-riddled face was in the mud. Della Osa then pulled down Casiano's pants to expose the dead boss's ass.

"George, you got the card?" the new boss asked Lyman.

Lyman didn't answer. He was staring and appalled by what he saw. Casiano...dead, his blown-away face lying in the mud, his pants were pulled down and his ass was sticking out. He couldn't believe the disrespect that was being shown to someone so deeply admired by these three men... these three men that had just killed him.

"Hey! *You got the card?*" Sal barked.

Lyman jumped and said, "Yeah," as he reached into his blood stained jacket, "Yeah...here it is."

He walked over to Sal and handed him a brand new Visa card. Sal looked at it. Even in the dark, he could see the shiny gold letters that spelled out *Rocco Casiano*.

Casiano never had a credit card in his life. Lyman got it from a contact in Queens.

To make the plan more plausible, the card was obtained through an insider from Gotti's people. It would undoubtedly be traced back to their credit card counterfeiting operation...adding more to the Gotti factor.

The card had another purpose. When and if the police found Casiano's body, it would be so mutilated and decomposed that the card would let them know who it was.

Sal took it, wiped off Lyman's fingerprints and slid it in the crack of the dead man's ass. Then he turned the body over, pulled up the pants, closed the zipper and buckled the belt.

He opened the body-bag, lifted the nearly-200-pound ex-boxer and dropped him in. As the body hit the ground, Della Osa saw the devastation that was done to his former boss's face and he quickly turned around to vomit.

It angered him that the other men had seen this.

Once the body-bag was zippered, he called over his two accomplices. They donned gloves from the trunk and carried the corpse to a small concrete blockhouse on the edge of the swamp. A padlock was used to secure it once Casiano's body was dumped inside, then Della Osa threw the key into a nearby stream of murky water.

As the key sank into the mud the transition of power had begun. Tommy Dolan said to Salvatore Della Osa, "You're the boss now."

And he was. Salvatore Della Osa was now the boss.

They stood motionless for a few moments, their feet wallowing in mud and their clothes and faces splattered with the blood of a beloved comrade-in-arms that they had just assassinated. This was not where one expected a coronation or crowning to take place.

But that was this business.

Before Dolan and Della Osa walked to their cars, which had been parked there hours before the hit, Sal said to George Lyman, "Get rid of your car before sunrise. I never want to see that fuckin' thing again. You hear me?"

There were no handshakes. There were no kisses or hugs. There were just three men...covered in mud, blood and rain.

Within an hour, Lyman's Lincoln was in a Newark salvage yard under the Jersey Turnpike. It was shredded into strips of unidentifiable metal and by sunrise it was on a barge filled with garbage on its way to be dumped several miles out into the Atlantic Ocean.

As they each drove home, Salvatore Della Osa and Tommy Dolan wept. That was Thursday, May 5, 1988.

I was in my basement studio when Al Nucci called on Wednesday, May 11.

"Hey kid. Have you heard from him lately?"

Just by the way he said it, I knew he meant Casiano.

"No, why? Is he asking if I've called about the tapes yet?"

"No. That's not the problem," Al said. "*Nobody's* heard from him since last Thursday."

I thought for a second and answered, "That's when he was h--" and then I shut up. I wasn't going to say *anything* over the phone. "You, uhm... you want me to stop by?"

"Yeah. Yeah, kid. As soon as you can."

And then he hung up.

Less than an hour later I walked through the front door of Al's tailor shop and was immediately stopped and frisked by a guy I had never seen before.

Al saw me and yelled, "No! No! He's okay! Leave him alone!"

He came over and we hugged and kissed.

"What's going on, Al?" I asked as I was led downstairs.

"Around a week ago, Rocco went missing. After a couple of days, his wife went to the Bayonne police and filed a Missing Persons report. He was supposed to be at his attorney's office the other day for depositions, but when he didn't show...the Feds got involved. Now it's all over the papers. It was even on television last night."

Except for four or five men that I had met at Casiano's party for me, Al's basement was filled with unfamiliar faces. All of them sat in small groups drinking coffee, smoking cigarettes, speaking in whispers and reading the various newspapers out of Hudson, Bergen, Essex and Passaic Counties. Even the New York dailies were covering the story of the mobster that had gone missing.

I leaned forward and whispered in Al's ear, "What do *you* think happened?"

He shrugged his shoulders, shook his head and said, "Don't know. Maybe the Federal trial got to him and he didn't want to go to jail. Maybe he took a couple of suitcases and he's sittin' on an island in the South Pacific. I don't know."

I picked up one of the local papers to see the headline on page 6: GENOVESE MOB NO HELP IN CASIANO SEARCH, COPS SAY. The article started off with, "Reputed members of the Genovese crime family are refusing to cooperate with authorities in their search for Rocco Casiano, said to be a family member and boss of the Hudson County waterfront, who was reported missing several days ago."

Farther down, I read, "New York City police, commenting on the theory that Casiano may have been murdered, said that any 'hit' on Casiano would probably have been ordered by his Genovese comrades."

I put the paper down and looked around at the people I was sitting in the midst of.

How do I get myself into these situations?

I continued reading.

"'There have been problems between the Gambino and Genovese families, but the rift between leaders John Gotti and Vincent 'The Chin' Gigante has been straightened out. If Casiano was murdered by a rival family, like the Gambinos, it probably would start a war' said one city police source."

Paragraph after paragraph...I couldn't believe what I was reading...but I read on.

"Law enforcement authorities in both states agreed that the Genovese family's only motive for murdering Casiano would be unhappiness with the attention he has been receiving from both the media and the investigators."

Then, in the next paragraph I saw a name that I recognized all too well.

"Among the reputed Genovese members and associates quizzed this week by Bayonne police were Armand 'Mondu' Guardino, Richard 'Dickie' Pignatello, George Lyman and Thomas 'Tommy The Irishman' Dolan."

Dolan.

I looked around the room. He wasn't there. Neither was Salvatore Della Osa. Seeing as they were Rocco's people...Rocco's *closest* people...one would have thought...?

I found Al in the crowd and whispered, "Where's Dolan and Sal? Why aren't they here?"

"Until Rocco turns up, Sal's runnin' things. He's out there doin' what he has to do. Dolan's too hot right now...I'm *glad* he's not here."

"Is there anything I can do, Al?"

He moved even closer to me and whispered, "From listening to those tapes...do you know anything? Did he say anything about who would want to do this to him? Did he think there was someone out to get him?"

"Nope...not that *I* heard. And I *listened*. When he came to me with the tapes, I saw how nervous he was. I really wanted to help him. But I couldn't find anything that would've done him any good. I'll be honest with you, Al...the Feds were gonna get him. He was sayin' shit on those tapes like, '*Bayonne is mine!*' and that he was pissed off because *some guy* from New York wasn't showing him the respect he deserves for his position and was tryin' to come into Jersey."

Al shook his head. He knew Rocco was referring to John Gotti.

I continued, "Most of the phone conversations were only a couple of minutes long with nothing specific being said. It was all pretty cryptic... even for me. A lot of, 'I'll meet you at *that place*,' or 'You go to that *other* place and meet so-and-so'...it didn't sound like he was concerned about getting whacked...either by the Gambinos or his *own* people."

We said our goodbyes, and as I walked out of the tailor shop I took my time slowly looking at the pictures that lined the walls...then checked my hair in one of the tri-sided mirrors.

Once I got home, I took all of Rocco's cassettes and the transcripts and put them in the big box. Then I taped it closed and put it away...far into the back of a closet in the studio.

I had a feeling Rocco Casiano didn't need them anymore.

On Friday morning, May 27, my father walked into my room with a cup of coffee and woke me.

"Drink this...and then get down to The Tailor's. He just called and asked that you come by. And listen to me...stay away from Sal Della Osa."

And then he walked out.

My mind was still in a fog from the partying I did the night before, so I gulped down the coffee and took a shower.

As soon as I got to Al Nucci's, he asked, "Did you see this morning's paper?" as he handed it to me before I had a chance to look at the pictures on the wall.

I was hoping to see a headline that read: JOHN LENNON ALIVE! THE BEATLES PLAN REUNION!

But instead, the banner across the front page said, CASIANO IS FOUND IN RIVER.

I stared at it. I couldn't bring myself to read the article.

Sure...we all suspected he was dead. Though we all wanted to believe

Al's theory that Rocco was sitting on a beach in Bora Bora...we knew that wasn't the case.

But to see the reality of it in print was more than I could take.

I walked into Al's office and poured a cup of coffee, then sat at the desk and started to read.

"The body of reputed mobster Rocco Casiano, who had been shot at least five times, was found stuffed in a mortician's bag floating in the Hackensack River. The body was found Thursday morning, about 9:30AM at the Sportplex Marina in Carlstadt, authorities said."

I raised my head and momentarily stared out the window before I continued.

"The badly decomposed body was pierced by bullets fired by a professional killer whose hiring was sanctioned by Casiano's former boss, Genovese crime family chieftain Vincent 'The Chin' Gigante of Manhattan."

I began to get pale as I read on.

"Also found in the bag with Casiano was a Visa credit card bearing the name of the victim, who reputedly was among the family's highest earners until his death. Federal authorities say, 'The card was left to serve as an identification tag.'"

I shook my head in disbelief...but continued to read, "Despite being a moneymaker for the crime family, his persistent conflicts with Genovese family leaders and flair for grabbing media attention at his recent trial destroyed his reputation among those leaders."

The article made reference to various reasons the body suddenly surfaced, but none were certain. "'If they didn't want the body to be found, it would never be found,' said one Federal investigator. 'It was probably buried somewhere and dug up so he could be discovered.'"

Just then, Al walked over. So I asked, "After three weeks? Why do you think his body turned up in Carlstadt, right on the other side of the Hacky from Secaucus?"

He leaned toward me, spoke very softly and said, "His mother."

As he backed away I gave a confused look.

Again, he came close and whispered, "His mother was falling apart. She's eighty-something years old, for Christ sake. She'd never gone so long without hearing from him. He practically still lived with her in that house in Bayonne. Rocco has a mansion down in Monmouth County, but the fuckin' guy was *Hudson County*. He wouldn't leave this place."

Al began to get emotional, having been a close friend of Casiano's since the fifties.

"Anyway," he continued, "His mother wanted to know if her son was dead...and if he *was*, she wanted to bury his body."

I sat there shaking my head in disbelief as he continued.

"What I heard was that last week she went to go see *the big guy*. I've known her for years. The old broad's got *balls!*" he said. "And I can actually believe she'd get a ride over to Little Italy and go to the social club where everybody knows he holds court. Then she gets there, goes to the front door and tells some guy she wants to talk to..."

Al stopped speaking and rubbed his chin. That was the hand-sign used to represent Vincente 'The Chin' Gigante. It was a name those who knew him knew he didn't want mentioned for fear of FBI taps. But the rubbing of one's chin surely sufficed.

He continued his story without missing a beat.

"Apparently, it worked...because he saw her. She told him that whatever the reasons were for her son dying, they weren't important anymore...all she wanted was to bury his body. The big guy probably listened, then told her he didn't know what she was talking about. Then he had whoever did the hit go dig him up and dump him in the river someplace easy enough to be found...just to show respect to that little old Italian mother."

I looked down at the paper and continued reading the lengthy article.

The final paragraph quoted an Assistant U.S. Attorney.

"'He was not the kind of guy to take orders easily. He must have angered some of his bosses. I think Rocco Casiano has now been tried by a jury of his peers.'"

"Yes," I said to myself as I sat back in the chair. "Yes, he has."

Once again...it was the end of an era.

Rocco Casiano...the person who had taken me under his wing and made it possible for me to go anywhere in New Jersey knowing I was safe in the arms of my Italian heritage...was gone.

I called Jerry from a payphone in Hackensack.

"Rocco's dead," I whispered.

He softly cried as I told him some of the details from the article.

Then we hung up.

Epilogue

Rocco Casiano's memorial service was a somber event.

For obvious reasons, he was cremated. There was no way his body could be laid out in a casket for viewing.

His mother, wife and daughter cried throughout the service as mourners came to pay their respects. I was there for the whole thing...I remember it all.

During a quiet moment, Tommy Dolan and Salvatore Della Osa asked me to take a walk outside with them.

I never mentioned it to anyone, but I always had a feeling about Tommy and Sal...ever since I put two-and-two together about Rocco meeting Dolan for dinner the night he went missing.

But some things are better left unsaid...and I kept my thoughts and feelings about it to myself.

It was a wise choice.

With one on each side, they towered above me as we walked around the block in near darkness. I could almost hear the shutters clicking from all of the cameras that were pointed at us from rooftops and through darkened windows of unmarked cars and vans.

"Sal tells me you're the person I should talk to about a situation I gotta deal with," Dolan said in his gruff Bayonne way and between drags on a cigarette.

I looked at Sal as The Irishman continued, "We all know how good you are with tape recordings."

My stare didn't leave Sal as Dolan put his arm around my shoulder and said, "I have a tape I need you to listen to."

I finally turned and looked at him as he said, "I need to know if those magical fuckin' ears of yours can hear something. 'Cause if *you* can hear it… then *they* can hear it. Can you do that for me?"

"Sure," I innocently answered, then asked, "What do *they* say is on it?"

"Beats the shit out of me," Dolan said, waving his long arms into the air. "I can't hear shit…but I need to know if the Feds can."

"Whatdya mean? Didn't they give you a transcript with it?"

"*Look!*" Sal angrily broke in, "There *ain't* no transcript!" His voice suddenly went to an angered whisper, "We had one of *our* people get us a copy of it from inside. They haven't even transcribed it yet."

"Inside where?"

Sal answered sternly, "Where the fuck you think? Newark…FBI Headquarters."

Great. Now I was going to listen to a tape that was swiped from the FBI. How did I get *into* these situations?

Oh…that's right. Family. Tradition. Honor. Respect.

Mistakenly, I had assumed that with Jerry gone and Rocco dead, my enlistment was over.

It wasn't.

I started to ask, "How did…? What if…? Why were…?" but kept cutting the questions short. They were questions I didn't *want* answers to.

But Sal gave a response anyway.

"This way we'll know exactly what they're gonna be comin' at us with so we can start puttin' our legal defense together. Okay? Happy you asked?"

No…I wasn't. But I wasn't going to tell *him* that.

"So I want you to do me a favor and be at Tommy's house tomorrow," Sal ordered.

It didn't sound like a favor I had the option to say "No" to.

"Any idea what's on the tape?" I asked.

"That's what *we* wanna know," Sal answered. "We listened but couldn't hear anything that could be considered incriminating. Just be at Tommy's tomorrow afternoon…and keep your mouth shut about this. Capice?"

Nothing more was said about it.

I somehow was able to shut my car door as I managed to balance the heavy Eumig cassette deck in my arms with a big, bulky pair of headphones wrapped around my neck. The assorted cords and jacks hung between my legs as I walked up to the house door.

With an extended pinky, I rang the bell.

George Lyman greeted me and led me into the living room. Once I put the equipment down I was embraced by Della Osa and Dolan.

"What's that?" Dolan asked.

"It's the deck I used for Rocco's stuff. I figured you wouldn't have anything in your house that would be studio-quality, so if I want to hear what's on the tape...I'll hear it with *this*."

Sal smiled and said, "You're good! I knew we could count on you."

Dolan asked, "What about speakers? I wanna hear it, too!"

"Don't need 'em." I held up the headphones and said, "I'll hear it better...in here."

"But *I* wanna hear what *you're* hearing."

There seemed to be a thread of suspicion in his voice.

I reassured him with, "Don't worry about it. If I hear something...I'll let you know."

I plugged the power cord into the wall and asked for the tape.

Della Osa handed it to me as if it were made of gold, then said, "Since we're not gonna be able to hear anything, I want you to tell us *exactly* what you're hearin'...when you hear it. I want to know everything that *anybody* can possibly hear on that fuckin' tape. Got that?"

I nodded, gave a thumbs-up and slipped on the headphones.

The tape started with two men speaking softly...*very* softly. So softly that I couldn't distinguish who they were or what they were saying. A few moments later, I heard other people enter. Then, at a regular volume, Sal and another man, who I didn't recognize, greeted Dolan and Lyman.

I told this to the men sitting in front of me as I stared at the meter levels while hitting a switch or two to filter out certain frequencies.

It didn't help...the sound was still very low.

"Yeah...we heard that, too. There's nothing in that section that can hurt us," Dolan confidently said.

After the four men sat down, the volume of their discussion quickly went so low that it again became inaudible.

Except for when someone stood to leave or had entered the room, all the dialogue was incomprehensible.

I told them I heard Dolan say, "What's this about, Sally?" and then nothing else for a few moments until the person I didn't recognize said, "I think *that* is something Salvatore wants to speak to you privately about.

I'll be back in a few minutes." It was followed by footsteps walking away. Then, once again...the sound became muffled.

My hands cupped the big headphones against my ears and I sat there as if in a deep trance, trying to hear something...anything. Every few minutes I'd just shake my head as I listened to nothing but the low murmur of unidentifiable voices and unintelligible dialogue.

After sitting through a few more hushed conversations, I heard footsteps, followed by the unknown voice asking, "So...is the *first* problem taken care of?" followed by, "And the *other* matter?" before it again became an inaudible mumble.

A few minutes later, the unknown voice rose from the table and left. The remainder of the tape was silent.

The quality of the recording was terrible. It was the worst surveillance tape I had ever heard...and until I packed up Casiano's box of cassettes and stored them deep into a closet, I had listened to a *dozen* interesting and well-recorded surveillance tapes.

What I didn't know was that as Tommy Dolan and George Lyman sat in front of me watching my reactions and listening as I told them what I was hearing...or not hearing...Salvatore Della Osa stood behind me with the silencer-barrel of a .22 caliber automatic inches from my head.

Had I actually heard something that would have made me aware that these three men were plotting to kill Casiano and Gotti...I would have to be killed.

Immediately.

Sal knew that the .22 would leave less of a mess and make less noise than his .45.

Fortunately, I didn't hear anything that was incriminating.

So, without my knowing it...I was allowed to live.

I was alive because the government did a terrible job of recording.

In actuality, though these wiseguys didn't know it...during their sit-down with Musarra they were doing the right thing.

They *whispered*.

They spoke so quietly throughout the entire meeting that the small microphone hanging a few feet above their heads had no way of picking it up. Only when someone spoke up or rose from the table were their words audible.

As I rewound the tape and took off my headphones, I looked at Dolan and said, "I'm sorry. But except for a couple of times where I heard you guys get up or down, I didn't hear shit. There's no conversation on this tape that anybody can use."

"You sure?" Dolan asked.

"Positive."

The three of them gave a collective sigh.

At that point, Sal lowered the pistol and slid it back into the holster under his jacket.

Then I said, "Wanna listen?"

"Yeah!" the big Irishman said, almost as if he didn't believe me.

I sat him in front of the deck, put the headphones over his head and told him to press them against his ears...and listen. Then I hit the PLAY button.

As Dolan sat there listening, Della Osa said, "Come with me."

The two of us walked through the kitchen and into the backyard.

He stopped short, turned to me and quietly said, "I'm the new boss."

I didn't know what to say. I didn't even know why he was saying it to me.

He opened his arms, so the obvious thing to do was to hug and kiss him.

I didn't say anything. I guess I was still in shock that Rocco Casiano was dead. What I didn't know was that I had just embraced the man who had killed him.

But being raised under the same beliefs and rules as Jerry, I knew that this was the man we, my family, were now bound to. He was the new boss...and he was to be shown respect.

Time passed. Things happened.

About a year after he was murdered, I dug Casiano's box of tapes and transcripts out of the closet and dropped it off at Andrew Herschfeld's office. I didn't want them in the house anymore.

The plot against John Gotti never got off the ground. It seems that The Commission had no problem with Casiano's disappearance, and when the press made the point of The Chin disciplining his biggest earner for stepping out of line...it brought order throughout the ranks. It showed everyone that the big bosses wouldn't take shit from anybody.

Dolan didn't get Staten Island. He *did* go to prison for nearly five years for his racketeering charges, and when he was released in the early '90s, he was home for only a few months before he died of cancer.

Sal did get to be the boss for about a year, then the Feds went after him for tax evasion...and they got him. In 1989 he was convicted and sentenced to 12 years in prison. After all he had done...he went to jail for tax evasion.

Then, from prison, on March 30, 1994, Salvatore Della Osa admitted to killing Rocco Casiano...along with naming his two accomplices.

In September of 1994, I was passing through Secaucus and ran into Tony Romano in my favorite local bar, *The Other Place*. As we sat having a couple of martinis, we started to discuss Della Osa's now-admitted hit on Rocco.

"I can tell you this because I know you're a stand-up guy," he said as he sipped his martini, "I got this from Mondu Guardino." He looked around to make sure no one was listening, then continued, "Sal fucked up, and there was no way anybody upstairs was gonna help him."

"No shit?"

"I heard it was 'cause of the piece he used," he whispered.

"The gun?" I whispered back.

"Yeah. He was given a .38 for the job. But somebody high up read in the papers that the autopsy and ballistic report said Rocco was killed with a .45...and *everybody* knew Sally carried that monster around with him."

"So...what's the difference what gun he used?"

"When you're given an order to use something by these people...and you don't follow it...you just fucked yourself. And that's what he did. He didn't follow orders. He never woulda been tied into the .38 if they ever found it. Sally didn't get rid of *his* gun like he should have after the hit, like he *would have* with the .38. And when the Feds picked him up on the tax charges, he had his cannon on him. One thing led to another...and the heat was on. Those tax-evasion charges were bullshit. The Feds just needed a reason to get into his house and seize everything so they could try to find some evidence that would lead to the Casiano hit. And since Sally didn't do what he was told...there was no way The Commission was going to protect him if the Feds found anything." Tony took a mouthful of the martini, then continued, "They must have found *something*, 'cause they--"

"So...why'd he admit to whacking Rocco?" I interrupted and naively asked, "Why didn't he let them try him in court to prove it?"

"He cut a deal," Romano answered as he took another swallow of his martini. "The Feds had a shitload of charges on him. At least two other murders, extortion, fraud, theft, arson...he was facin' a hundred fuckin' years in the joint. I guess he figured if he admitted to killing Rocco...along with naming Dolan and George Lyman...they'd cut him a deal."

I was a little shocked hearing that it was the three of them. I quickly recalled my FBI tape-listening session...and it gave me chills. *Bad* chills.

"Dolan's dead...so I can understand Sal turning *his* name in," I said. "But why Lyman? Why'd the fuck Sal do that?"

"To add to the deal," Tony responded, "But you don't think it ended there, do ya? By admitting that it was a sanctioned hit, he implicated people higher up the fuckin' totem pole. Believe me, they ain't too happy...I can tell you that."

"Jeez!"

"There's even talk that Sal was plannin' on whackin' Gotti, for Christ sake."

"What about Lyman?" I asked.

"Well, if *I* was Lyman, I'd be pissed off *and* scared shit," Tony laughed. "For the last six years the Feds *never* had him involved in the hit. They never had any idea! Except for Sally and Dolan, nobody else really knew Georgie was there. Once Dolan died, Lyman only had Sal to worry about... and he believed that Sally, being the *Italian*, would do the right thing...that he wouldn't talk." Then Tony shook his head, finished his drink and said, "Georgie was wrong."

Suddenly, his attitude changed and a look of anger came across his face.

"That fuck, Sal...he didn't even have the balls to face Rocco when he killed him. What kind of man is that? Not one of *ours!* Lyman...Dolan... they weren't Italian...they ain't got no fuckin' code of honor...so I can understand *them* doin' it that way."

Because of the martinis, Tony's voice began to get louder as he continued, "But Sally? If he can kill his own boss, then take his territory... and not even *face* the guy...how the fuck you expect him to do the right thing and not give up *your* name and everybody *else's* name down the line?"

I had to calm him down and remind him where we were. The Other Place was a local bar, and not a place where it was okay to raise one's voice about such things.

After the waitress brought another round, he leaned close to me and continued, this time a little calmer and softer, "Georgie's gonna have some big fuckin' problems if he goes to the joint. Ya gotta remember, before he was Dolan's muscle...he was Sergeant George Lyman of the Hudson County Police Department. You got any idea what it's like in a Federal prison being an ex-cop?"

He looked at me for a response.

I shook my head and whispered, "It ain't gonna be like a day at the shore."

"The guards sure-as-shit ain't gonna do anything to protect you...and the hard-timers inside can't wait to kick the shit outta some guy who used to wear a uniform. No...I wouldn't wanna be George when *that* trial comes around."

"Whatdya think'll happen to Sal? Will he get out?"

"I guess you're outta the loop now, huh, kid?"

I furrowed my brow and asked, "Whatdya mean?"

He let out a short loud laugh.

"The Feds reneged. They fucked Sally. After they got him to admit to killing Rocco and droppin' names...they *charged* him with the hit and he's gonna be in there for a long fuckin' time...if he gets out at all."

I took a healthy swallow of the vodka and vermouth, sat back in the booth and drifted from the conversation. It was too much.

Thanks to the martinis, I flashed back on the last 19 years.

I remembered that first night...August 29, 1975.

My twenty-second birthday.

I threw the dice to the far end of the crap table and lost thousands of dollars, only to be told I was, "...*doin' just fine!*" by my Godfather.

I recounted the fun and excitement I had for the next twenty-six months...until that morning when I was told I was being measured for a hole in the desert.

I remembered the first time I met Casiano in Al Nucci's tailor shop as I looked at the photo gallery along the walls.

I thought about the day I returned from L.A. and was whisked to a party to be given my official mob name, and the night Della Osa put the gun he would eventually murder the boss with...up to my head.

Jerry was still in Palm Springs and enjoying life in the desert.

Vinnie Caputo was dead.

Casiano was dead.

Dolan was dead.

Sal was in a Federal prison…and it didn't look like he was going to be getting out anytime soon.

Six years after the fact…George Lyman now had to defend himself for being an accomplice to the murder of Rocco Casiano.

I lost touch with Mike Caruso and haven't seen him in years. Occasionally, I'd stop in to see Taz whenever I would pass one of his motels.

Al Nucci still had his tailor shop and had recently opened a gym for boxers and began promoting matches.

I hadn't seen Louie Calderone or Bobby Grant since Casiano's memorial service.

Over the years, Lady Millicent became a fond and happy memory.

I still stayed in touch with Linda Rossi…I'm not *crazy*.

In 1985, when I was 32 years old, I had left the music business. It was time for me to find another life. The musical styles of the time were far from the rock-and-roll I enjoyed playing…and there was a new and different 22-year-old *kid* breathing down my back at every session. It was time to move on.

I lived off of my savings for a few years, and went looking for a new direction…I had to decide what I wanted to be…now that I had to grow up.

By the early '90s, I was working for a large insurance company making presentations to municipalities, counties and unions for payroll deduction insurance programs. I wore a suit and tie every day, and parted my corporate haircut on the side.

Christ! So much had changed.

The phone rang in my Ramsey, New Jersey, home in August of 1995.

"Hello?"

"Juan?"

"Hey, Jer! How you doin'?"

"I thought you'd want to know…we're moving, and besides…I wanted to wish you--"

"Back here, Jer? You're moving back here?" I interrupted and excitedly asked.

"No. But I think you'll get a kick out of this," he paused and laughed, "We're moving to Vegas."

The line went quiet.

I said nothing.

"Juan? You there?"

"Yeah. Yeah, I'm here. But..."

Again, I went silent.

"But what?" he asked.

"Can you *go* there?"

"That was a *long* time ago. Besides, I wasn't even involved when the shit hit the fan. Remember? Nineteen years in Palm Springs is enough for *anybody*. I want to go someplace with a bit more action."

"Yeah...but--"

"Don't worry. I'm gonna live there. It's not like I'm checking into a hotel. Those days are long gone," he said with confidence.

"Yeah...well, *I'm* not gonna take that chance. I haven't been back, and I have no intention on *goin'* back. Now, what were you gonna say before I interrupted you?"

"Oh! I wanted to wish you Happy Birthday!"

I'm sure he heard my happiness as I answered, "Thanks, Jer. Thank you very much."

"Shit. Twenty years ago today we were in Vegas together, huh? That's makes you forty-two, for Christ sake."

"Yeah...and that makes you..." I did some quick math and continued, "Fifty-eight."

"Don't remind me," he yelled. "*Jesus!* I remember the day you were born. And your christening. It doesn't seem like that long ago."

"But you made them great years for me, Jerry. You know that, don't you?" I couldn't believe that after all these years I was actually saying his name over the phone...and it didn't faze him in the least.

He gave me his new address and phone number in Vegas and told me to come out whenever I had the chance. Then he wished me Happy Birthday again...and told me he loved me.

I smiled when we hung up. I missed him...and I guess I missed the old times a little, too.

It was only because of my job that I eventually and reluctantly went to Vegas on October 9, 1998, to speak at a union convention. It would have been John Lennon's fifty-eighth birthday.

I made it a point to call Jerry as soon as I checked into my room, and took him, his wife and mother out to dinner on my expense account, and then I took them back to my nineteen-hundred-dollar-a-night penthouse suite at The Mirage.

"You still know how to live good in Vegas...and you still make sure somebody else picks up the tab, don'tcha, Juan?" he asked as I showed them around.

I put my arms around him...tight, and said, "*You* taught me how. *You* made some of the best times of my life happen. You gave me memories that I'll *always* remember."

After I had finished my gig at the convention, I spent the next few days with Jerry before I flew back to Jersey...this time without worrying that I had to get out with only a minute to spare.

And he *still* wouldn't tell me why he left Jersey.

During the evening of a very cold Monday, December 28, as I sat in front of the fireplace of my Bergen County home, the phone rang. When I answered it, I couldn't make out what the male caller was saying until he coughed to clear his throat.

"Juan?"

"Jer?"

"Yeah. How you doin'?"

"What's the matter? You sick?" I asked.

"Yeah, You could say that. Busy?"

"No. Why?"

"Can you take a drive?"

"For you? Sure. Whatdya need?"

"Can you come into the city?" he asked.

"What city? New York? Why? Where are you?"

I laughed to myself as I realized that we had ended each response with a question. It was just like old times.

He gave me an address of an uptown brownstone and a phone number, then he said, "And don't forget to *come around* sometime."

I immediately drew a double ended arrow over the address and the last four digits of the phone number...just like the old days.

"What are you doing there?"

"When I see you," his voice was growing weaker as he continued, "And don't tell anyone I'm here. *Anyone*. Not even family. Nobody knows I'm here but you."

I told him I'd be there in an hour and hung up the phone.

It was frigid outside as I drove my Lincoln Mark VIII over the George Washington Bridge. Because of the time of year, traffic into the city wasn't so bad and I was there right on time.

I brought the Mark VIII, Lincoln's idea of a sports car, because I wanted to hear Jerry give me his age-old lecture about two-door cars.

He always hated them.

He'd say, "You'll *never* get me in the back of a two-door. There's no way out. They're too easy to get whacked in. At least with a four-door you have a chance of gettin' out if somebody walks up to the car and starts shooting. A two-door? Forget about it. That's why you'll never see me in one."

That's why I had a four-door Continental at home in the garage, too.

When I rang the bell to the brownstone, Jerry's wife answered the door. She looked terrible.

"Carol! What's the matter? What's going on?" I asked before going inside.

"Jerry's sick," she answered as tears filled her eyes. Once she regained her composure, she said, "He was in Sloan-Kettering Hospital over Christmas. We've been here since last week. It's my niece's place." She started crying. "They took tests. He's got cancer. Lung cancer. It's bad. They say he's going to die." She couldn't speak anymore.

We embraced and cried in the doorway.

As I walked inside, I asked, "Where is he?"

"Sleeping. He wanted to be awake when you got here, but he was in so much pain that he needed to take his medicine. It makes him very tired. He'll be asleep for about another hour or so. Can you stay?"

"Of course I'll stay! Just tell me what's going on...*please?*" I asked.

Apparently, a month earlier, he started to have pain in his left arm and chest. He finally went to a doctor and was sent to a hospital in Vegas. After they took some tests, they recommended that he immediately go to New York's Sloan-Kettering.

And he did.

She began to cry again as she said, "They say he's got about a year-and-a-half to live."

I fell back into the couch as the color drained from my face and all energy left my body.

We sat staring at the walls until the bedroom door slowly opened and my Godfather appeared. He was in a heavy robe and had lost almost thirty pounds since I had seen him nearly three months earlier. He still wore his gold chains, but no rings, bracelet or watch, as his wrists and fingers had gotten too skinny.

I didn't know what to say...but he did.

"Hello, Juan."

I jumped up from the couch and hugged him, tight. But this time I could feel his bones. He felt brittle.

He sat down and we talked for a bit before he said, "Do you have any free time before I go back to Vegas?"

"Sure. Why?"

"I'd like to take a drive. Can you--"

I interrupted and said, "Whatever it is...of course I will. Where you wanna go?"

"It's been twenty-two years. I think it's time. Besides, everybody's gone. I wanna see Jersey...just one more time," he said as tears filled his eyes.

The next day, I took the Continental out of the garage, drove into the city and picked up Jerry and his wife.

We returned to Jersey through the Lincoln Tunnel so the first thing he'd see would be Hudson County. I drove him past the house he grew up in on 23rd Street in Union City, and into Secaucus to drive by Al Nucci's Custom Tailor shop. Then we went to their old house in Ridgefield before we headed to the cemetery in Paramus where his father's ashes rest.

Jerry lost his father in December of 1989, and my father passed away in January of '94, leaving us the *men* of our families, and with the responsibility of looking after our Italian mothers.

Throughout the ride he sat next to me with the seat reclined to its fullest extent and his head resting into the leather as he listened to the cassette mixed with a compilation of songs from the '50s, '60s and '70s.

"What's the name of this tape, Juan? There's a lot of good music on it," he asked over The Dell Vikings singing *Come Go With Me*.

"It's one of mine," I matter-of-factly answered.

"What do you mean?"

"I make 'em. I buy the CDs and record what songs I want onto the cassette. Then I make the labels on my computer. See?" I handed him the cassette box while negotiating the highway traffic.

As one song faded and The Dave Clark Five's *Because* started, he asked, "You put this whole thing together?"

"It's easy."

His mind started racing as he looked at me.

"I got a guy who can run these off by the hundreds. You make the masters and the labels and I got another guy that can sell 'em. We can make some nice money doin'--"

A couple of days earlier he was told he had a year-and-a-half left to live, yet here he was trying to pull off just one more scam.

"You can't do that, Jer!" I innocently laughed and interrupted. "You gotta get permission and license the rights for each tune first."

"And if we didn't?" he slyly asked.

"We'd have a problem with copyright infringements. We'd get in a lot of trouble. That's Federal."

He put his head back and smiled.

"You know, Juan...that was always the difference between you and me."

I again turned my attention from the road, looked at him and asked, "Oh yeah. And what's that?"

He stared out the front window and said, "You never knew how to turn a felony into a misdemeanor." Then he slowly turned his head, smiled at me and continued, "Maybe that was a good thing, huh?"

His hand reached over and held mine.

I took him to my home in Ramsey for dinner before we returned to the city...and he returned to Las Vegas to greet the New Year.

On Tuesday, March 9, 1999, I flew to Los Angeles on business, so I thought a visit to Jerry would be in order. I drove to Vegas on Thursday.

His wife answered the door, and I could see the wear and tear that Jerry's illness was having on her. When I brought my suitcase inside I saw Jerry sitting in a chair. He didn't have the strength to get up to greet me.

It was very hard for me to see him like that, but I tried to keep our spirits up as we spoke about the D'Amore family back in New Jersey.

I stayed for a few days before business forced me to return to L.A., but before I left I sat with him for a few private moments as he rested in bed.

"I have a favor to ask of you, Jerry."

He looked at me...as if ready for anything and willing to take on whatever my request would be.

"I want to write a book," I said.

His eyebrows went up.

"I want to write about what happened in Vegas. It was a fantastic time. It was the most exciting time of my life...and I want to write about it."

Still, he said nothing.

I continued, "They're all gone. Vinnie, Casiano, Dolan, Della Osa... they're gone. They're either dead or in jail."

"And I'll be gone soon, too," he sarcastically said.

"But *before* you go...I want you to do something for me."

Again, he just looked at me...but this time he smiled.

I went into my briefcase and handed him a box.

"This is the best and easiest-to-use micro-cassette deck out there."

I took out 10 blank tapes and laid them on the night-table as I continued, "I want you to talk to this thing as if you were talking to me. I want you to tell me what happened. I want you to tell me about the things you think would be interesting. I want you to tell me about Frank DeNike, my dad, the Vegas scam...Dolan...Casiano...Sal. Tell me the things I don't know. Tell me about Vinnie Caputo. Tell me why, nearly twenty-three years ago...you left New Jersey."

"There's a lot of stories there, Juan."

"So? Tell 'em to me! While you're sitting in bed...just turn the deck on and ramble. Fill in the blanks and I'll tell *your* story along with mine and Casiano's. Tell me the things I was a part of...but didn't know what went on behind-the-scenes."

"You won't do anything with them until after I die...right?"

"You have my word," I assured him.

He leaned toward me, put his lips to my ear and said, "You always were the one to do the right thing, Jon."

"For you, Jer. For you," I whispered.

And then he kissed me.

As we held each other, he said, "The doctors were wrong, you know, when they first said I had eighteen months. Last week they told me I have about two months...and that's it."

It wasn't what I wanted to hear Jerry say. I sat in front of him and started to cry. There was nothing I could do to hold back the tears.

I had spent my entire life doing anything and everything for Jerry...my cousin...my Godfather. But no matter how many *right things* I may have done before...nothing I could do was going to help him now.

We held each other for a long time. I didn't want to let him go.

Not long after I returned to Jersey, I stopped into Al Nucci's tailor shop to let him know about my cousin's illness.

"Did you hear the news last week?" Al asked after we hugged and kissed.

I shrugged my shoulders and shook my head.

"George Lyman committed suicide."

"Get the fuck outta here!"

"His trial for Rocco's murder was scheduled for this week...eleven fuckin' years after they killed him...and Lyman knew he was going to wind up in jail. So the fuckin' guy has a few drinks, takes a couple of sleeping pills, goes down into his garage, starts his car and goes to sleep. That's it. There was no way he was gonna do time. No way."

I stood silent.

"You know, kid. A lot's changed over the years," said Al, who was by now in his late 60s. "There don't seem to be the same breed of guys that there used to be. These young Turks...they run by different rules...a different code. Their idea of *la famiglia*, of *respect*...it's all different. Even the new boss...wanna meet him?"

My answer was quick and sure.

I smiled, took a step back and respectfully said, "No. No thanks. I don't think I want to play anymore. Most of the guys we knew ain't even around for one reason or another. I'd rather not know anything about *any* of the new guys. My old man was never too thrilled that I did what I did in Vegas. I was only in it because of Jerry...and those days are gone. *Long* gone."

Then we kissed and hugged, but before I left I looked at the pictures on the wall...and checked my appearance in the mirror.

By April, I made plans to leave New Jersey behind and move to where I always wanted to live, Los Angeles, California.

On Saturday, May 1, 1999, I packed my Mark VIII full of clothes, cassettes and some weed and began the drive west.

By Tuesday, May 4, I pulled into Vegas around 9:30PM. Jerry was bedridden and could barely speak.

I sat at his side for hours, trying to joke with him...trying to do whatever I could to make him smile.

"I know I've told you this before," he strained to say. "But you were always the one--"

I cut him off and laughed, "Yeah...I know...the one to do the right thing."

When we said goodbye the following morning, we knew it would be the last time we'd see each other.

He hung on for another month, and then on the morning of Sunday, June 6, four months and seven days after he was diagnosed and told that he'd have a year-and-a-half to live, my Godfather Jerry died at his home in Las Vegas.

His daughter called me in L.A. shortly after it happened. I sat by the phone...speechless...numb...and crying.

When I finally got myself together, I drove to the same spot in Malibu that I went to after I watched The MGM go up in flames, then again when John Lennon was killed. I sat on the beach and looked off into the distance...to where I decided long ago to have my ashes spread when *my* time comes.

Two weeks later, I flew to Vegas for Jerry's memorial service. When we returned to his house, his wife said there was something she wanted to talk to me about...privately.

"Jerry wanted me to have you take care of a few things for us," she said.

I looked at her...I didn't know what it could be.

She handed me a small box.

"I don't know what's inside. But he said I was to give it to you after he..."

She couldn't bring herself to say the word.

I took the box and opened it. It was the micro-cassette recorder and seven of the ten tapes. Now *my* eyes began to fill with tears.

Then she held two urns in her hands. One was full of ashes. The other was empty.

She poured a small amount of ashes into the empty one. Then she handed me the other and said, "Jerry always wanted his ashes spread in the ocean off of Malibu. I can't bear to lose all of him...I have to keep some. But we knew we could count on you to do it for him...for *us*."

I was speechless. I went weak in the knees.

"I don't believe it," I said through the tears that filled my eyes.

"What do you mean?"

"I had no idea *that* was where he wanted to be, because...because..." I couldn't catch my breath, "Because that's where *I* want *my* ashes spread. How could we *both* want to be in the same place? How did he know? We never talked about it."

"He *didn't* know. He's wanted that since he first went to Malibu in the early seventies," she answered. "It was just a place we drove through...he said he thought the Pacific looked peaceful from there...and it was what he wanted when the time came."

"But how--" I started to ask.

"Because you were more than cousins. You were more than *family*. In your hearts you were the closest that two people could be...the two of you were the same. You loved and respected one another in a way most people would never understand. *Where* the two of you wanted your ashes spread was just *another* similarity...a uniqueness the two of you shared. And who knows? Maybe there...you'll always be connected." Then she looked into my eyes and asked, "Will you do this for me? Will you do this for Jerry?"

No words needed to be said as I held her.

When we finally composed ourselves, she pulled out her last request.

She pushed a small black suitcase in front of me and said, "There's no one else in the family who'd know what to do with this, and Jerry would have wanted you to have it." Then she said no more about it.

I lifted the suitcase and was surprised at how heavy it was.

I could see by her expression it wasn't something she wanted to see, so I took it to the guest room and opened it.

It was his pieces. His guns. .22s, .22s with silencers, .25s, a snub-nosed .38, a .44 magnum, a 9mm Beretta and a couple of police revolvers.

There were also two pairs of soft black leather gloves and gun cleaning equipment.

So much for *flying* back to Los Angeles.

The following morning, I rented a car, loaded my suitcases into the trunk, and put Jerry's ashes and the tape recordings in the front seat with me.

Then I slowly and cautiously drove west.

I held onto the ashes for another ten weeks, then called my friend Steve, owner of the Cara Mia, a 45' yacht that he docked in Marina del Rey. I made arrangements for a late afternoon cruise on Sunday, August 29, my forty-sixth birthday, and brought along Linda Rossi, John Phillip Law, Patsy's wife Rose, my cousins Phyllis and Joey, and a select group of my closest Los Angeles friends.

There wasn't a cloud in the summer sky and a mild breeze drifted across the calm sea as we left the marina.

I brought out a case of chilled Dom Perignon and filled everyone's glass as I recounted stories about Jerry...a man all those onboard, except my family, knew nothing about. As I spoke of him, my eyes illuminated with enthusiasm and admiration.

Once we were off the Malibu coast, the Cara Mia turned west...into the setting sun.

Soon, spirits were very high and everyone was having a wonderful time.

At some point, Steve shut the engines and yelled from the bridge, "We're about five miles offshore, directly west of Malibu."

Slowly, I took a piece of paper from my pocket. I had prepared some words over the past few days about my Godfather...and I thought that I'd assemble everyone on the bow and say something before releasing his ashes from the urn. Something personal...something solemn.

But solemn wasn't our style.

Jerry always kept my excitement meter on *high* and the energy *up*. There was no need to bring down this magical feeling that I just shared with the people onboard.

I quickly turned away from everyone and decided that what I had to say to and about my Godfather...would be said just between *us*.

I put the paper back into my pocket, and as everyone ate from the buffet in the cabin, I slipped a cassette into the deck and walked to the bow with everything I needed in order to say goodbye to my closest cousin...a bottle of Dom, a champagne flute, the black briefcase and the urn.

I sat on the deck with my legs hanging over the edge and my body resting along the railing as the music from the cassette started to play. It was the fully produced and orchestrated version of *Can You Feel The Sun Go Down*, the song I wrote back in 1975 while sitting at the piano in the living room of Patsy D'Amore's Studio City home.

Then I filled the long thin glass with champagne.

As I took a drink, a sudden feeling of dread overwhelmed me.

I felt I couldn't go through with what I had promised to do...and I knew why.

The reason was simple.

I didn't want to.

I didn't want to acknowledge that the person responsible for the most endearing memories and extraordinary adventures of my life...was gone.

And most of all...I didn't want to admit that another era had ended.

I cursed myself for not being strong enough to do it.

"You promised!" I said to myself.

For an instant, I even thought I heard Jerry say, "Relax Juan, you're doin' great. I know you'll do the right thing. You always do."

And he was right.

I always did.

The music and the thoughts inside my head were the only things I could hear.

I took a deep breath, picked up his urn, looked at it...and gave it my best shot.

"You have any idea what you meant to me, Jerry?" I asked, happy that no one was around to see me speak to the brass container of ashes. "You opened a door and guided me through something I'll remember forever. Twenty-four years ago *today*, you allowed me to see a side of life few people *ever* see, much less *experience*. You gave me a fuckin' Wonderland better than Alice's...because mine was real. It really...*really* happened."

I took a long, slow drink from the flute.

"And...you always looked after me."

My eyes filled with tears, and after another deep breath, I continued. "You made sure that even when you were thousands of miles away...I was still safe. You were *more* than a cousin, Jerry."

The tears began to run down my face.

"I'll always have the memories of you...the things you did for me...the things we did together. My love and respect for you...and yours for me."

I couldn't go on. My lips trembled from the pain of missing him.

I looked down at the water and opened the urn.

The chorus of the song began to build to a crescendo and the melodic lyrics repeated the refrain "Can you feel the sun go down," just as the bottom of the sun touched the horizon.

As his ashes landed onto the peaceful blue surface, tears were streaming down my face. I said softy, "Someday, Jerry...Someday we'll be here together...Someday."

And then, one at a time...I dropped each of his pistols into the sea.

I was sure I heard him whisper in my ear, "Happy birthday, Juan."

It was the end of another era.

My days as one of the boys...and as *The Kid*...were finally over.

Oh yeah, and today...my picture is on the wall at
Al Nucci's Custom Tailors.
In between two of Sinatra's.

The End

The Cast of Characters
in alphabetical order

Jon D'Amore

The author. *a/k/a The Phantom Of The Grand; Juan; The Kid.*

Antonio

Patsy D'Amore's long time friend and maître 'd at The Villa Capri.

Barbie

A classy hooker in Las Vegas.

Carmen Basilio

Two-time (welterweight & middleweight) 1950s era world boxing champion.

Louie Calderone

Tommy Dolan's right hand man.

Vinnie Caputo

Jerry D'Amore's hitman.

Carl

A pit boss at The MGM Grand.

Mike Caruso

Jerry's right hand man. *a/k/a Big Mike.*

Rocco Casiano

Started as Frank DeNike's bodyguard. Became successor to Frank DeNike's territory. *Aka The Boss; Rocco.*

Tony Costa

Jerry's *other* right-hand man. *a/k/a Taz.*

Frank Costello

Right-hand man to Lucky Luciano, and heir apparent to Luciano's family, until he was wounded by Vincente Gigante. Then he turned the family over to Vito Genovese.

Angelo Cutillo

Benny Petrillo's uncle. *a/k/a The Collector; Uncle Angelo.*

Ann D'Amore

Jon's mother.

Carmine D'Amore

Jon's father, former Textile Workers Union of America official. *a/k/a Rocky.*

Dominic D'Amore

Jon's uncle, Carmine's brother, Jerry's father, Frank DeNike's brother-in-law. *a/k/a Geil*.

Franklyn D'Amore

Patsy's older brother. His birth name was Dominic Francesco D'Amore.

Gerald D'Amore

Jon's cousin and Godfather. Dominic's son. Carmine's nephew. Frank DeNike's nephew and Godson, Underboss to Rocco Casiano. *a/k/a Jerry; The Beard*.

Pasquale D'Amore

Rocky and Dominic's cousin, famous Los Angeles restaurateur and Franklyn's younger brother. *a/k/a Patsy*.

Rose, Phyllis & Joey D'Amore

Patsy's wife, daughter and son (respectively).

James Dean

Famous actor from the 1950s.

Salvatore Della Osa

Rocco Casiano's bodyguard.

Frank DeNike

Dominic's brother-in-law. The boss of Lucky Luciano's North Jersey territory. Married to Dominic's wife's sister. An official for the International Brotherhood of Pipefitters.

Nicky DePasquale

A stupid loanshark. *a/k/a Dion*.

Thomas Dolan

Rocco Casiano's childhood friend and underboss. *a/k/a The Irishman; Tommy; Wally Gazzulo*.

Carlo Gambino

The head of the Gambino family, and *capo di tutti capi* during the 1960s and '70s.

Vito Genovese

Took over Lucky Luciano's family after a failed attempt on Frank Costello's life. The family then changed its name to the Genovese family.

Vincente Gigante

The head of the Genovese family until the 1990s. *a/k/a The Chin*.

John Gotti

The head of the Gambino family during the 1980s and into the '90s.

Bobby Grant

A member of Dolan's inner crew.

Armand Guardino

A messenger for The Commission. *a/k/a Mondu.*

Heather

A 22-year-old Manhattan model that Jon took to the Bahamas for New Years.

Andrew Herschfeld

Rocco Casiano's attorney.

Joe Koonce

Casino Manager for The Tropicana.

Vito Lanni

Undercover cop who infiltrated Benny Petrillo's crew. *a/k/a Special Agent Robert Testa, of the New Jersey State Police.* See Robert Testa.

Petey LaVeglia

Assistant to Vinnie Caputo. *a/k/a Big Petey.*

John Phillip Law

Actor. Appeared in *Barbarella*, *The Russians Are Coming The Russians Are Coming*, *The Spiral Staircase*, and dozens more.

Charles Luciano

The first *capo di tutti capo. a/k/a Lucky.*

George Lyman

Tommy Dolan's enforcer and driver. A former Sergeant in the Hudson County Police Department.

Cosmo Manzi

He borrowed money from Jerry, and didn't expect to pay it back.

Arthur McCormick

An FBI Agent.

Michele, Jeanette & Sharon

Three women in their early 40s that Jon meets at The MGM Grand pool during his first trip to Vegas.

Roberto Musarra

Northern New Jersey Consigliere for the Genovese family.

Al Nucci

Longtime friend of Rocco Casiano and Jerry D'Amore. *a/k/a The Tailor.*

Lady Millicent Overton

Second cousin to the Queen of England, and a lot of fun to be with.

Patty, Debbie & Sandy

Sandy is a blackjack dealer at The Trop and friends with Patty and Debby.

Benny Petrillo

Angelo Cutillo's nephew. *a/k/a Cheap Benny.*

Dickie Pignatello

Middleman for The Commission.

Sonny & Marco Ranouro

Underbosses of Casiano.

Rick Rogers

One of Tommy Dolan's gamblers, from Newport Beach, California. *a/k/a Newport.*

Tony Romano

Father of a high school friend of Jon's. He turns out to be part of Rocco Casiano's crew.

Mickey Rooney

Famous stage and screen actor.

Linda Rossi

A friend of Phyllis', and eventually Jon's.

Tony Salerno

Head of the Genovese Family after the death of Vito Genovese. In the mid-1970s he retired and handed over the reins to Vincente 'The Chin' Gigante. *a/k/a Fat Tony.*

Frank Sinatra

Famous Italian singer from Hoboken, Hudson County, New Jersey. Met Franklyn and Patsy D'Amore in the late 1940s and became friends and a regular at their Hollywood restaurants.

Mr. Smith

Supposedly a representative from the Casino Security Investigation Board.

Stefano

The maitre 'd at the Italian restaurant in The MGM Grand.

Steve

Owner of the yacht '*Cara Mia.*'

Robert Testa

See Vito Lanni.

Mrs. Todisco

Neighbor's home where Casiano had his extra garage and escape route.

Dave & Patricia Toma

Patricia is Carmine's sister, Jon's aunt and Godmother. She married Dave Toma, a Newark cop who became the basis for two TV cop shows: *Toma* and *Baretta*.

John Travolta

Budding television star of *Welcome Back, Kotter*. A Bergen County native.

Mr. & Mrs. Waite

The American guardians of Lady Millicent; from Barrington Hills, Illinois.

Bill Zitane

Jon's high school friend who relocated to San Francisco in the early 1970s to attend college. Jon stayed at his apartment when working there.

Photograph Credits
in alphabetical order

Photos 3, 4, 9, 11, 12, 14, 15, 16, 17, 18, 21, 25, 27, 28 & 29 *Courtesy of the Ann & Jon D'Amore Collection*

Photos 8, 10 & 13 *Courtesy of the Joseph D'Amore Collection*

Photos 6 & 26 *Provided with love by Lynne & Jennifer Flora*

Photos 1, 2 & 5 *Courtesy of the Peter Flora Collection*

Photos 23 & 24 *From the private collection of Eileen & George Herberger*

Photo 20 *Courtesy of Patricia Hurley*

Photo 19 *Courtesy of Dawn Law*

Photo 7 *Courtesy of the Diane Lombardi-Fleming & Charles Lombardi Collection*

Photo 22 *Courtesy of the Jamie Todisco Collection*

Additional photos donated but not used *Courtesy of the Philip Bracco Collection, Courtesy of the Pamela Canzano Collection, Courtesy of the Michael D'Amore Collection, Courtesy of Ashley Rogers* and *Photo by Harold Sherrick.*